CHRISTIANITY AND THE NEW EUGENICS

Should we choose to have only healthy or enhanced children?

Calum MacKellar

INTER-VARSITY PRESS
36 Causton Street, London SW1P 4ST, Englan
Email: ivp@ivpbooks.com
Website: www.ivpbooks.com

First published 2020

British Library Cataloguing-in-Publication Data
A catalogue record for this book is available from the British Library.

ISBN: 978-1-78359-913-4
eBook ISBN: 978-1-78359-914-1

Set in 10/13.25pt Minion Pro
Typeset in Great Britain by CRB Associates, Potterhanworth, Lincolnshire
Printed in Great Britain by Ashford Colour Press Ltd, Gosport, Hampshire

Inter-Varsity Press publishes Christian books that are true to the Bible and that communicate the gospel, develop discipleship and strengthen the church for its mission in the world.

IVP originated within the Inter-Varsity Fellowship, now the Universities and Colleges Christian Fellowship, a student movement connecting Christian Unions in universities and colleges throughout Great Britain, and a member movement of the International Fellowship of Evangelical Students. Website: www.uccf.org.uk. That historic association is maintained, and all senior IVP staff and committee members subscribe to the UCCF Basis of Faith.

Contents

1	**Introduction**	1
	Learning from the past	6
	Looking to the present	8
2	**Eugenics in its historical context**	11
	The history of eugenics in Germany	12
	The history of eugenics in the UK	15
	The history of eugenics in the USA	20
3	**A Christian enquiry into the new eugenics**	23
	Creation and the image of God	26
	Procreation, love and unconditional acceptance	44
	The new eugenics and the equality of all	80
	Other arguments relevant to the new eugenics	101
4	**Presentation of different eugenic procedures**	125
	Reproductive eugenics through the selection of partners	125
	Reproductive eugenics through selecting to have many, few or no children	128
	Eugenics through selective adoption	129
	Eugenics through sex selection	132
	Eugenics through egg and sperm selection	134
	Eugenics through prenatal genetic selection	139
	Eugenics and embryonic selection	143
	Eugenic selection through human cloning	148
	Eugenic selection through infanticide	152
	Eugenics through genome and germline modifications	156
5	**Conclusion**	177
	God's creation of the child	180
	Unconditional acceptance in procreation	181

The immeasurable worth and value of all individuals created in the same image of God 183
The ethics of the new eugenics 185
Risks of discrimination 187
The value and worth of life versus the quality of life 192

Further reading 198
Glossary 200
General index 208
Index of Scripture references 212

1
Introduction

Society is on the brink of a biomedical revolution in the development of novel reproductive procedures enabling the selection of certain kinds of children. A new age of reproduction that will have a profound impact on humanity, though most members of society, including Christians, are unaware of this brave new eugenic dawn. Moreover, little extensive Christian study has yet taken place seeking both to understand and to find a way forward in the complex future of reproductive selection. In addition, many Christians do not comprehend why, if given the choice, they should not be able to decide what kind of children they want. Why, they ask, should they not be able to choose to have only healthy children? Why not avoid bringing a child into existence with a serious disorder? Why not prevent the significant suffering a disabled child, and his or her parents, may experience?

Of course, the Bible does not specifically mention whether it is acceptable to select what kinds of children should be brought into existence, but this does not mean that it cannot provide guidance on the topic. As with many modern technologies, it just means that Christians need to examine these new possibilities by digging deeper into the overarching principles of Christianity revealed in the written word of God. In so doing, they must also inform themselves of the latest philosophical and scientific developments while considering what lessons can be learned from history.

It was the Englishman Sir Francis Galton (1822–1911) who first coined the term 'eugenics' in 1883 as 'the science of improving stock' through 'all influences that tend in however remote a degree to give to the more suitable races or strains of blood a better chance of prevailing speedily over the less suitable than they otherwise would have'.[1] The word 'eugenics'

[1] F. Galton, *Inquiries into Human Faculty and Its Development* (London: Macmillan, 1883), p. 25, n. 1.

derives from two Greek roots, *eu* (meaning good) and *genesis* (meaning offspring or bringing into life). It characterizes the practice of producing human life that is good at birth (or a noble heredity) based on the belief that human beings can be improved from a genetic perspective. More specifically, eugenic developments describe selection strategies or decisions aimed at affecting, in manners considered to be positive, the genetic heritage of a child, a community or humanity in general.[2] From this perspective, Galton sought to organize and apply new information about the evolution of animals provided by the theory of his cousin Charles Darwin (1809–82) in the latter's influential book, published in 1859, *On the Origin of Species*. In so doing, Galton developed his own proposals by applying this theory to humankind in his 1869 book *Hereditary Genius*,[3] in which he argued:

> [T]hat a man's natural abilities are derived by inheritance, under exactly the same limitations as are the form and physical features of the whole organic world. Consequently, as it is easy . . . to obtain by careful selection a permanent breed of dogs or horses gifted with peculiar powers of running, . . . so it would be quite practicable to produce a highly-gifted race of men by judicious marriages during several consecutive generations.[4]

Thus, it was through the success of the breeding of farm animals, and the suggestion that human beings should not be considered differently from other animals, that modern eugenic ideas were developed. These became relatively popular at the end of the nineteenth and beginning of the twentieth centuries. A number of prominent figures supported eugenic selection, including Sir Winston Churchill (1874–1965), the wartime prime minister of the UK, who was openly disappointed, on the grounds of civil liberties, when Britain resisted positive eugenic action. In 1910 Churchill wrote to the then prime minister Herbert Asquith (1852–1928) to express his support for a bill that proposed to introduce a compulsory sterilization programme in Britain, indicating:

---

2 C. MacKellar and C. Bechtel (eds), *The Ethics of the New Eugenics* (New York: Berghahn, 2014), p. 3.

3 F. Galton, *Hereditary Genius* (London: Macmillan, 1869), v.

4 Ibid., p. 1.

> The unnatural and increasingly rapid growth of the feeble-minded and insane classes, coupled as it is with a steady restriction among the thrifty, energetic and superior stocks, constitutes a national and race danger which it is impossible to exaggerate . . . I feel that the source from which the stream of madness is fed should be cut off and sealed up before another year has passed.[5]

However, despite the many benefits eugenic proposals seemed to promise humanity, they remained on the margins of serious scientific disciplines because a number of subjective elements were believed to be at the centre of many of the policies. These included positions that could lead to a form of discrimination between certain categories of individuals – something that eventually culminated in the atrocities of Nazi Germany in the first half of the twentieth century. Because of these crimes, eugenic proposals were then condemned as coercive, restrictive or genocidal after the Second World War, resulting in many societies completely rejecting any resemblance to such policies.

At the beginning of the twenty-first century, however, the old eugenic dreams are beginning to resurface, with an increasing number of new selective reproductive procedures being developed. For example, children are already being born who have been selected for good genetic endowments through careful screening programmes of embryos, sperm and eggs. Some scientists have even predicted that in the near future it will become common for parents to select specific characteristics in their offspring. Thus, a new eugenic impetus has begun in society, even though many still believe that past eugenic activities were unacceptable. The Danish ethicist Lene Koch, in 2009, put it well:

> Today eugenics is something few would want to see realised, but we should appreciate that it was originally a focus of a widely held hope for a better and healthier population. The definition of 'better and healthier' may no longer embrace the elimination of socially, morally, and genetically undesirable elements as defined by the early eugenicists, but the hope for better health still underpins the rationale for genetic applications.[6]

---

5 Quoted in M. Lind, 'Churchill for Dummies', *Spectator*, 24 April 2004.

6 L. Koch, 'Eugenics', in P. Atkinson, P. Glasner and M. Lock (eds), *Handbook of Genetics and Society: Mapping the New Genomic Era* (London: Routledge, 2009), pp. 437–447 (p. 446).

This is also something that American scientist James Watson, who won the 1962 Nobel Prize in Physiology or Medicine for his discovery of deoxyribonucleic acid (DNA), developed when he argued in 1995 that:

> Our growing ability to unscramble human genetic destinies will increasingly have an impact on how humans view themselves and justify their behaviour toward others. Our children will more be seen not as expressions of God's will, but as the results of the uncontrollable throw of genetic dice that do not always give us the results we want. At the same time, we will increasingly have the power, through prenatal diagnosis to spot the good throws and to consider discarding through abortion the bad ones.
>
> But to so proceed flies in the face of the long-cherished idea that all human life is sacred and intrinsically worthwhile. So there is bound to be deep conflict between those persons who want to maintain revered values of the past and those individuals who wish to have their moral values reflect the world as now revealed by observations and experiments of modern science. In particular, we are increasingly going to be accused of unwisely 'playing God' when we use genetics to improve the quality of either current or future human life.[7]

In this context Christians need to consider carefully whether such eugenic developments should be welcomed, rejected or considered neutral. For example, they will need to ask whether it would be acceptable, from a Christian perspective, to choose to have only healthy children and, if so, what arguments should be used. They would also have to examine, as a matter of urgency, the potential advantages as well as the risks for society of such choices. In 1922 the English Christian writer and philosopher Gilbert K. Chesterton (1874–1936), who was opposed to eugenic ideology, published his prescient *Eugenics and Other Evils*, where he indicated:

> The wisest thing in the world is to cry out before you are hurt. It is no good to cry out after you are hurt; especially after you are

[7] J. Watson, 'Values from Chicago Upbringing', in D. A. Chambers (ed.), *DNA: The Double Helix Perspective and Prospective at Forty Years* (New York: New York Academy of Science, 1995), pp. 194–197 (p. 197).

> mortally hurt. People talk about the impatience of the populace; but sound historians know that most tyrannies have been possible because men moved too late.[8]

In pondering all the possible arguments in favour of and against eugenic policies, a number of different kinds of procedures may also be examined that reflect the eugenic aims of those who are considering them. Sometimes the goal may be clear but at other times concealed, even to the person making the reproductive decision. These include the following aims.

1 Negative (or preventative) eugenics: strategies or decisions that seek to avoid or reduce what is considered to be an undesired genetic heritage in a child, community or humanity in general, such as:
   (a) compulsory sterilizations of undesirable persons capable of reproduction
   (b) marriage restrictions of undesirable persons capable of reproduction
   (c) selecting-out undesirable embryos or foetuses because they are affected by disorders
   (d) immigration controls preventing certain kinds of people from entering a country or
   (e) extermination of certain undesirable persons.
2 Positive (or progressive) eugenics: strategies or decisions aimed at promoting what is considered to be a desired genetic heritage in a child, a community or humanity in general, such as:
   (a) the selection of desirable sperm in a sperm bank
   (b) certain forms of marriage counselling or
   (c) promoting increased birth rates in couples who are deemed to be biologically desirable parents.

The distinction, however, between positive or negative eugenics is not clear-cut. For example, some procedures, such as the genetic selection of embryos and certain forms of marriage counselling, allow participants to make a choice based on genetic characteristics widely viewed as either positive and desirable or as negative and undesirable. Similarly, a

[8] G. K. Chesterton, *Eugenics and Other Evils* (Seattle: Inkling, 2001), ch. 1, p. 13.

distinction can usually be made between 'enhancement' and 'healing', though it may sometimes be difficult to draw a line between the two concepts and is related to the definitions of other terms as well as cultural norms and values.[9] In this regard the concept of 'enhancement' (or augmentation) usually represents activities (whether biological or not) through which an individual is transformed to exceed what is normal in order to improve his or her natural function.[10] The concept reflects the idea of using technology to increase the human functioning of a healthy individual beyond the norm for that person and in the absence of any identified dysfunction.[11] However, an enhancement does not generally include the creation of capacities in new living beings that have never previously existed in humanity. The aim is simply to improve on the norm but not to surpass a pre-existing, natural state or capacity in humanity. The concept of 'healing', on the other hand, reflects the idea of restoration and may be defined as the removal of certain disorders relative to a recognized standard of an average healthy human being.

Learning from the past

Interestingly, many who work in the field of genetic selection often seek to avoid using the term 'eugenics' in their discussions since they recognize that it is loaded with meaning and tarnished by the abuses that took place during the Nazi regime in Germany in the first half of the twentieth century. As a result, alternative terminology such as 'human enhancement' or 'therapeutic selection' is considered to be more appropriate, though the consequences may be similar and the changes may only be cosmetic. Thus, many of those who support selection procedures argue that using the term 'eugenics' is detrimental to recognizing scientific progress and its predictive capacity.

---

[9] For some, an intervention may be a therapy; but for others, the same intervention may be an enhancement, leaving a grey area in between. Moreover, it can be unclear whether therapies whose primary purpose is curing diseases but that have a secondary potential of improving performance should be classed as enhancements or treatment.

[10] P. Moore, *Enhancing Me: The Hope and the Hype of Human Enhancement* (Chichester: Wiley, 2008).

[11] J. Harris, *Enhancing Evolution* (Princeton: Princeton University Press, 2007), p. 9. Cf. British Medical Association (2007), 'Boosting Your Brainpower: Ethical Aspects of Cognitive Enhancements'; retrieved 27 August 2010 from <www.bma.org.uk/images/Boosting_brainpower_tcm41-147266.pdf>.

British scientist Francis Crick (1916–2004), who received the Nobel Prize with James Watson, indicated in 1971 that the Nazis had simply given eugenics 'a bad name', adding, 'I think it is time something is done to make it respectable again.'[12] In addition, many present commentators seek to avoid using the word when future parents undertake the selection decision voluntarily in order to make sure that their future child is not affected by a serious biological disorder.[13] Indeed, respect for patients' wishes and their autonomy in reproduction have become dominant positions in contemporary society.

But honesty demands that the different selection procedures already taking place in society are described as 'eugenic' if lessons are to be learned from history. There is no way around this reality, and it is inherently deceitful to undertake an exercise in 'vocabulary cleansing'. Many of the historical eugenicists believed that the establishment of a voluntary eugenic system in conjunction with widespread education and accessibility were the best ways of preventing the birth of people they considered degenerate.[14] For example, even Galton was opposed to any coercion in the implementation of eugenic policies.[15] In short, eugenic policies are about the selection of human persons based on genetics, regardless of the different forms in which such a selection may take place.

Furthermore, it is unfortunate that use of the word 'eugenics' elicits such a defensive reaction from so many supporters of selection procedures who generally articulate (rightly) deep offence at being compared to Nazi policy sympathizers. Such a reaction disregards the important historical fact that most past supporters of such eugenic procedures were not considered to be moral monsters, but normal people influenced by similar contemporary trends and aspirations to those that exist today. In addition, eugenic sympathizers in Nazi Germany, who did not stop the abuse implemented by their government, were not all that different from those who existed at the time in other European countries. This means that taking the moral high ground by suggesting that such unethical and abusive eugenic programmes could never take place today reflects a

---

12 F. Crick, Letter to Dr John T. Edsall on 10 June 1971; retrieved 6 February 2020 from <https://profiles.nlm.nih.gov/ps/access/SCBBNH.pdf>.

13 D. B. Paul, *Controlling Human Heredity: 1865 to the Present* (Amherst: Humanity, 1998), pp. 3–4.

14 Ibid., p. 135.

15 D. King, 'The Persistence of Eugenics', *Human Reproduction and Genetic Ethics* 5.2 (1999), pp. 31–35.

profound lack of humility and sense of reality. Perception also requires a rejection of the belief that 'It cannot happen here', 'It cannot happen again' or 'It cannot happen to us'. Society can never believe that it is free from the abuses of the past.

Looking to the present

It is important therefore to seek to learn from history and what went wrong in the past. This is because even at the beginning of the twentieth century eugenic ideology was driven by the aim of maximizing what is considered to be good, from the perspective of a relentless quest for health and the avoidance of suffering – an aim that resonates today in relation to the expected health and quality of life outcomes for a future child. As the American scientist Lee Silver asked in 1999:

> Why not seize this power? Why not control what has been left to chance in the past? Indeed, we control all other aspects of our children's lives and identities through powerful social and environmental influences . . . On what basis can we reject positive genetic influences on a person's essence when we accept the rights of parents to benefit their children in every other way?[16]

Some bioethicists are already arguing that parents should feel obliged to seek to bring the best possible children into existence.[17] Thus, it is suggested that medical technologies should be used to dispense with disability and disease.

At the same time the accumulation of many single voluntary decisions by parents will eventually have a significant, though unintended, impact on the whole of a population. For example, if most parents choose to avoid a certain disability, an accumulation of such decisions may have a significant eugenic impact on a societal group. As the ethicist Cynthia Cohen puts it, 'Individual decisions taken collectively, if promoted and supported as a matter of public policy, could amount to a new form of eugenics.'[18]

---

[16] L. M. Silver, *Remaking Eden* (London: Phoenix [Orion], 1999), p. 277.

[17] J. Savulescu, 'Procreative Beneficence: Why We Should Select the Best Children', *Bioethics* 15.5–6 (2001), pp. 413–426.

[18] C. B. Cohen, 'Designing Tomorrow's Children', in A. R. Chapman and M. S. Frankel (eds), *Designing Our Descendants* (Baltimore: Johns Hopkins University Press, 2003), pp. 296–310 (p. 305).

Similarly, Silver indicates, 'For while each individual use of the technology can be viewed in the light of personal reproductive choice – with no ability to change society at large – together they could have dramatic, unintended, long-term consequences.'[19]

Concerns also exist that eugenic developments may result from an unrestrained market encouraged by consumer choice as well as unavoidable social expectations. The American bioethicist Diane Paul states:

> The real problem is not the one we most fear: a government program to breed better babies. The more likely danger is roughly the opposite; it isn't that the government will get involved in reproductive choice, but that it won't. It is when left to the free market that the fruits of genome research are most assuredly rotten.[20]

This means that any selection procedure that is heritable would alter the genetic make-up of the resulting children and future generations, which may have unforeseeable effects. Moreover, if it is eventually possible to alter a person's genes and those of his or her descendants to remove or change attributes such as a predisposition to disorders, it may also be possible to change just about any other attribute.

Because of these developments, grave concerns have been expressed as to the consequences for society when it becomes possible to decide what kinds of children are brought into existence.[21] When a system of 'quality control' is applied to human procreation, and especially to the resulting children, careful reflection becomes necessary. Ever since the English writer and philosopher Aldous Huxley (1894–1963) published his dystopian science fiction book *Brave New World* in 1932,[22] describing a society in which individuals are genetically created to fit into social hierarchies, considerable anxiety has existed relating to the prospect of creating a similar society – one established with different groupings of people designed to fulfil different roles. Silver explains with respect to the new eugenic risks that:

---

19 Silver, *Remaking Eden*, p. 11.

20 D. B. Paul, 'Eugenic Anxieties, Social Realities, and Political Choices', in C. F. Cranor (ed.), *Are Genes US? The Social Consequences of the New Genetics* (New Brunswick: Rutgers University Press, 1994), pp. 142–154; quoted in Silver, *Remaking Eden*, p. 249.

21 C. MacKellar and C. Bechtel (eds), *The Ethics of the New Eugenics* (New York: Berghahn, 2014).

22 A. Huxley, *Brave New World* (New York: Harper 1932 [repr. 1998]).

> It is individuals and couples who want to reproduce themselves in their own images. It is individuals and couples who want their children to be happy and successful. And it is individuals and couples . . . who will seize control of these new technologies. They will use some to reach otherwise unattainable reproductive goals and others to help their children achieve health, happiness, and success. And it is in pursuit of this last goal that the combined actions of many individuals, operating over many generations, could perhaps give rise to a polarized humanity more horrific than Huxley's imagined Brave New World.[23]

In this regard, though Huxley's book was set in the year 2540, new developments in reproductive eugenic procedures have brought his dystopian future a lot closer, meaning that the ethical implications of such a world now need to be considered. But before doing so it is necessary to try to learn some of the lessons from the history of eugenics.

---

[23] Silver, *Remaking Eden*, p. 10.

2

Eugenics in its historical context

Selective eugenic procedures were mentioned at least as early as the Greek philosopher Plato (427–347 BC), who believed that human reproduction should be controlled by government.[1] He argued that '[t]he best men must have intercourse with the best women as frequently as possible, and the opposite is true of the very inferior'.[2] But even before Plato, the ancient city of Sparta had allegedly developed a radical eugenics programme by leaving babies outside city borders for a certain amount of time to test their survival strength, with those who were too weak then dying from exposure.[3]

With the growth of Christianity in the West, however, which condemned practices such as abortion, infanticide and the intrusion of third parties into the sexual life of married couples, many selection procedures were rejected as immoral. Only during the 1860s and 1870s was eugenics, as a specific discipline, re-examined with the aim of improving the genetic heritage of society.

On this account, Galton indicated that only through clear social policies could society be saved from degeneration towards mediocrity.[4] One of his interests was to reproduce 'eminent men' who were 'well known to persons familiar with literary and scientific society' and for whom 'the

---

1 D. J. Galton, 'Greek Theories on Eugenics', *Journal of Medical Ethics* 24.4 (1998), pp. 263–267.

2 Plato, *Republic*, Book 5, in A. Bailey, S. Brennan, W. Kymlicka, J. Levy and A. Sager (eds), *The Broadview Anthology of Social and Political Thought: From Plato to Nietzsche*, vol. 1. (Peterborough, Ont.: Broadview, 2008), p. 87.

3 '[A]nd whose infants, if they chanced to be puny or ill-formed, were exposed in a chasm . . . and left to die' (W. Berns, *Making Patriots* [Chicago: University of Chicago Press, 2001], p. 12).

4 F. Galton, 'Typical Laws of Heredity', *Nature* 15 (1885), pp. 492–495, 512–514, 532–533. Galton's parade illustration of this reversion is the rarity of giants: 'Giants marry much more rarely than medium men, and when they do marry they have but few children. It is a matter of history that the more remarkable giants have left no issue at all' (p. 492).

whole intelligent part of the nation mourns when they die'.[5] When Galton himself died in 1911, he was the recognized leader of eugenics, and with nearly fifty years of interest in the subject had become convinced that the future of respectable society depended on some form of eugenic selection.

At the beginning of the twentieth century, therefore, many European countries[6] as well as Canada and the USA had examined and even developed eugenic policies independently of any political ideology. This included programmes for the sterilization of individuals deemed unfit for procreation in certain countries, in order to address concerns of social degeneration.[7] Interestingly, a number of studies have also demonstrated how some religious leaders actively supported the eugenics movement at the time, such as in the UK and the USA.[8]

In order to be brief, however, the following section will present only eugenic developments that have taken place in Germany, the UK and the USA.

The history of eugenics in Germany

Eugenic ideology was present in Germany long before the National Socialists, led by Adolf Hitler (1889–1945), were elected in 1933. The first professor of eugenics was nominated in 1923 at the University of Munich, where some of the topics studied included the desirability of Nordic traits while seeking to discourage the propagation of those considered inferior. More surprisingly, however, it seems that many in the German Christian clergy embraced eugenic ideology as soon as the Nazis came to power.[9] As a result, once Hitler was elected, a new eugenic impetus began, having as its aim the protection of a 'pure' race through selection policies

[5] F. Galton, *Hereditary Genius* (London: Macmillan, 1869), pp. 5, 11.

[6] This included a number of Nordic countries, such as Denmark, Sweden, Norway and Finland. See MacKellar and Bechtel, *Ethics of the New Eugenics*, pp. 21–24.

[7] For more information, see A. Bashford and P. Levine (eds), *The Oxford Handbook of the History of Eugenics* (Oxford: Oxford University Press, 2010).

[8] C. Rosen, *Preaching Eugenics: Religious Leaders and the American Eugenics Movement* (Oxford: Oxford University Press, 2004); G. J. Baker, 'Christianity and Eugenics: The Place of Religion in the British Eugenics Education Society and the American Eugenics Society, *c.*1907–1940', *Social History of Medicine: The Journal of the Society for the Social History of Medicine* 27.2 (2014), pp. 281–302.

[9] E. W. Lutzer, *Hitler's Cross* (Chicago: Moody, 1995); S. F. Weiss, *The Nazi Symbiosis: Human Genetics and Politics in the Third Reich* (Chicago: University of Chicago Press, 2010); G. Broberg and N. Roll-Hansen (eds), *Eugenics and the Welfare State: Norway, Sweden, Denmark, and Finland* (East Lansing: Michigan University Press, 2005).

that encouraged 'racial hygiene'.[10] This started with a previous proposal to legalize the sterilization of certain kinds of individuals, which was brought into force in 1934. However, the voluntary element of prior legislative proposals was expanded to include the involuntary sterilization of 'hereditary and incurable drunkards, sexual criminals, lunatics, and those suffering from an incurable disease which would be passed on to their offspring'.[11] From 1934 to 1939 the Nazi regime compulsorily sterilized up to 350,000 German citizens whom they viewed as mentally and physically 'unfit' so that, among other reasons, they would not be able to have children.[12]

Eugenic ideology was also put into practice through the euthanasia programme initiated in 1939. This empowered certain physicians to grant 'mercy killing to those deemed incurable according to the best available judgement of their state of health'.[13] The basis for this eugenic initiative had been developed with the concept of a 'life unworthy of life' that first appeared in 1920.[14] This kind of thinking became an important component of the Nazi ideology with, for example, the making of the 1939 propaganda film *Existence Without Life; Mentally Ill.* Hitler wrote in his 1925 autobiography, *Mein Kampf*:

> The demand that defective people be prevented from propagating equally defective offspring is a demand of the clearest reason and, if systematically executed, represents the most humane act of mankind. It will spare millions of unfortunates undeserved sufferings, and consequently will lead to a rising improvement of health as a whole.[15]

---

10 D. Wikler, 'Can We Learn from Eugenics?', *Journal of Medical Ethics* 25.2 (1999), pp. 183–194 (p. 185).

11 'Sterilisation of the Unfit, Nazi Legislation', *The Guardian*, 26 July 1933; retrieved 26 July 2011 from <http://century.guardian.co.uk/1930-1939/Story/0,6051,126942,00.html>.

12 D. B. Paul, *Controlling Human Heredity: 1865 to the Present* (Amherst: Humanity, 1998), pp. 89–90; R. Evans, 'How Hitler Perverted the Course of Science', *The Telegraph*, 2 December 2008; retrieved 1 July 2009 from <www.telegraph.co.uk/science/science-news/3540339/How-Hitler-perverted-the-course-of-science.html>; J. Glad, *Future Human Evolution: Eugenics in the Twenty-First Century* (Schuylkill Haven: Hermitage, 2008), p. 57.

13 Correspondence from Adolf Hitler to Reichsleiter Bouhler and Dr Karl Brandt in October 1939, backdated to 1 September 1939. Quoted in German National Ethics Council, *Opinion: Self-Determination and Care at the End of Life* (Berlin: Nationaler Ethikrat, 2006), p. 33.

14 A. Hoche and K. Binding, *Die Freigabe der Vernichtung Lebensunwerten Lebens* (Leipzig: Felix Meiner, 1920).

15 A. Hitler, *Mein Kampf*, vol. 1, tr. R. Manheim (Boston: Houghton Mifflin, 1943), p. 255; quoted in E. Black, *War Against the Weak* (New York: Thunder's Mouth, 2004), p. 274.

Trying to understand the barbarism present during the National Socialist regime is challenging and many questions remain. Overall, the euthanasia programme ended with the death of some 70,000 German patients in psychiatric institutions. But the Nazis were proud to have, among other reasons, a scientific foundation for their policies while avoiding the high cost of care for the disabled.

Nonetheless, strong opposition to the Nazi euthanasia programmes did occur, especially from Catholic clergy such as the Bishop of Münster, Clemens August Graf von Galen (1878–1946). In a Sunday sermon he condemned the deportation and euthanasia of mentally ill people, arguing that 'These are people, our brothers and sisters; maybe their life is unproductive, but productivity is not a justification for killing.'[16] In other words, he indicated that such actions could be considered a form of murder, which violated both the law of the land and the law of God.[17]

Many of the euthanasia programmes in Germany at the time were a form of negative eugenics – genetic purification by means of elimination. But the Nazis also sought to implement positive eugenic policies with, for instance, the development of initiatives seeking to reproduce 'racially pure' children. For the sole purpose of producing superior children German men certified as biologically fit and racially pure were encouraged to reproduce with women who had similar characteristics. The aim was to develop a 'master race'.[18] From 1943 until the end of the war providing an abortion to an 'Aryan' (especially Nordic) woman became a capital offence in Nazi Germany unless it could be demonstrated that the child would be born with a disorder. But 'non-Aryan' women were encouraged to have abortions.

As a result of the atrocities committed in the name of eugenic ideology in Nazi Germany any procedure even hinting at such a way forward became almost universally condemned after the end of the Second World War in many of the countries where it had once been popular. In response to the Nazi atrocities most post-war politicians denounced the notion of any inherent inequality between human beings. More importantly,

---

[16] P. Löffler (ed.), *Bischof Clemens August Graf von Galen: Akten, Briefe und Predigten 1933–1946* (Paderborn: Ferdinand Schöningh, 1996), p. 874.

[17] B. A. Griech-Polelle, *Bishop von Galen: German Catholicism and National Socialism* (New Haven: Yale University Press, 2002).

[18] D. Crossland, 'Himmler Was My Godfather', *The Times*, 6 November 2006; retrieved 30 June 2009 from <www.timesonline.co.uk/tol/news/world/europe/article626101.ece>.

legislative bodies throughout the world, while seeking to construct an ethical framework preventing any repetition of such atrocities, sought to learn the lessons from the abuse that had taken place.

The history of eugenics in the UK

As already noted, it was in the UK that the first eugenic proposals were considered at the end of the nineteenth century with, among a number of factors, the publication of Galton's writings. In 1907 the UK Eugenics Education Society (EES) was created in order to influence public opinion and voice concerns relating to the perceived demographic predicament arising from less gifted individuals having too many children. The elderly Galton even served, a year later, as its first honorary president.[19] The first issue of *The Eugenics Review*, published by the EES in 1909, expressed its objectives as follows:

- To set forth the national importance of eugenics in order to modify public opinion and create a sense of responsibility in bringing all matters relating to human parenthood under the domination of eugenic ideals.
- To spread a knowledge of the laws of heredity in order to affect the improvement of the race.
- To further eugenic teaching, at home, in the schools, and elsewhere.[20]

Interestingly, in the same issue of this first journal published by the EES, an Anglican professor of divinity at Cambridge University, the Reverend William R. Inge (1860–1954), who became dean of St Paul's Cathedral in London in 1911, gave a kind of official 'seal of approval' of eugenic practices, from a Christian perspective, indicating:

> Humanitarian legislation, or practice, requires to be supplemented, and its inevitable evil effects counteracted, by eugenic practice, and ultimately by eugenic legislation. The need is more urgent when, as

[19] D. Wikler, 'Can We Learn from Eugenics?', *Journal of Medical Ethics* 25.2 (1999), pp. 183–194.

[20] *The Eugenics Review* 1.1 (April 1909), inside front cover. Mentioned in Baker, 'Christianity and Eugenics', pp. 281–302 (p. 283).

> in our own country [the UK], the constitution of society favours the multiplication of the unfit and the elimination of the higher types.[21]

However, he then went a lot further by condemning Christians who oppose eugenic policies:

> But if there is any scourge which does not strike the guilty only, which ruins innocent lives by thousands, and which is responsible for an incalculable amount of degeneration in the town populations of all civilised countries, then I say to those who would gladly leave things as they are, in the supposed interests of Christian morality, that their views are as false to the recorded teachings of Christ as they are repugnant to the common dictates of humanity and the future welfare of mankind.[22]

The science historian Graham Baker indicates that such a statement from Inge was 'an important religious endorsement for the [EES] society',[23] which perceived the poorer classes as having few positive qualities worth passing on to future generations. It even labelled them as the 'residuum': the unwanted leftovers. Thus, one of the first aims of the EES was to seek to reduce the relatively high birth rates of the lowest and poorest classes in society so that these people would ultimately disappear. A general improvement of the whole of society would then follow as the middle and upper classes eventually regained a majority of the population.

Amid its many proposals the EES suggested the enforced isolation of individuals whose reproduction could threaten what it believed were positive social goals. This eventually resonated among some UK politicians with the passing of the UK *Mental Deficiency Act 1913*, which legalized the compulsory detention of people labelled 'idiots', 'imbeciles', 'feeble-minded' or 'morally defective'. Among other reasons, the aim was to control their reproduction by segregating them into special colonies, asylums, sanatoriums and hospitals. The EES also initiated a campaign in

[21] W. R. Inge, 'Some Moral Aspects of Eugenics', *The Eugenics Review* 1.1 (1909), pp. 26–36 (p. 29).

[22] Ibid., p. 33.

[23] Baker, 'Christianity and Eugenics', p. 284. Baker also notes that 'Inge's contribution to the first issue of the *The Eugenics Review* certainly endorsed the potential power of eugenics' (ibid., p. 285).

the 1920s to legalize the sterilization of those it considered to be unworthy of having children, but this was opposed by an increasing resistance to eugenic ideology both in the UK and internationally. For example, in 1930 Pope Pius XI (1857–1939) published a strong statement supporting the freedom of marriage, which was being debated in countries such as the UK. He denounced eugenics as 'that pernicious practice' and explicitly declared the inappropriateness of any civil body attempting to regulate human reproduction.[24] In particular he stated:

> Public magistrates have no direct power over the bodies of their subjects; therefore, where no crime has taken place and there is no cause present for grave punishment, they can never directly harm, or tamper with the integrity of the body, either for the reasons of eugenics or for any other reason.[25]

In other words, one of the main motives for the UK government's reluctance to introduce eugenic policies was the strength of the Roman Catholic lobby and the fear of those in power of adopting controversial and contentious legislation.[26]

The EES and other organizations supporting eugenic ideology did, however, have some success in convincing prominent members of British society of the advantages of selection. As already indicated, Sir Winston Churchill was an ardent supporter of eugenic policies. In 1912 he even attended the First International Eugenics Congress in London and agreed to become its vice-chairman.

Other past prime ministers, such as Arthur Balfour (1848–1930), who gave the opening speech at the first international conference on eugenics in 1912, and Neville Chamberlain (1869–1940), were also supportive of eugenic proposals.[27]

In 1926 the EES changed its name to the (British) Eugenics Society but lost many supporters after the Second World War. In 1989 it changed its

---

24 Pope Pius XI (1930), *Casti Connubii*, §§ 68–71; retrieved 7 February 2020 from <www.vatican.va/content/pius-xi/en/encyclicals/documents/hf_p-xi_enc_19301231_casti-connubii.html>.

25 Ibid., § 70.

26 G. R. Searle, 'Eugenics and Politics in Britain in the 1930s', *Annals of Science* 36 (1979), pp. 159–169.

27 D. J. Kevles, *Au nom de l'eugénisme* (Paris: Presses Universitaires de France, 1995), pp. 88, 162.

name again to the Galton Institute, which still exists and has continued to attract prominent personalities. As a result, eugenic ideology did not completely disappear after the war. For example, Welsh legal scholar Glanville Williams (1911–97) suggested in 1957 that certain persons with congenital disability should be sterilized:

> The obvious social importance of preventing the birth of children who are congenitally deaf, blind, paralysed, deformed, feeble minded, mentally diseased, or subject to other serious hereditary afflictions, and the inadequacy of contraception for this purpose, has naturally given rise to the proposal to use sterilisation of the unfit as a means of racial improvement . . . by keeping alive mentally and physically ill-equipped children, we are opposing natural selection.[28]

Similarly, Francis Crick proposed that certain groups of people should be encouraged to be sterilized through a payment. In 1970 he wrote:

> My . . . suggestion is . . . an attempt to solve the problem of irresponsible people and especially those who are poorly endowed genetically having large numbers of unnecessary children. Because of their irresponsibility, it seems to me that for them, sterilization is the only answer and I would do this by bribery. It would probably pay society to offer such individuals something like £1,000 down and a pension of £5 a week over the age of 60. As you probably know, the bribe in India is a transistor radio and apparently there are plenty of takers.[29]

Moreover, the older brother of Aldous Huxley, Sir Julian Huxley (1887–1975), who was a professor of physiology at Kings College in London as well as the first director of the United Nations Educational, Scientific and Cultural Organization (UNESCO) and the president of the British Eugenics Society from 1959 to 1962, wrote, 'Once the full implications of evolutionary biology are grasped, eugenics will inevitably become part

[28] G. Williams, *The Sanctity of Life and the Criminal Law* (New York: Knopf, 1957), pp. 80–81.

[29] F. Crick, Letter to Dr B. Davis 22 April 1970; retrieved 21 June 2019 from <https://profiles.nlm.nih.gov/ps/access/SCBBPG.pdf>.

of the religion of the future, or whatever complex of sentiments may in future take the place of organized religion.'[30]

Reflecting on his belief, which was relatively common at the time, that the lowest classes in a society should not reproduce too quickly, he also indicated:

> The lowest strata, allegedly less well-endowed [*sic*] genetically, are reproducing relatively too fast. Therefore . . . they must not have too easy access to relief or hospital treatment lest the removal of the last check on natural selection should make it too easy for children to be produced or to survive; long unemployment should be a ground for sterilization, or at least relief should be contingent upon no further children being brought into the world.[31]

Those who were assumed to have limitations caused by genetic factors were considered as holding back society on its road to improvement. The very value and worth of a human being could be sacrificed to improve society.

A final example, after the Second World War, of a prominent personality supporting eugenic procedures was the 2010 English Nobel Prize winner for Physiology or Medicine, Robert Edwards (1925–2013), who developed in vitro fertilization (IVF). In 1999 he said, 'Soon it will be a sin for parents to have a child that carries the heavy burden of genetic disease. We are entering a world where we have to consider the quality of our children.'[32] Recent documents have shown that Edwards served as a trustee for the Galton Institute on three separate occasions until 1997.[33] Edwards also implies a link between IVF and eugenic tendencies when commenting on the twenty-fifth anniversary of the first birth through IVF in 1993, indicating that initiating IVF 'was about more than infertility . . . I wanted to find out exactly who was in charge, whether it was God himself or whether it was scientists in the laboratory'. Edwards then concludes,

30 J. S. Huxley, 'Eugenics and Society', *The Eugenics Review* 28.1 (1936), pp. 11–31 (p. 11).
31 Ibid. p. 24.
32 Quoted in J. Quintavalle, 'Better by Accident than Design', in Institute of Ideas (compiled E. Lee), *Designer Babies: Where Should We Draw the Line?* (London: Hodder & Stoughton, 2002), p. 73.
33 O. K. Obasogie, 'The Eugenics Legacy of the Nobelist Who Fathered IVF', *Scientific American*, 4 October 2013.

'It was us.'[34] In more recent times a number of scholars have suggested that even the decriminalization of abortion with the UK *Abortion Act 1967* may have been motivated partly by a willingness to eradicate the disabled and unwanted based on eugenic ideology.[35]

The history of eugenics in the USA

One of the first recorded eugenic experiments in the US took place in the perfectionist community of Oneida in the state of New York. The leader of the community, John Noyes (1811–86), was a theologian and utopian visionary who believed that Christians had a responsibility to promote moral perfection. Central to this mission was the selective breeding of human beings considered to have attained an approximation of perfection.[36] Noyes organized a campaign between 1869 and 1879 encouraging high-quality members of the community to become parents, resulting in the birth of fifty-eight children. Community members involved in the programme were selected on the basis of a number of characteristics, including intelligence, physical traits and commitment to Noyes's vision.[37] The children born from the programme were studied and judged to be superior in physique and intellect.

Eugenic ideology seems to have flourished in the USA at the beginning of the twentieth century. It was even supported by a significant number of Christians, including Protestant clergymen, who, because of their religious convictions, believed they had a responsibility to encourage what they considered to be a superior form of humanity. For example, about 200 Protestant pastors refused to marry couples who lacked a medical certificate proving that they were both mentally and physically healthy, with many more accepting the policy as desirable even though they would not implement its rigours.[38] Even on the state level, some thirty US states

---

34 Ibid.

35 A. Farmer, *By Their Fruits: Eugenics, Population Control, and the Abortion Campaign* (Washington, D.C.: Catholic University of America Press, 2008), pp. 150–151.

36 M. L. Carden, *Oneida: Utopian Community to Modern Corporation* (Syracuse: Syracuse University Press, 1998), p. 61.

37 Ibid., p. 63.

38 For a discussion relating to the interaction of Christian beliefs and eugenics, see G. J. Baker, 'Evolution, Eugenics and Christian Mission; Health and Welfare in Transition: London and New York, c.1865–1940', *Wellcome History* 40 (2009), pp. 12–13. See also C. Rosen, *Preaching Eugenics: Religious Leaders and the American Eugenics Movement* (Oxford: Oxford University Press, 2004).

had enacted eugenic marriage laws, by 2014, restricting certain kinds of people, such as those deemed 'epileptic, imbecile or feeble-minded' from marrying or by declaring their union invalid.[39] But on the national federal stage eugenic concerns also emerged as a topic for debate. Theodore Roosevelt (1858–1919), president of the USA from 1901 to 1909, wrote in 1913:

> I wish very much that the wrong people could be prevented entirely from breeding; and when the evil nature of these people is sufficiently flagrant, this should be done. Criminals should be sterilized and feeble-minded persons forbidden to leave offspring behind them . . . The emphasis should be laid on getting desirable people to breed.[40]

As a result, eugenic regulations were implemented though legislation, such as a 1917 government statute excluding from immigration to the USA 'all idiots, imbeciles, feebleminded persons, epileptics, [and] insane persons'.[41] This was then developed with the US Congress passing the *Immigration Restriction Act 1924*, which sought to reduce the number of undesirable immigrants to the USA by 15 per cent compared to previous years. In an attempt to maintain clear genetic heritage, the Act also strengthened existing laws prohibiting the mixing of race. Senator Ellison DuRant Smith (1864–1944) of South Carolina said during the discussions on this Immigration Act in 1924:

> Thank God we have in America perhaps the largest percentage of any country in the world of the pure, unadulterated Anglo-Saxon stock; certainly the greatest of any nation in the Nordic breed. It is for the preservation of that splendid stock that has characterized us that I would make this not an asylum for the oppressed of all countries, but a country to assimilate and perfect that splendid type

39 Black, *War Against the Weak*, p. 146; D. J. Kevles, *In the Name of Eugenics* (Cambridge, Mass.: Harvard University Press, 1995), pp. 99–100.

40 T. Roosevelt, *Outlook* (3 January 1914); quoted in E. A. Carlson, 'The Eugenic World of Charles B. Davenport', in J. A. Witkowski and J. R. Inglis (eds), *Davenport's Dream: 21st Century Reflections on Heredity and Eugenics* (Cold Spring Harbor: Cold Spring Harbor Laboratory Press, 2008), pp. 59–76 (p. 59).

41 Black, *War Against the Weak*, p. 188.

of manhood that has made America the foremost Nation in her progress and in her power, and yet the youngest of all the nations.[42]

Overall, eugenic policies continued to affect many American citizens, though this happened primarily through measures such as forced sterilization programmes.[43] The 1907 *Compulsory Sterilization Law* of Indiana was the first to be enacted, though the public was generally unaware of this initiative.[44] According to this law, every institution that housed 'confirmed criminals, idiots, rapists and imbeciles' could authorize medical personnel 'to perform such operations for the prevention of procreation'.[45] This legislation was then replicated by other states to such an extent that by 1927 an estimated twenty-four states had enacted forced sterilization laws. By 1940 more than 35,000 men and women had been castrated or sterilized in the USA.[46] American sterilization policies and practices continued with little opposition until the 1970s. Indeed, it was only after the beginning of the twenty-first century that their abusive nature was generally recognized in the USA.[47]

Finally, it is worth noting that American influence on international eugenic policies was significant. In fact, the Nazi government in Germany often looked to the USA for evidence of favourable results of sterilization policies, which were portrayed as being both feasible and humane.[48]

---

42 Speech by Ellison DuRant Smith, 9 April 1924, *Congressional Record, 68th Congress, 1st Session, 1924* (Washington, D.C.: Government Printing Office, 1924), 65, 5961–5962.

43 By 1940 35,878 men and women had been sterilized and castrated in the USA; see Black, *War Against the Weak*, p. 123.

44 Ibid., p. 67.

45 State of Indiana, *Acts 1907 – Laws of the State of Indiana, Passed at the Sixty-Fifth Regular Session of the General Assembly* (Indianapolis: William B. Burford, 1907), pp. 377–378.

46 Black, *War Against the Weak*, p. 123.

47 J. Schoen, 'From the Footnotes to the Headlines: Sterilization Apologies and Their Lessons', *Sexuality Research and Social Policy* 3 (2006), pp. 7–22.

48 D. Kevles, *In the Name of Eugenics: Genetics and the Uses of Human Heredity* (Berkeley: University of California Press, 1985), p. 169; Black, *War Against the Weak*, p. 400.

3
A Christian enquiry into the new eugenics

As already noted, in examining the new selective procedures from a Christian perspective, it is essential to learn from the abusive history of eugenic movements. But knowledge of the past is not sufficient to make wise judgments about twenty-first-century ethical questions. For example, it may be possible to ask whether eugenic selection is wrong in all circumstances or whether it is just the earlier abuse that was unacceptable. In so doing it should also be noted that eugenic proposals have always been seen as controversial because of their association with very sensitive issues such as race, disability and the relative worth or value of individuals and the way they are considered by society.[1] The eugenic movements of the past did not hide their beliefs that some human beings could be considered genetic threats to society and that sterilization and euthanasia could be seen as appropriate. For example, in 1969 Francis Crick in his personal letters expressed his belief that all human beings are not equal:

> As far as I remember I said that the biological evidence was that all men were *not* created equal, and it would not only be difficult to try to do this, but biologically undesirable. As an a[s]ide I said that the evidence for the equality of different races did not really exist. In fact, what little evidence there was suggested racial differences.[2]

Of course, many of these past eugenic programmes are now seen as unacceptable and are rightly condemned as deplorable. Unfortunately,

---

1 D. Kevles, *In the Name of Eugenics: Genetics and the Uses of Human Heredity* (Berkeley: University of California Press, 1985), pp. 300–301.

2 F. Crick, Letter to Lord Snow, 17 April 1969; retrieved 7 February 2020 from <https://profiles.nlm.nih.gov/SC/B/B/C/G/_/scbbcg.pdf> (emphasis original).

however, concerns relating to eugenic procedures are almost exclusively relegated to such historic abuses, with comparisons to existing practices being dismissed as naive and inappropriate. However, such a sense of security in what is perceived as the respectable present is fragile. This is because many of the current selection procedures are uncomfortably similar to those present at the beginning of the twentieth century, though they are no longer compulsory. Even in the Christian context many similarities exist between past and present discussions. For instance, there is already support in the Christian community to make sure that certain kinds of children, such as those who would have short lives of suffering owing to significant disability, are not brought into existence, which is clearly a eugenic position. The American Protestant theologian Ted Peters wrote in 2003:

> The problem with the status quo is that it is filled with human misery, some of which is genetically caused. It is possible for us to envision a better future, a future in which individuals would not have to suffer the consequences of [defective] genes . . . [O]ur ethical vision cannot acquiesce with present reality; it must press on to a still better future and employ human creativity with its accompanying technology to move us in that direction.[3]

Moreover, there is an increasing willingness among some in the Christian community to consider the enhancement of certain genetic traits, which is made all the easier because of the difficulty of distinguishing therapy from enhancement. The argument is that the child's best interests should be the central reason behind eugenic considerations. If it were possible to make sure that only the 'right' kinds of children were brought into existence, and that other ethical Christian concerns, such as those related to the destruction of embryos, were addressed, then many Christians would likely question why some forms of selection should not be supported.

On the other hand, an increasing sense of apprehension concerning current eugenic procedures exists because of the complexity of some of the arguments both supporting and opposing the proposals. But this is

---

[3] T. Peters, *Playing God? Genetic Determinism and Human Freedom*, 2nd edn (New York: Routledge, 2003), p. 150.

not just a concern with the science behind the different procedures. The unease, in a way, recognizes that when society crosses the eugenic line it is in uncharted and dangerous waters and that it would be difficult to return to the safety of present ethical values. It is, therefore, extremely important for Christians to examine and unpack the arguments both in favour of and against the new eugenics from a biblical perspective in order to consider whether the proposed procedures should be welcomed or rejected. In other words, the promise of a better or even perfect world should not be used by Christians to cut ethical corners. As the British Christian writer C. S. Lewis (1898–1963) indicates in *The Screwtape Letters*, first published in 1942, in a fictional dialogue between an old, experienced, demon and a younger one concerning human beings:

> They will not apply themselves steadily to worldly advancement, prudent connections, and the policy of safety first. So inveterate is their appetite for Heaven that our best method, at this stage, of attaching them to earth is to make them believe that earth can be turned into Heaven at some future date by politics or eugenics or 'science' or psychology, or what not.[4]

In this context of an attraction and even temptation towards eugenics, the different positions of the various Christian denominations should also be examined despite the reality that, unfortunately, little has yet been published on the topic. This is especially the case from a Protestant and Orthodox perspective, while Roman Catholic positions require further development.

On this basis the study will begin by discussing the complex concept of the *imago Dei*, the 'image of God', what it means and why it is crucial in developing any understanding of the equal value and worth of all possible future as well as existing human beings. To better understand human procreation the investigation will then continue by examining the manner in which God created humankind. In so doing, a discussion will be developed concerning whether parents should always seek to bring their children into existence in a context of unconditional love and acceptance. A final theme, which has become relevant with the advent of new procedures to edit the genome (the complete genetic make-up) of human

[4] C. S. Lewis, *The Screwtape Letters* (New York: Macmillan, 1976), pp 130–131.

beings, concerns the possibility of accepting germline modifications from a Christian perspective. These would enable genetic positive changes to be passed down from an individual to his or her descendants.

Creation and the image of God

When couples and other individuals seek to bring a child into existence through strategies aimed at affecting in a manner considered positive the genetic heritage of the child, eugenic factors become relevant. But before studying the key ethical challenges in making such choices, it is necessary to examine what individuals are seeking to achieve in having children in the first place. From a Christian perspective this becomes even more significant because of the wonderful concepts of God's creation and the parents' procreation, which will now be explored.

What does 'creating' mean?

For Christians, only God is the creator and he alone can create something out of nothing (*ex nihilo*) and without being subject to an outside agenda. The term *ex nihilo* becomes important for Christians in order to distinguish creation from shaping or forming something out of something else. Genesis 1:1–3, 26–28 states:

> In the beginning God created the heavens and the earth. Now the earth was formless and empty, darkness was over the surface of the deep, and the Spirit of God was hovering over the waters.
>
> And God said, 'Let there be light,' and there was light . . .
>
> Then God said, 'Let us make mankind in our image, in our likeness, so that they may rule over the fish in the sea and the birds in the sky, over the livestock and all the wild animals, and over all the creatures that move along the ground.'
>
> So God created mankind in his own image,
> in the image of God he created them;
> male and female he created them.
>
> God blessed them and said to them, 'Be fruitful and increase in number; fill the earth and subdue it. Rule over the fish in the sea and the birds in the sky and over every living creature that moves on the ground.'

From a theological perspective, God's creation denotes the specific initiation or activity of God that only he can undertake and in which word and act of creation are one (Gen 1:1; Ps. 148:5). Interestingly, it was through God's speech, rather than through painting or sculpting, that creation was brought into existence. This may reflect the fact that spoken words expect a response even though this may be one of silence. Furthermore, God is apparently answering his own questioning when at the end of each day he announces that what he has spoken into existence is good.[5]

The word and act of creation by God of humanity is characterized by the special Hebrew verb *bārā'*, which is also used when God created the universe, to indicate that God's creative works were new, incomparable, good and perfect. Indeed, a comprehensive examination of the use of *bārā'* leads to the conclusion that in nearly all cases[6] it refers to an activity uniquely performed by God and includes both the concept of command and execution[7] as well as (1) the performance of bringing forth and (2) making a new subject or object.[8] Moreover, when God created humankind in this specific manner, it was the only time that he looked back to his image in order to create. Genesis 1:26 states, 'Then God said, "Let us make mankind in our image, in our likeness . . ."'. Therefore, a specific, powerful and intrinsically divine act of creation is found in the creation of human persons, who were the crown of God's divine creative action. When God created humanity, it should also be noted that it was not only the Father who participated in this action but all three persons of the Trinity, unified by the three relationships of love between them. In other words, creation resulted from both (1) the three persons, and (2) the three relationships of love between the persons of the Trinity. At the same time, God creates from the wholeness and exclusivity of his Trinity. He gives of himself completely, as a whole being, and does not share the creation act of his human creatures with any other god or human being – though, as explained later, human beings can procreate. Because of this his human

5 B. Waters, *This Mortal Flesh: Incarnation and Bioethics* (Grand Rapids: Brazos, 2009), p. 170.

6 God is generally the subject of the verb *bārā'*, though in a very few verses in the Old Testament man is also the subject of the verb, such as in Josh. 17:15, 18 and 1 Sam. 2:29, although in these cases *bārā'* is not translated as 'create'.

7 D. Fergusson, *The Cosmos and the Creator: An Introduction to the Theology of Creation* (London: SPCK, 1998), pp. 7–8.

8 T. J. Finley, *Dimensions of the Hebrew Word for 'Create'*, *Bibliotheca Sacra* 148.592 (October–December 1991), pp. 409–423.

creatures reflect and image the wonderful wholeness, love and completeness of the Trinity.

Furthermore, when God created the world and humanity a deep sense of belonging came into being between himself and his human creatures, bonded by a profound reality of love. Even when humankind rebelled against this relationship and was estranged from him through sin, God did not abandon his creation to go and create another and better universe. The mystery and awesome reality of creation belonging to God because he created it can be understood only in its profoundest sense by the events that took place on the cross.[9] This also means that the lives of God's human creatures belong only to him, though they can be seen as stewards and are accountable to him for their manner of life. Human beings are thus expected and trusted to use their lives appropriately, while being restrained by certain limits. They are also expected to recognize their immeasurable and equal-to-one-another value in the eyes of God and of each other. But this can be developed only when studying some of the elements of the image of God, a theme that is central to the value of all human life as well as being the foundation of the equal worth of all persons.

The image of God

Ever since the Christian church came into being, ethical debates have taken place relating to (1) the value and worth of human beings, (2) whether they are equal to one another, and (3) the manner in which they should be considered. In this context it was natural for the early Christian scholars to build on their Jewish roots in seeking to understand the uniqueness and special importance of humankind as arising from their being created in the image of God. Indeed, it is impossible to understand the moral status of human beings from a Christian perspective without also examining this wonderful theme.

Moreover, even though the concept of the image of God is deeply complex, this does not mean that it is unimportant or that it cannot be described, to some degree, when examined from different angles giving various insights into its nature. Some of these may even be more relevant than others in confirming that all persons reflect this image and that they do this in absolutely the same way. This means that it is essential to avoid

[9] C. MacKellar, *The Image of God, Personhood and the Embryo* (London: SCM, 2017).

reducing the image of God only to one standpoint. A more careful perspective is obtained when all these non-competing angles are brought together all at once.

Different aspects of the image of God

Early church theologians and biblical scholars have always been inquisitive about what makes humanity so special in the eyes of God. Many volumes have been prepared discussing the importance and implications of his image being reflected in humanity. But the use of the term 'image' in the Bible together with its origins and development as a word with complex meanings makes any interpretation challenging. This led to numerous interpretations in the Christian tradition of the way human beings reflect the divine image, while also emphasizing the unique character of humanity. For example, some of the most important concepts of the multifaceted image of God have been understood to express the following:

- God created human beings in a unique and very special way;
- human rationality and autonomy;
- humanity's responsibility to rule over and care for creation;
- the relational capacity of human beings, since God is inherently relational;
- the substantive human elements in persons.

To be sure, it is likely that the image of God reflects all these different ideas and many others besides since, as already emphasized, it is a multifaceted concept. This means that all these perspectives should be considered as interdependent as well as reinforcing and supporting each other.

It is also important not just to understand God's image with whatever human traits society believes are essential, such as a capacity to reason or human functions including ruling over creation. Moreover, it is impossible to present an exhaustive definition of the image of God in human beings since the very essence of this image reflects something of God, who is outside humanity's complete understanding. However, it is true to say that the theology of the image of God and personhood has fundamentally shaped the Christian understanding of humanity. It is also accepted that only Jesus Christ, the incarnate Son of God, perfectly reflects the image of God.

The image of God from a biblical perspective

The creation accounts in Genesis cannot be fully appreciated without noting the crucial words of Genesis 1:26–27:

> Then God said, 'Let us make mankind in our image, in our likeness . . .'
>
> So God created mankind in his own image,
> in the image of God he created them;
> male and female he created them.

On this account, if the term 'likeness' is considered to be synonymous with 'image', then 'image' is repeated four times in these two verses.

Interestingly, there are only two other passages in which the image of God is mentioned in Genesis. These are Genesis 5:1–2 and 9:6. Genesis 5:1–2, which is somewhat similar to the passage in Genesis 1, indicates that '[w]hen God created mankind, he made them in the likeness of God. He created them male and female and blessed them. And he named them "Mankind" when they were created'. In Genesis 9:6 the image of God is used to prohibit murder because 'in the image of God has God made mankind'. Outside Genesis the expression is found only rarely but its importance far exceeds its frequency. It has been characterized by the French Protestant theologian Henri Blocher as 'the most concise summary of biblical anthropology',[10] with the Scottish Protestant theologian David Cairns (1904–92) commenting, 'The subject of the image of God in man is really the great subject of the Christian doctrine of man.'[11]

Significantly, two narratives of creation are presented in Genesis; namely, in 1:1 – 2:3 and 2:4 – 3:24. Though these two passages reflect different aspects of God's creation, it is likely that they were both considered as complementary portrayals of the creation account. As such, they not only attest to the history of God's creation but are theological in nature, while presenting the way God is implicated in his creation. These two narratives will now be examined in the order in which they appear in Genesis.

---

[10] H. Blocher, *In the Beginning* (Leicester: Inter-Varsity Press, 1984), p. 79.

[11] D. Cairns, *The Image of God in Man* (London: SCM, 1953), p. 16.

Genesis 1:1 – 2:3

In Genesis 1 God brings creatures into existence in a rising order of importance, ending with human beings created in his image (1:26–27). It is worth observing that in all these stages of creation God simply commands the different beings into existence. It is only when creating human beings that God appears to deliberate within himself the bringing into existence of such beings who reflect his image. This depiction of God's pondering within himself the creation of humanity emphasizes that he is not simply initiating another stage of creation but is doing something completely new and very special. Indeed, because human beings are created by God in his image, in his likeness (Gen. 1:26–27), they are totally different from all the other animals and the rest of creation.

Different views exist about how best to translate the expression in Genesis 1. In the Hebrew there is no conjunction between the terms 'image' and 'likeness'. This means that a proper translation of the expression is 'let us make man in our image, after our likeness'. This contrasts with translations that insert the word 'and' between the two terms, implying that 'image' and 'likeness' reflect two different features. But most scholars now agree that the words for 'image' and 'likeness' express the same meaning in Hebrew, with the expression 'after our likeness' being a similar expression to 'in our image'. Indeed, in the whole of the Bible, including in Genesis, the two Hebrew words appear to be used interchangeably.

Genesis 2:4 – 3:24

The order of creation in Genesis 2:4 – 3:24 is different from that of Genesis 1 in that it begins with man, continuing with plants and animals, and concludes with the woman, who is presented as man's companion. This man is also seen as being brought into existence from the dust of the earth and as having been created in a different way from the rest of creation. Moreover, the manner in which man is created from the earth is highlighted by a play on words, since in Hebrew the word for 'man' (*ʾādām*) sounds like and may be connected to the Hebrew for ground (*ʾădāmâ*). Therefore, human beings are presented as being part of the material, the earth, from which this world is created. Man became a living soul, an animated being (*nepeš* in Hebrew), only when God breathed into the shaped earth the breath of life (*rûaḥ* in Hebrew), which is presented as the origin of all life (see Gen. 1 – 2).

New Testament

The 'image of God' expression is used infrequently in the New Testament to depict what is so special about human beings. It is also employed a number of times to portray the unique status and divine sonship of the incarnate Word of God. In Colossians 1:15 Christ is described as 'the image [*eikōn*] of the invisible God'; in Hebrews 1:3 as 'the exact representation [*charaktēr*] of [God's] being'; and in 2 Corinthians 4:4 as 'the glory of Christ, who is the image of God'.[12]

The expression of the image of God is further used to describe the outcome of salvation, as in Colossians 3:10, where the new identity of Christians is depicted as 'being renewed in knowledge in the image of its Creator'. In this respect, human beings are not seen as the original: they merely reflect an image of God, the real source of this image. In addition, the New Testament addresses the image of God in passages dealing with the restoration of the image, which has been hidden by sin, in the redemptive work of Christ.

The image of God from a historical perspective

What the image of God represents and whether it makes all human beings equal in value to each other has been the source of complex debates throughout the history of theology, with a number of important discussions taking place throughout the centuries.[13] One of the earliest Christian theologians to discuss the image of God was Irenaeus (c. 130 – c. 200), who was born in Asia Minor (now Turkey) and became Bishop of Lyons (now in central France) in the year 177. He was one of the first to make a distinction in Genesis 1:26 between 'image' and 'likeness'. For Irenaeus, God created human beings in the beginning in his image and likeness, but then, through the fall, the likeness of God in all human beings (their original righteousness and supernatural graces that make them godlike) was lost, though the image of God (the natural qualities of human beings, such as their rational and free nature, that make them resemble God) remained.[14] In the early church such a position had a number of other supporters, including the North African Tertullian (c. 160 – c. 225), who

---

[12] Ibid., p. 41.

[13] For a detailed discussion of the different interpretations of the *imago Dei* throughout Christian history, see S. Grenz, *The Social God and the Relational Self: A Trinitarian Theology of the Imago Dei* (Louisville: Westminster John Knox, 2001).

[14] Irenaeus, *Against Heresies* 5.6.1.

believed that God created human beings in his image, which could never be destroyed, but the likeness of God could be lost through sin. It is also thought that Irenaeus believed that the likeness of God (lost at the fall, but which can be regained through redemption) is being restored in Christians.[15]

However, the position, associated with Irenaeus, that the likeness of God was lost through the fall, with the image remaining, is now generally considered inappropriate. Instead, and as already indicated, it is believed 'image' and 'likeness' reflect the same meaning – a position also supported by the medieval Italian theologian Thomas Aquinas (1225–74), though he did accept that the two words could be used in different ways.[16] Aquinas also argued that the image of God is reflected in all human beings (even after the fall) and could be defined as a certain endowment that all human beings possess rather than the ability to express this endowment.[17] For Aquinas, this image was also related to humanity's ability to reason.[18]

The image of God and the Reformation

The distinction, first proposed by Irenaeus, between image and likeness was one that many early Protestant theologians sought to maintain in some form. For example, the German reformer Martin Luther (1483–1546) sought to develop this difference by suggesting that there was a 'public' and 'private' image. He believed that while the public image was present in all human beings, the private image was reflected only in Christians. Luther also argued that fallen humanity retained a 'relic' (a remnant reflection) of the original image of God. He might have done this because he sought to maintain a distinction between a 'given' for all human beings and a 'potential' for those who are redeemed in Christ.

The French theologian John Calvin (1509–64), being influenced by Luther's earlier work, also considered two aspects of the image of God. The first was grounded in the presence before God of all human beings, the originator of the image, and the second was based on the divine purpose for human beings. For Calvin, therefore, there was something that always remained of immense value in a human being, even in the greatest of wretchedness, and this was the image of God. Calvin followed Luther

15 A. A. Hoekema, *Created in God's Image* (Grand Rapids: Eerdmans, 1986), pp. 33–34.

16 Thomas Aquinas, *Summa Theologica* 1.93.9.

17 Hoekema, *Created in God's Image*, p. 37.

18 Aquinas, *Summa Theologica* 1.93.2–6.

in using the notion of a 'relic' that retains the image of God in sinners to highlight the importance of continuing to respect them as persons with special worth and value.[19] For Calvin, moreover, human beings are in the image of God in so far as they reflect back God's glory to him. The picture of a mirror is the principal one in Calvin's mind.[20] But in contrast to a number of church fathers and other medieval theologians, Calvin argued that there was no difference between the likeness and the image of God.[21]

The image of God in contemporary Christianity

In discussing the concept of the image of God, contemporary Christian scholars generally agree that human beings have been created in the image of their creator (Gen. 1:26–27). This means that humanity has special value, though the distinction between the creator and the creature remains. In other words, the image of God found in humankind reflects in some way his own being and nature. These scholars, however, suggest many different aspects of this reflection of God's nature in humankind, which for them is the reason why human beings are so unique and special.

In the following section a study will be attempted to understand the image of God from five of the most relevant perspectives, but because they overlap it will sometimes be impossible to completely separate their positions. These five perspectives will be (1) the concept of creation and (2) the doctrine of the incarnation, as well as (3) substantive, (4) relational and (5) functional aspects of the image of God. Again, it should be stressed that this study is not exhaustive. There are certainly other ways of understanding the *imago Dei* in human beings.

The image of God and creation

One of the aspects of the image of God that has probably been most overlooked in theology is the notion that this image can be transmitted through the very act of creation itself. This is important because it expresses the reality that it was God who created humanity in his image. Had it been some being other than God who had created humanity, then human beings would not have been created in the image of God.[22] This is

---

[19] Cairns, *Image of God in Man*, 2nd edn, p. 146.

[20] T. F. Torrance, *Calvin's Doctrine of Man* (London: Lutterworth, 1949), p. 36.

[21] J. Calvin, *Institutes of the Christian Religion*, ed. J. T. McNeill, tr. Ford Lewis Battles (Philadelphia: Westminster, 1960), 1.15.3.

[22] MacKellar, *Image of God*.

highlighted in that when God created humankind in his image, there was a reflecting back to himself of his image: 'Then God said, "Let us make mankind in our image, in our likeness"' (Gen. 1:26). Specifically, there was something of the image of God in his human creatures because he created them.

This also means that each human person is created from, and equally reflects, both the beautiful unity of all three persons of the Trinity and also the amazing love that binds them in communion. It is also worth noting that God gives of himself completely and equally in love in creating each of his human creatures. In short, it is because (1) God created human beings (2) in a specific manner that they bear without exception his image. In other words, a special kind of God-reflecting divine creative activity takes place in the creation of human beings that brings them all into a special relationship with their creator. In this way the image of God not only defines human beings but also expresses the creative manner in which God made them different from the rest of creation.[23]

This implies that the image of God is equally reflected in all human beings because they are created by God in the same way. Whatever characteristics human beings may have, they are all made as God's counterparts and in his image, in a special similar manner. This is highlighted by the Anglican theologian Christopher Wright, who argues that:

> We should not think of the image of God as an independent 'thing' that we somehow possess. God did not give to human beings the image of God. Rather it is a dimension of our very creation. The expression 'in our image' is adverbial (that is, it describes the way God made us), not adjectival (that is, as if it simply described a quality we possess). The image of God is not so much something we possess, as what we are. To be human is to be the image of God.[24]

By recognizing that each human being is a reflection of who God really is, it is then possible to emphasize how important and equally valuable each person is before God.

---

23 Claus Westermann indicates, 'There can be no question that the text is describing an action, and not the nature of human beings' (C. Westermann, *Genesis 1–11: A Commentary* [London: SPCK, 1984], p. 155).

24 C. J. H. Wright, *Old Testament Ethics for the People of God* (Leicester: Inter-Varsity Press, 2004), p. 119.

How this creation of every human being by God takes place will always remain a mystery. But it does take place and will continue to take place even if the individual is disabled or lives only a short time. Thus, the very definition of a human person is a being who reflects the image of God, an image that is present because it was God who created this individual out of his love. It also means that the wonderful love of God is always present when a new person comes into existence. As the British Protestant physician and bioethicist John Wyatt indicates:

> [I]n Christian thought, the dignity of a human being resides not in what you can do, but in what you are, by creation. Human beings do not need to earn the right to be treated as Godlike beings. Our dignity is *intrinsic*, in the way we have been made.[25]

This means that the image of God expresses a divinely bestowed status that is equal to all and is independent from any functionality or capacity that, as discussed later, is very relevant in discussing a Christian consideration of eugenic selection.

The image of God and the incarnation

The incarnation is central to any understanding of the value and worth of human beings because it has a profound theological meaning for the whole of creation. As already indicated, that 'the Word became flesh' (John 1:14) is not an addition but a confirmation of creation by God: it is his stamp of approval for all he has made. The incarnation affirms the worth and value of the whole of creation while revealing the significance of creation. It forms what the Scottish Protestant theologian Thomas F. Torrance (1913–2007) calls 'the great axis of God's relation with the world of space and time, apart from which our understanding of God and the world can only lose meaning'.[26]

The incarnation is of central importance because it is God's affirmation of his creation. God, the creator, became part of creation. In Christ the divine Word entered this world to redeem and restore what was originally 'very good' and has never ceased to be the object of his love.

---

[25] J. Wyatt, *Matters of Life and Death, Today's Healthcare Dilemmas in the Light of Christian Faith* (Leicester: Inter-Varsity Press, 1998), p. 55 (emphasis original).

[26] T. F. Torrance, *Space, Time and Incarnation* (Oxford: Oxford University Press, 1969), p. 68.

Of course, seeking to understand the incarnation is a challenge but is also fundamental to any reflection relating to humanity and what it means to be a person, while being central in many theological applications such as in gaining insights into the equality in worth and value of all human beings.

The incarnation is also God's affirmation that his human beings are above all other beings in creation. Though all life forms are to be respected, it is because the Word of God took on humanity that human beings have been confirmed as uniquely valued by God. As the 2007 General Assembly Report of the Free Church of Scotland explains, 'God showed the great value of human life by sending his own Son, Jesus, to give us eternal life. The incarnation, life, death, resurrection and ascension of Christ certify for us the worth of human life in God's sight.'[27] In more specific terms, Jesus Christ stands as God's decisive Word on humanity by reflecting human life as God intended it to be.[28]

The image of God and substantive aspects

Unfortunately, substantive aspects of the image of God in humanity are not easy to identify. The *Oxford English Reference Dictionary* definition of 'substantive' reflects 'the essential material forming a thing'.[29] From this perspective, and as already noted, the substance or essential material from which humanity is formed is nothing else than the dust of the earth. As the British Roman Catholic bioethicist David A. Jones and others indicate:

> Often in the Scriptures the forming of the child in the womb is described in ways that echo the formation of Adam from the dust of the earth. This is why Psalm 139 describes the child in the womb as being formed 'in the depths of the earth'. (Ps 139:15)[30]

But the *Oxford English Reference Dictionary* also indicates that the concept of 'substantive' can express the meaning of a 'separate and independent

27 2007 General Assembly Report of the Free Church of Scotland.

28 A. R. Rollinson, 'The Incarnation and the Status of the Human Embryo', MLitt. thesis, Religious Studies Department of Newcastle University, 1994, pp. 216–217.

29 J. Pearsall and B. Trumble (eds), *The Oxford English Reference Dictionary*, 2nd edn (Oxford: Oxford University Press, 1996), p. 1439.

30 D. A. Jones, et al., 'A Theologian's Brief on the Place of the Human Embryo Within the Christian Tradition, and the Theological Principles for Evaluating Its Moral Status', in B. Waters and R. Cole-Turner (eds), *God and the Embryo* (Washington, D.C.: Georgetown University Press, 2003), pp. 190–203 (p. 194).

existence'. In a certain way, therefore, the substantive aspects of humanity may express what is important in the *Homo sapiens* species from the perspective of its physical human nature or substance in whatever manner this may be considered. For example, this may reflect the human body or the human genetic heritage but would, generally, not relate to any human capacities. On the other hand, it may reflect human nature, in its constitution, structure and form. For instance, the Greek philosopher Aristotle (384–322 BC) believed that the substantial form of a human being consists in the essential properties of this being. But a clearer description of these substantive aspects that make human nature so important is difficult to characterize.

Regrettably, this is also the case from a theological perspective, where the substantive aspects of the image of God are hard to define, with different understandings of these aspects developing throughout history. For example, the notion of 'substance' has been considered to mean that a kind of 'mirror image' of God's essential nature may exist in human beings, or that they have a spiritual dimension which reflects that of God. In addition, a substantive understanding of the image of God may suggest that some quality or faculty is uniquely present in human beings, something expressed in their nature. In the past this substance was characterized by humanity's capacity to reason, express free will or have a relationship with God. Characteristics that, to some extent, are necessary to understand the relational and functional aspects of the image of God, which we will now consider.

The image of God and relational aspects

Throughout history the possibility of forming relationships between persons has been one of the most important aspects used in seeking to define both the image of God and what it means to be a person. Relationships between persons are crucial in Christian theology because they enable interactions of love to exist – a love that confers value and meaning on the relationship. This is as true of the love that exists between human beings as it is for the love that exists between God and his human creatures.

From the very beginning of Genesis there is a strong reflection of who God is in the relational character of creation. The statement 'Let us make mankind in our image' (Gen. 1:26) reflects, in some way, the creational relationship in love of a Godhead-in-community – a love existing from all eternity in personal relationship between the persons of the Trinity that expands to his human creatures. Not surprisingly, therefore, each time the image of God is mentioned in Genesis it is always associated with relationships. To be created in the image of God is to be created as a person in a community of relationships with God and with others. For example, in 2002 the International Theological Commission of the Holy See indicated that 'human persons are created in the image of God in order to enjoy personal communion with the Father, Son and Holy Spirit and with one another in them'.[31]

This means that the divine image in human beings has both vertical and horizontal dimensions.[32] The 'vertical image' can be expressed by a relationship in which a dialogue exists, which was initiated by God and enables human beings to become beings-in-partnership with him. But it is also a vertical relationship supported by love. As the American Protestant bioethicist John Kilner says, 'Complete conformation to Christ's image . . . entails not only experiencing God's love but also loving God in return [Rom. 8:28–29].'[33] In other words, one of the most important ways in which the relational aspect of humanity's renewal according to God's image is expressed in Scripture is in terms of loving (*agapē*) relationships with God. This is why Jesus Christ is the perfect reflection of the image of God: he perfectly reflects the love coming from the Father, while returning this love to him. Fallen humanity, on the other hand, only partially reflects the perfect image of God because of sin.

The horizontal aspect of the image expresses the fact that persons are persons-in-community. This originates from the model found in the Trinity, which is a community of persons in which the notions of being a person and relationships are interdependent. This means that Father, Son and Spirit are not only discrete and independent individuals, but persons in relation and persons only through relation.[34] In the Bible this horizontal dimension is best described in Genesis 1:27, where the image of God is clearly expressed in the face-to-face relationship between a man and a woman:

---

31 International Theological Commission, *Communion and Stewardship: Human Persons Created in the Image of God* (Rome: The Vatican, 2002), para. 4.

32 A full exposition of this theme is given in A. I. McFadyen, *The Call to Personhood* (Cambridge: Cambridge University Press, 190).

33 J. F. Kilner, *Dignity and Destiny: Humanity in the Image of God* (Grand Rapids: Eerdmans, 2015), p. 298.

34 McFadyen, *Call to Personhood*, p. 27.

> So God created mankind in his own image,
> in the image of God he created them;
> male and female he created them.

This all means that it is only through a relationship of love with God and with others that the image of God can be understood.

Moreover, a number of contemporary theologians have suggested that the image of God can refer to the notions of both status and standard. They explain that the concept of status reflects what human beings actually are. In other words, the image of God is not something that can ever be lost or taken away from the individual and is not dependent on any function or capacity.[35] This strong concept of status affirms that human beings are the image of God (1 Cor. 11:7). On the other hand, considering the image of God in terms of a standard means looking at what human beings should be as well as how they should live. This standard is what God intends human beings to become through their renewal and transformation (Eph. 4:24; Rom. 8:29). Thus, while all humans have exactly the same status in being created in God's image, giving them their inherent value and equality, the extent to which they measure up to the standard of that image differs among them.[36] As the American Protestant bioethicist Ben Mitchell and others argue:

> The significance of the Fall for the image of God does not rest in any damage done to the image . . . but rather in the fact that those created with the status of God's image no longer measure up to the standard of what God's image should look like – even though they retain the status of being the images of God.[37]

By considering the image of God as both a status and a standard it is also possible to understand these concepts as being unrelated to the effects of sin. This is important, as Mitchell and others again emphasize:

> A common feature of both the image as status and the image as standard is that they are thoroughly positive and uncompromised.

---

[35] C. Gunton, *The Triune Creator: A Historical and Systematic Study* (Grand Rapids: Eerdmans, 1998), p. 204.

[36] C. B. Mitchell, E. D. Pellegrino, J. Bethke Elshtain, J. F. Kilner and S. B. Rae, *Biotechnology and the Human Good* (Washington, D.C.: Georgetown University Press, 2007), p. 70.

[37] Ibid., p. 74.

> Accordingly, theological claims that the image of God is 'tarnished' or 'diminished' after the Fall are biblically inaccurate and therefore misleading. Nowhere does the Bible indicate that either the image as status or the image as standard can be compromised.[38]

As Kilner further explains, 'The dignity of all who are in God's image, humanity's dignity, neither depends on particular human attributes nor diminishes with sin.'[39] Thus, while the image of God may be hidden or no longer be fully reflected because of sin, it is never diminished. This is again very important for understanding the equality in value and worth of every human being.

The image of God and functional aspects

The *Oxford English Reference Dictionary* defines functional as 'serving a function', with the concept of 'function' being characterized as 'an activity proper to a person'.[40] On this basis, functional aspects are expressed through a capacity to do or be something. But because a capacity to do something is often seen as enabling an individual to be something, these two aspects can generally be examined together.

In considering the functional aspects an individual may express in reflecting the image of God, it may be useful to study the different capacities or functionalities seen as important in past Christian discussions. Indeed, ever since the beginning of the Christian church some scholars have proposed that the image of God must express spiritual qualities or capacities such as reason (or intellect), free will and self-consciousness. For instance, one highly influential interpretation of the image of God in the Christian tradition came from the North African theologian Augustine (354–430), who argued that, since God is a Trinity, some derivative trinitarian structure may be found in humankind. He reviews a number of possible suggestions; in particular 'the memory, understanding and will',[41] which enable human beings to reason.

Interestingly, more modern theologians are also attracted to humanity's ability to reason. This includes the German Protestant theologian Walther Eichrodt (1890–1978), who suggested that a human being's likeness to God

---

38 Ibid., pp. 70–71.

39 Kilner, *Dignity and Destiny*, p. 314.

40 Pearsall and Trumble, *Oxford English Reference Dictionary*, p. 561.

41 Augustine, *De Trinitate* 10.12.

is principally 'in his capacity for self-consciousness and self-determination; in short, in those capacities which we are accustomed to regard as typical of personality'.[42] But rationality was not the only human function to be considered, for many other capacities were used to interpret the divine image. For example, the English Protestant theologian John Stott (1921–2011) writes:

> Some think [the image of God] means that human beings are God's representatives, exercising dominion over the rest of creation in his place. Others conclude that God's image alludes to the special relationship that he has established between himself and us. But if we see the expression both in its immediate context in Genesis and in the broader perspective of Scripture, it seems to refer to all those human qualities or capacities that render us unlike the animals and like God.[43]

Stott goes on to enumerate some of these human qualities:

1 Rationality and self-consciousness,
2 A capacity to discern what is moral and having a conscience to do what is perceived to be right,
3 Creativity which reflects a similar capacity in the Creator to make beautiful things,
4 Sociability and the ability to establish authentic relationships of love reflecting the reality that God is love, and
5 Spirituality which makes humanity hunger for God.[44]

All these functional aspects make human beings, in general, unique in being able to decide, create and celebrate their love for God and others. But none of them may be sufficient on their own to characterize the image of God, since they are unable to reflect the more important defining elements of humankind. As the American theologian Noreen Herzfeld explains, 'Identifying a quality or set of qualities as the image of God implies a hierarchy of traits within the human person, a hierarchy that

42 W. Eichrodt, *The Theology of the Old Testament II* (London: SCM, 1961), p. 60.
43 J. Stott, *Through the Bible Through the Year* (Oxford: Lion Hudson, 2006), p. 18.
44 Ibid., p. 18.

has generally been detrimental to the Christian view of the body.'[45] Similarly, the Swiss Protestant theologian Karl Barth (1886–1968) simply calls them 'symptoms of humanity' or, more specifically, observations that can be understood only once one is in possession of the full text.[46]

Some scholars even argue that the emphasis given by many Christian writers on the capacity to reason may in fact reflect only their own preferences as to what is important.[47] Moreover, although the faculties of reason, freedom and discernment are undoubtedly qualities that many human beings can express and may also be considered as manifestations of the divine image, such an image can never be reduced to these characteristics.[48] Indeed, if the image of God was especially related to functional aspects, such as reasoning, it would mean that every human being would reflect the image of God to a different degree. This is one of the dangers of examining only functional characteristics. Because they are all differently expressed in each human being, this may lead some to believe mistakenly that human beings are unequal in value and worth.

The image of God: conclusion

In bringing all these different aspects of the image of God in humankind together, it is possible to agree with the Greek theologian Gregory of Nyssa (AD 335 – c. 395) that it is impossible to determine completely what this image represents since it reflects something in God, who is beyond our understanding. He maintained, 'One of the characteristics of the Godhead is to be in its essence beyond our understanding, and so the image should also express this.'[49]

Moreover, it is possible to conclude that the fall hides but does not destroy the image of God. Kilner explains, 'While the Bible consistently avoids indicating that the image of God is either lost or damaged in human beings – now or in any day – all too many people are learning

45 N. L. Herzfeld, *In Our Image: Artificial Intelligence and the Human Spirit* (Minneapolis: Fortress, 2002), p. 19.

46 K. Barth, *Church Dogmatics* (Edinburgh: T&T Clark, 1957–75), III/ 2, pp. 83–157.

47 G. Wenham, *Genesis Chapters 1-15*, Word Biblical Commentary (Waco: Word, 1987), p. 30.

48 P. Matthews, 'Discerning Persons: How the Early Theology Can Illuminate Contemporary Bioethical Approaches to the Concept of Person', PhD thesis, Saint Mary's University College, 2010, pp. 143, 160.

49 Gregory of Nyssa, ' On the Creation of Man' 2, *Patrologia Graeca* 44, 153D, 156B; retrieved 7 February 2020 from <https://epdf.pub/patrologia-graeca-44-st-gregory-of-nyssa.html>.

today that such loss or damage has occurred.'[50] Adding, 'The result has been an understanding, influential in Protestant circles, that sinful human beings have virtually lost God's image.'[51] For Kilner this is regrettable, since recognizing the full image of God in all human beings (though hidden by sin) provides the greatest defence against any destruction of human persons.[52]

In addition, by considering the central Christian concept of the image of God it is possible to examine how fundamental doctrines such as the creation by God of humanity can be used to confirm the immeasurable as well as absolute equality in value and worth of all human beings. As Wyatt explains, 'our creation in God's image implies . . . a radical equality . . . In the human community, we are surrounded by other reflections of God who are different but fundamentally equal in dignity to ourselves.'[53] This, as will be discussed, is one of the central themes that can be used to frame the discussion relating to a Christian understanding of the new eugenics.

It is also worth noting that human beings do not simply *bear* the image of God: they *are* the image of God. Every human person should be recognized as having a distinctive yet equal moral status (Gen. 9:6). Moreover, the image of God in human beings is not just reflected in their 'earthly' existence but in what Christians will become after death. This is a destiny that is in the presence of Christ filled with the love of Christ and clothed with the righteousness of Christ. As the British Roman Catholic ethicist Pia Matthews concludes, 'The teaching of the image of God in humans then is principally a theological message of creation, relationship and salvation.'[54] Human beings are made in the image of God with the aim that they will accept being his children for ever in love.

Procreation, love and unconditional acceptance

Having examined the central Christian doctrine of God's creation and the significance of the image of God, equally reflected in every person, it

50 Kilner, *Dignity and Destiny*, p. 174.

51 Ibid., p. 164.

52 Ibid., p. 21.

53 J. Wyatt, *Matters of Life and Death: Human Dilemmas in the Light of the Christian Faith*, 2nd edn (Nottingham: Inter-Varsity Press, 2009), p. 61.

54 Matthews, 'Discerning Persons', p. 160.

is now important to examine whether a Christian understanding of procreation may exist.

What does procreation mean?

Procreation is the process by which new human beings are brought into existence by two parents through a loving relationship. As the American Protestant bioethicist Gilbert Meilaender explains, '[I]n distinctively human procreation the child is not simply a product of the will or choice of its progenitor. It is, instead, the internal fruition of an act of marital love.'[55] At the same time, the American physician and bioethicist Leon Kass indicates, 'How does begetting differ from making? In natural procreation, human beings come together, complementarily male and female, to give existence to another being who is formed, exactly as we were.'[56] Moreover, in the word 'procreation' *pro* in Latin means 'on behalf of' or 'for'. Thus, children are not only procreated 'for' the parents but also 'for' the child's sake, since he or she is begotten and endowed with the same moral status as the human procreators. In addition, children are begotten 'for' others so that they can love and be loved by these others.

The traditional use of the term 'procreation' to denote the bringing into existence of children is also based on the reality that it is God who created humanity. Human beings have, therefore, perceived their involvement in bringing forth children in terms of God's overall creation.[57] As already mentioned, in the Christian church it is recognized that God is the creator and Lord of all life. The initiative rests with God and the act of creation originates and finds its fulfilment only within the existence of love in the Holy Trinity, which is poured out through the creation of human beings by God who are, therefore, created from love, to be loved and to love. As Pope John Paul II (1920–2005) said:

> God is love (1 Jn 4:8) and in Himself He lives a mystery of personal loving communion. Creating the human race in His own image and continually keeping it in being, God inscribed in the humanity of

55 G. Meilaender, 'Human Dignity and Public Bioethics', *The New Atlantis* 17 (summer 2007), pp. 33–52; retrieved 2 June 2008 from <www.thenewatlantis.com/publications/human-dignity-and-public-bioethics>.

56 L. R. Kass, 'The Wisdom of Repugnance', *The New Republic* 216.22 (2 June 1997), pp. 17–26 (p. 23).

57 L. R. Kass, *Toward a More Natural Science* (New York: Free, 1985), p. 48.

> man and woman the vocation, and thus the capacity and responsibility, of love and communion. Love is therefore the fundamental and innate vocation of every human being.[58]

Similarly, the British Protestant theologian Colin Gunton (1941–2003) explained, 'God creates freely, out of love, but it is a love which leaves the creature something to be and to do: to live in time, to praise its Creator and to return, perfected, to the one who made it.'[59] Children then can be seen both as the true offspring of their parents and as new human beings created by God. But this participation by the parents in God's creation of both the soul and the body of his human creatures will always remain a mystery.

Furthermore, God always intended men and women to express their love and communion through the act of bringing into existence, with him, a symbol and reality of their union in a child. Though it would have been possible for God to create, from the very beginning, millions of sterile, sexless human persons on earth, he chose to share the nature of his creative love by making it possible for a man and a woman to procreate with him new children. In this way he lets these human parents experience and share some of the wonder of bringing a child into existence with him, giving the human act of procreation incredible dignity and grandeur.

Children should, therefore, be procreated out of, while reflecting, the communion of love between their two human parents while being created out of, while reflecting, the communion of love existing in the Trinity. At the same time, a child should be brought into existence out of the communion of love between all three actors (God, the human father and the human mother) participating in bringing this child into existence while also becoming, for these actors, the collective focus of new relationships of love. The act and gift of procreating then become one of the most wonderful and mysterious expressions of real unifying love. Indeed, procreating a child is one of the most extraordinary and exciting participatory acts that can ever be contemplated by human persons and one that is also the most divine.

---

[58] Pope John Paul II, Apostolic Exhortation *Familiaris Consortio* (1981); retrieved 7 February 2020 from <www.vatican.va/content/john-paul-ii/en/apost_exhortations/documents/hf_jp-ii_exh_19811122_familiaris-consortio.html>.

[59] C. Gunton, *Christ and Creation* (Carlisle: Paternoster, 1992), p. 77.

The very source and origin of procreation should therefore be seen as the love that should exist between the parents in their communion with God. This was re-emphasized by Pope Benedict XVI:

> Human generation can never be reduced to the mere reproduction of a new individual of the human species, as happens with any animal. The arrival of each person in the world is always a new creation. The words of a Psalm recall this with profound wisdom: 'For it was you who created my being; knit me together in my mother's womb . . . my body held no secret from you when I was being fashioned in secret' (Ps 139[138]:13, 15).[60]

The Protestant ethicist Brent Waters further develops this idea by indicating that '[a] child is not the outcome of a reproductive project, but exhibits an unfolding familial love. Thus, a child is not a means of self-fulfilment, but the impetus of an expansive and loving fellowship.'[61]

Procreation is therefore not only an expression of the love that exists in the Trinity and between the parents but generally entails the presence of a relationship of love between the procreators (parents) and the Creator, which, again, expands towards the procreated being. In Christianity, it is also the case that only persons made in the image of God can participate in his creation of another person. Only a person can procreate a person: only images of God can procreate other images of God. Non-persons cannot procreate persons. Again John Paul II develops this Christian understanding of procreation when he wrote:[62]

> A certain sharing by man in God's lordship is also evident in the specific responsibility which he is given for human life as such. It is a responsibility which reaches its highest point in the giving of life through procreation by man and woman in marriage. As the Second

---

60 Address given by Benedict XVI to the Members of the Pontifical Academy for Life on the occasion of the 15th General Assembly, Consistory Hall, Saturday 21 February 2009; retrieved 20 September 2010 from <www.academiavita.org/template.jsp?sez=AssembleaGenerale&pag=2009/rel2009/benxvi/discbenxvi&lang=english>.

61 B. Waters, *Reproductive Technology* (London: Darton, Longman and Todd, 2001), p. 51.

62 John Paul II, *Evangelium Vitae* (1995), paragraph 43; retrieved 3 December 2007 from <www.vatican.va/holy_father/john_paul_ii/encyclicals/documents/hf_jp-ii_enc_25031995_evangelium-vitae_en.html>.

> Vatican Council teaches: 'God himself who said, "It is not good for man to be alone"' (Gen 2:18) and 'who made man from the beginning male and female' (Mt 19:4), wished to share with man a certain special participation in his own creative work. Thus he blessed male and female saying: 'Increase and multiply' (Gen 1:28).[63]
>
> By speaking of 'a certain special participation' of man and woman in the 'creative work' of God, the Council wishes to point out that having a child is an event which is deeply human and full of religious meaning, in so far as it involves both the spouses, who form 'one flesh' (Gen 2:24), and God who makes himself present. As I wrote in my Letter to Families: 'When a new person is born of the conjugal union of the two, he brings with him into the world a particular image and likeness of God himself: the genealogy of the person is inscribed in the very biology of generation. In affirming that the spouses, as parents, cooperate with God the Creator in conceiving and giving birth to a new human being, we are not speaking merely with reference to the laws of biology. Instead, we wish to emphasize that God himself is present in human fatherhood and motherhood quite differently than he is present in all other instances of begetting 'on earth'. Indeed, God alone is the source of that 'image and likeness' which is proper to the human being, as it was received at Creation. Begetting is the continuation of Creation.[64]

It is also important to recognize that it is from his existing love that God creates his human beings, whom he loves through the participation of the love of the parents. American Christian ethicist Paul Ramsey (1913–88) commented on Ephesians 5:

> It is out of His love that God created the entire world of His creatures ... Of course, we cannot see into the mystery of how God's love created the world. No more can we completely subdue the mystery (which is but a reflection of this) contained in the fact that human acts of love are also procreative ... Nevertheless, we

[63] Pastoral Constitution on the Church in the Modern World, *Gaudium et Spes*, 1965, para. 50.

[64] Letter to Families *Gratissimam sane* 9, *Acta apostolicae sedis* 86 (1994), p. 878; cf. Pius XII, Encyclical Letter *Humani Generis, Acta apostolicae sedis* 42 (1950), p. 574.

> procreate new beings like ourselves in the midst of our love for one another, and in this there is a trace of the original mystery by which God created the world because of His love. God created nothing apart from His love and without the divine love was not anything made that was made.[65]

This means that God's love is always behind the creation of a human child and always continues towards this child no matter how healthy or unhealthy, suffering or flourishing and how long or short his or her life may be. There is never a moment in all the existence of any child (from the beginning of his or her life) when he or she is not unconditionally loved by God. In procreation, moreover, parents give of themselves completely to each other but also to the child, just as the persons of the Trinity give of themselves completely to each other and to the child when he or she is created. In this way God always intended parents to share, and recognize a glimpse of, the wonder and celebration of his creation of his human creatures through their ability to procreate their own children. On this basis the bringing into existence of children should always be from a relationship of mutual, exclusive and unconditional love between the parents. This love then 'expands' onto and towards the child and into a new bond of mutual belonging and unconditional love.

Because of this, children want to be reassured that they were unconditionally procreated by their parents while recognizing that they are both the fruit and the representation of the love of the parents – a love that also ties them to their parents. The children may then be overcome with wonder when they realize that they are actually the result and an expression of all the amazing love that exists in God's triunity as well as the love of their parents. This is wonderfully expressed by David when he reflects on his creation by God and his procreation by his parents:

> For you created my inmost being;
>   you knit me together in my mother's womb.
> I praise you because I am fearfully and wonderfully made;
>   your works are wonderful,
>   I know that full well.

---

65 P. Ramsey, *Fabricated Man – The Ethics of Genetic Control* (New Haven: Yale University Press, 1970), p. 38.

> My frame was not hidden from you
> when I was made in the secret place,
> when I was woven together in the depths
> of the earth.
> Your eyes saw my unformed body;
> all the days ordained for me were written
> in your book
> before one of them came to be.
> (Ps. 139:13–16)

Thus, from a Christian perspective what is particularly significant about this 'procreation' – this 'creation for' – is that it is a creation not only 'for' the sake of parents, the sake of the child or the sake of others, but ultimately 'for' the sake of God, the creator of all things. Procreation should, therefore, be an act of love for God in which parents bring a child into existence, whom they, but also God and all his other created human beings on earth and in heaven, can love for all eternity (and not just during this short life on earth). The child becomes, in this way, an expression made flesh of (1) the unconditional love of his or her parents, (2) the unconditional love in the Trinity and (3) the unconditional love between the parents and God.

Why become a parent?

Becoming a parent may seem like one of the most natural things to do in the life of a couple. But when individuals are asked why they want to become parents, the reasons quickly become unclear and complex, even for Christians. For example, the American Protestant theologian Stanley Hauerwas wrote:

> [T]he question to begin with is why anyone should want to have children in the first place. We assume that such a desire is not arbitrary but based on our most profound moral convictions. Yet it has been my experience that when you ask people why they want children they usually become surprisingly inarticulate. They say it is fun (obviously these have never had children), that it is a manifestation of their love (but then what do you do with your children if the love fades), or it is to please the grandparents or to prevent the couple from being lonely (again less than good reasons, since then the child is being used for some purpose other than him – or

herself), or that children are our hope for the future (and then they always disappoint us).[66]

In other words, though an enumeration of several reasons may be suggested by hopeful parents for wanting children, the deep urge for childbearing can remain hidden. Even more surprisingly, the reasons why parents may want to have children have not been extensively investigated in academia.[67] It is important, therefore, to consider this question carefully before any attempt is made to understand reproductive eugenic selection.

To begin with, it may be useful to remember that one of the strongest urges faced by all societies is to '[b]e fruitful and increase in number' (Gen. 1:28), but does this urge relate to some biological trigger in the brains of the couples or persons, or does it satisfy needs they feel children could fulfil?

It has also been suggested that persons choose to have children for either social or personal goals.[68] However, though numerous reasons are often given by hopeful parents for wanting children, the deep urge for childbearing can remain hidden. Even if most parents acknowledge children as something positive to which they aspire, surprisingly some do not have any deeper or well-thought-out explanations. The philosophers David Benatar (from South Africa) and David Archard (from the UK) state, 'Bringing new people into existence raises many important ethical questions and it would thus be preferable if people at least thought about these before deciding to procreate.'[69] There is certainly a lot of confusion in the minds of prospective parents when asked about their reasons for wanting to beget a child, which has spilt over into academic and regulatory circles.

The concept of begetting

The meaning of 'begetting', from a Christian perspective, reflects the secular interpretation of bringing forth someone who is equal in moral

66 S. Hauerwas, *Suffering Presence: Theological Reflections on Medicine, the Mentally Handicapped, and the Church* (Notre Dame: University of Notre Dame Press, 1986), p. 145.

67 T. H. Murray, *The Birth of a Child* (Berkeley: University of California Press, 1996), pp. 1–14; M. Kettner and D. Schafer, 'Identifying Moral Perplexity in Reproductive Medicine: A Discourse Ethics Rationale', *Human Reproduction and Genetic Ethics* 4.1 (1998), pp. 8–17.

68 M. Marshall, 'Why Have Children?', *International Journal of Applied Philosophy* 3.4 (1987), pp. 1–13.

69 D. Benatar and D. Archard, 'Introduction', in D. Archard and D. Benatar (eds), *Procreation & Parenthood* (Oxford: Oxford University Press, 2015), p. 2.

status and nature. For example, though human parents beget children, God did not beget (but created) Adam in Genesis, since God and Adam were of a different nature (one is divine and the other human). John Paul II said that in the begetting of a new human being God remains present in a special way since he is the source of his image and likeness in the new human being through Adam (Gen. 1:26):[70]

> This is what the Bible teaches in direct and eloquent language when it reports the joyful cry of the first woman, 'the mother of all the living' (Gen 3:20). Aware that God has intervened, Eve exclaims: 'I have begotten[71] a man with the help of the Lord' (Gen 4:1). In procreation therefore, through the communication of life from parents to child, God's own image and likeness is transmitted, thanks to the creation of the immortal soul.[72] The beginning of the 'book of the genealogy of Adam' expresses it in this way: 'When God created man, he made him in the likeness of God. Male and female he created them, and he blessed them and called them man when they were created. When Adam had lived a hundred and thirty years, he became the father of a son in his own likeness, after his image, and named him Seth' (Gen 5:1–3). It is precisely in their role as co-workers with God who transmits his image to the new creature that we see the greatness of couples who are ready 'to cooperate with the love of the Creator and the Saviour, who through them will enlarge and enrich his own family day by day'.[73] This is why the [fourth-century] Bishop Amphilochius [of Iconium in modern-day Turkey] extolled 'holy matrimony, chosen and elevated above all other earthly gifts' as 'the begetter of humanity, the creator of images of God'.[74]

---

[70] John Paul II, *Evangelium Vitae* (1995), para. 43; retrieved 3 December 2007 from <www.vatican.va/holy_father/john_paul_ii/encyclicals/documents/hf_jp-ii_enc_25031995_evangelium-vitae_en.html>.

[71] In Hebrew, *qānâ*.

[72] Pius XII, 'Animas enim a Deo immediate creari catholica fides nos retinere iubet', Encyclical Letter *Humani Generis*, *Acta apostolicae sedis* 42 (1950), p. 575.

[73] Second Vatican Ecumenical Council, Pastoral Constitution on the Church in the Modern World *Gaudium et Spes*, 50; cf. John Paul II, Post-Synodal Apostolic Exhortation *Familiaris Consortio*, *Acta apostolicae sedis* 74 (1982), p. 114.

[74] *Homilies* 2.1; Corpus Christianorum: Series graeca (Turnhout: Louvain University Press, 1977–), 3, 39.

What is noteworthy here is that the two words used with respect to the fathering of Seth in the image and likeness of Adam are the same as those used in Genesis 1:26 when God says, 'Let us make mankind in our image, in our likeness . . .'. Moreover, because the author has just reaffirmed the creation of humanity in God's image in Genesis 5:1, using a shortened form of the expression 'in the likeness of God', an emphasis seems to be intended that, as humanity is in God's image, so is Seth in Adam's image (though humanity was not begotten, but created, by God, while Seth was begotten by Adam). This parallel suggests that in the same way that God sent his Son to die on the cross because of the wonderful and immeasurably powerful bonds of love he initiated with his created human beings, a similar and very strong bond exists between Adam and Seth – a bond that nothing can break. Adam will always be Seth's father in the same way that God will always be the father of humanity.[75]

However, the term 'begetting' can also be used in other instances in Christianity to express the special manner in which human parents cooperate with God, the Creator, to bring forth human children reflecting his image. When humans beget a child made in the image of God, that child is therefore never fully under their control. Some contingency remains in taking part in God's creation of this child, who can never be a product designed and controlled by the parents. Gilbert Meilaender further explains:

> In begetting we too give of ourselves and thereby form another who, though other, shares our nature and is equal to us in dignity. If, by contrast, we come to think of the child as a product of our reason and will, we have lost the deepest ground of human equality – and, perhaps as important, have missed the meaning of the human act of love.
>
> A child who is thus begotten, not made, embodies the union of his father and mother. They have not simply reproduced themselves, nor are they merely a cause of which the child is an effect. Rather, the power of their mutual love has given rise to another who, though different from them and equal in dignity to them, manifests in his person the love that unites them. Their love-giving has been life-giving; it is truly procreation. The act of love that

75 Kilner, *Dignity and Destiny*, p. 151.

> overcame their separation and united them in 'one flesh,' that directed them out of themselves and toward each other, creates in the child a still larger community – a sign once again that such self-giving love is by God's blessing creative and fruitful.[76]

Meilaender further indicates:

> In begetting we give rise to one like us, one with whom we share a nature equal in being and dignity. Since we do not transcend the child we have begotten, we do not give it worth and significance any more than we understand ourselves to have been given dignity by our progenitors.[77]

On this account, although children are brought into existence through the one-flesh unity of their parents, children cannot be seen as the parents' possessions. Instead, children and their parents belong together as a family without any consideration of ownership. Children should never be considered, therefore, as objects, instruments or products solely fulfilling the aims of the parents. This is because they are as precious as their parents.

Procreation out of unconditional love and acceptance

Ever since God's creation of human beings, parents have usually unconditionally loved and accepted their children regardless of biological characteristics when they were born. Moreover, whether or not this acceptance demanded a specific effort is unimportant. What is crucial to the present discussion is that human society has flourished while parents have considered their children as inherently valuable, either because they believe they reflect the image of God or for another reason. This is important because it means that eugenic ideology is inherently flawed, since it does not recognize that the concepts of procreation and unconditional acceptance are connected. Thus, with the new selective technologies now being developed, parents are in danger of considering their children as

---

[76] G. Meilaender, *Bioethics: A Primer for Christians*, 3rd edn (Grand Rapids: Eerdmans, 2013), p. 15.

[77] Ibid., p. 20.

possessions that must be assembled to certain quality standards in order to be accepted. In other words, there is now a conditional acceptance of the children which contradicts the reality that when parents procreate a child, they bring forth a person who, like themselves, is worthy of equal acceptance by all the members of human society and by God. Moreover, this acceptance of the child should never be something that needs to be earned, and should be independent of any biological traits.

Before the development of reproductive technologies, future parents were unable to change any of their future child's genetic characteristics. Consequently, if they were dissatisfied with the biological features of their child, the parents did not have any rational cause for regret. This is because they did not have any alternatives, since nothing could have been done to change their child's genetic constitution. A kind of 'natural humility' existed in which parents, in an attitude of uncontrolled openness to the unchosen, unconditionally accepted their child in the way he or she was born.[78] Christian theology indicates that the strongest forms of relationships between persons arise through the existence of self-denying *agapē*-love and unconditional acceptance that, as already noted, should always exist in procreation. As God shows unconditional love and acceptance towards his human creatures because he created them, Christians believe that all children, no matter who they are, should be loved unconditionally by their parents because they procreated them. Both creation by God and procreation by parents express in this way the love behind such actions.

In addition, Christian parents should remember that they not only bring a child into existence 'for this world' but do so for all eternity, so that God and his other children in heaven can have a wonderful relationship with him or her. As Pope Pius XI explained in 1930, 'men are begotten not for the earth and for time, but for Heaven and eternity'.[79] This is often forgotten when parents concentrate too much on 'this world' while seeking to give a child the best quality of life for this earthly existence. Indeed, from this eternal perspective whether or not the child is disabled or has any other characteristic cannot be seen as the most important factor. Thus, in the same way that unconditional love in procreation

[78] Cf. J. Malek, 'Use or Refuse Reproductive Genetic Technologies: Which Would a "Good Parent" Do?', *Bioethics* 27.2 (2013), pp. 59–64; Nuffield Council on Bioethics, *Genetics and Human Behaviour* (London: Nuffield Council on Bioethics, 2002), p. 155.

[79] Pius XI, *Casti Connubii* (1930), para. 69.

should exist between the parents, it is possible to argue that unconditional love should exist by the parents for the child.

It is also important to understand that procreation should always involve two complete and loving persons. It is the whole man, through his whole sperm (representing and imaging his whole embodied being), that unites with the whole woman, through her whole egg (representing and imaging her whole embodied being), to bring forth, through God's creation, a whole new person. In this way procreation takes place between two persons who give totally of themselves to each other (and to the child who may result) in their whole embodied souls and their whole ensouled bodies.

Of course, it should be noted that sperm and egg cells are not living souls, but represent the embodied souls and ensouled bodies of the man and woman from whom they originate.

As the Romanian Orthodox priest Dumitru Stăniloae (1903–93) explains, men and women have in their united seed not only a concentrated determination of their specific bodies, but a representation, as a united whole, of the body of each of them together with their living souls. And their living souls united by the union of their bodies bring forth not only a new body, but also a new living soul that is the work of God.[80]

On this account, when parents procreate, they do so from their exclusive 'whole'[81] as a couple but also from their 'whole' as individual embodied parents and do not involve other parties. The child then knows that he or she is procreated from the loving 'whole' that forms the couple made up from each of his or her parents. This means that only the two parents and their bodies should take part in the procreation of a child and another person's body parts, such as his or her reproductive cells, should never be involved.

That parents should create their children through unconditional love also finds strong support in international law. For example, Article 1 of the UN Universal Declaration of Human Rights states, 'All human beings are born free and equal in dignity and rights. They are endowed with reason and conscience and should act towards one another in a spirit of

---

[80] D. Stăniloae, *Chipul nemuritor al lui Dumnezeu (l'image immortelle de Dieu)*, vol. 1 (Bucharest: Cristal, 1995), p. 45, tr. J. Boboc, *La grande metamorphose; Éléments pour une théo-anthropologie orthodox* (Paris: Cerf, 2014), pp. 450–451.

[81] 'Whole' in this sense means that nothing has been taken out of the being that would result in a loss of its existence. It also relates to the notion of 'oneness'.

brotherhood.' This implies that all human life is to be seen as wonderfully valuable and equal without any exceptions. In other words, all children should be recognized as having inherent value and worth (in the same way as their parents).

But this situation, unfortunately, is slowly changing with some new reproductive procedures. In recent decades an openness to the idea that human life does not have inherent worth has been developing in society.[82] Some now indicate that what makes human life valuable is its quality, not its very existence, and that only human lives that meet specific quality standards are valuable and thus deserving of protection or acceptance.[83] Any human being (especially a foetus or infant who may be a possible future disabled child) who does not meet such requirements then loses any right to unconditional acceptance.[84]

Though many in society may continue to acknowledge the United Nations' principle that '[a]ll human beings are born free and equal in dignity and rights', some advocates of reproductive selection seem to want to add the stipulation 'but some lives are preferred over others', or, as the British author George Orwell (1903–50) put it in his 1945 book *Animal Farm*, all are equal but some are 'more equal than others'.[85] Consequently, many scientists, journalists, social workers and healthcare professionals, together with a number of outspoken ethicists, seem to support eugenic procedures in which one life is seen as being more valuable than another, making conditional selection something to be accepted. In the UK more than 90 per cent of foetuses diagnosed with Down syndrome are already being terminated.[86] Some prospective parents are also prepared to eliminate a foetus who may have a correctable disorder such as a cleft palate. Of course, these so-called eugenic abortions account for only 1 per cent of abortions in the UK, but the numbers indicate that the principle

---

82 E.g. J. Glover, *Causing Death and Saving Lives* (Harmondsworth: Penguin, 1977), pp. 39–59.

83 E.g. see P. Singer, 'Presidential Address: Is the Sanctity of Life Ethic Terminally Ill?', *Bioethics* 9 (1995), pp. 327–343; and H. Kuhse, *The Sanctity-of-Life Doctrine in Medicine: A Critique* (Oxford: Clarendon, 1987).

84 H. Kuhse and P. Singer, 'Individuals, Humans and Persons: The Issue of Moral Status', in H. Kuhse (ed.), *Unsanctifying Human Life: Essays on Ethics* (Oxford: Blackwell, 2002), pp. 188–198.

85 G. Orwell, *Animal Farm* (New York: Penguin, 1951), p. 114.

86 Anonymous, 'Harrison's Parents Chose His Name when He Was a 35-Week Foetus – Then They Were Offered a Termination', *The Telegraph*, 21 May 2006; retrieved 10 August 2011 from <http://tinyurl.com/telegraph-harrison>.

of unconditional acceptance is being undermined. This also means that such selection procedures may result in genocide by stealth of entire communities of persons with certain genetic traits.[87]

In addition, the prospect of setting specific preconditions for the existence of certain children makes it possible for these prerequisites to come between the parents and their child. Although long-term effects of eugenic selection procedures on a society are difficult to predict, the risks arising from such procedures to the parent–child relationship merit further analysis. Moreover, in order to examine all the different aspects relating to the concept of unconditional acceptance, it is important to differentiate those that may be related to the parents and those that may have an effect on the children brought into existence through selection. In this respect, the following review will start by exploring the parents' perspective and the reasons why they might seek to bring into existence a selected child.

The dangers of instrumentalizing the child

As already noted, from a Christian perspective children should be procreated out of the love of the parents for each other so that they can love their child together – a child who reflects the same moral status as them. Moreover, Christians and civilized society have always asserted that a child is neither an asset, a product with monetary value, nor an object. Unfortunately, however, the new eugenic procedures being developed may well be damaging to this general view. This is because, in some cases, selection procedures may enable future parents to begin to consider their children as products or instruments to satisfy their own desires and aspirations. Children may become the mere means to their parents' ends. Accordingly, such selection procedures may change society into one in which parents bring a particular kind of child into existence only to fulfil their preferences. Parents who invest significant financial and social capital into bringing a certain kind of child into existence may be more likely to consider him or her as a product or a means to achieve their own aspirations. They may even see the child as a kind of reward for their investment in time and money in bringing a healthy child into existence.

---

[87] N. Agar, *Liberal Eugenics, in Defence of Human Enhancement* (Oxford: Blackwell, 2004), p. 149.

Thus, it is possible to ask whether any use of selection procedures will encourage the 'instrumentalization' of the future child. In other words, whether such procedures could support the position that children are valuable only if they bring enjoyment to their parents. For example, when the two members of a couple choose one embryo instead of another in order to make sure that they have a girl instead of a boy, accusations of instrumentalization may be justifiable.

A 2010 case in Canada exemplified the concerns about the relationship between selection procedures and the instrumentalization of children. In this instance a couple had asked a surrogate to gestate their embryo, since the commissioning woman could not do so herself. However, when the couple eventually discovered that the foetus was likely to be affected with Down syndrome, they then requested the surrogate to undergo an abortion, resulting in significant distress in the gestating woman. In examining the case, Canadian bioethicist Françoise Baylis noted, 'The child is seen by the commissioning parents as a product, and in this case a substandard product because of a genetic condition.'[88] However, as already argued, this is an extremely distressing perspective, since a child should never be reduced to being seen as just an object. This is because a child always has an inherent value and worth equal to that of any other person.

In a similar way, selection procedures are likely to impose stereotypical expectations on a child who could turn out to be very different from the one who was planned. This may make it more difficult for parents to accept their child unconditionally. In other words, any intentional selection procedure of the prospective child's biological traits may reflect instrumentalization elements because prospective parents recognize that *they* would prefer some characteristic to others. That is to say, the way the parents seek to fulfil their own wishes through the child becomes important. The child is not unconditionally accepted as a human person with inherent worth, regardless of his or her characteristics. The concept of *conditional parenthood*, whereby individuals decide to be parents only if their child fulfils certain biological criteria, may then represent a significant misunderstanding of what it means to be a loving parent.

---

[88] T. Blackwell, 'Couple Urged Surrogate to Abort Fetus Due to Defect', *National Post*, 6 October 2010; retrieved 11 August 2011 from <http://tinyurl.com/NationalPost-Surrogate>.

The importance of unconditional love and acceptance by parents

So far in human history parents have usually loved and unconditionally accepted their child whatever his or her positive or negative biological traits. But with eugenic selection, parents will be able to choose what kinds of children they want based on a number of biological characteristics. This means that the concept of 'an acceptable child' becomes relevant, and the various possible aspects of what is considered 'acceptable' may have complex but profound consequences for the parent–child relationship. The way parents subsequently consider their children may then slowly change from one of unconditional acceptance to one of critical scrutiny.

On this account, as never before, future parents may bring their child into existence with the critical eye of a consumer, making sure that stringent expectations have been met. The compassionate, caring and loving relationship of unconditional acceptance of a child will then be a thing of the past. This also means that if a selection procedure is shown to be inaccurate and fails to produce the desired traits, parents will face the dilemma of aborting, giving up for adoption or parenting a child they do not want. If the child does not fulfil expectations, parental dissatisfaction and even rejection may then be expressed. Sociologist Barbara Katz Rothman asks pointedly:

> What does it do to motherhood, to women, and to men as fathers too, when we make parental acceptance conditional, pending further testing. We ask the mother and her family to say in essence, 'These are my standards. If you meet these standards of acceptability, then you are mine and I will love you and accept you totally. After you pass this [genetic] test.'[89]

Moreover, any disappointment with the biological quality of the child may be even more poignant than if natural conception had taken place. This is because the more reliable a selection process becomes, the greater the parents' distress if they eventually have a child with the 'wrong' characteristics.

---

[89] B. Katz Rothman, 'The Products of Conception: The Social Context of Reproductive Choices', *Journal of Medical Ethics* 11 (1985), pp. 188–192 (p. 190), mentioned in S. B. Rae, *Brave New Families: Biblical Ethics and Reproductive Technologies* (Grand Rapids: Baker, 1996), p. 209.

On this basis, the development of choice, investment and preconditions for the very existence of children raises questions about how parents will relate to the children they bring into existence through selection procedures. As the Argentinian legal ethicist Roberto Andorno argues with respect to a pregnancy:

> The ethical problem arises when, in order to obtain the birth of a healthy child, certain necessary 'quality' criteria are determined which the fetus must fulfill in order to have the right to be born, indeed this presupposes that children are no longer desired *for their own sake.*[90]

For instance, if a child was selected because of his or her health but then became injured after an imprudent accident he or she could have avoided, the parents might justifiably be angry about the child's recklessness. This is because the parents might have invested both financially and emotionally in the child's health. In order to continue to accept the child for who he or she is, the parents would have to withhold their anger (and distress) without communicating any disappointment to their son or daughter. They would also have to find new reasons for accepting the child or risk rejecting him or her because of the injury. However, with the shortcomings of human nature, it is doubtful the parents would be able to hide their disappointment from the child. As a result, the child might internalize the parents' distress and begin to believe that they no longer love and unconditionally accept him or her for who he or she has become. As in many other circumstances where no parental unconditional acceptance exists, the child might then find it difficult to accept himself or herself and, eventually, express unconditional love and acceptance to others, thereby perpetuating the predicament.

To be sure, there is no reason to believe that parents would withdraw their unconditional love and acceptance from their child even if he or she no longer reflects what they selected him or her to be. In the same way, parents may continue to accept unconditionally a child who does not express the traits they selected. However, when parents require certain

90 R. Andorno, 'Fondements philosophiques et culturels de l'eugénisme sélectif', in J. Laffitte and I. Carrasco de Paula (eds), *La génétique, au risque de l'eugénisme?* (Paris: Edifa-Mame, 2010), p. 130 (tr. C. MacKellar; emphasis original).

conditions to be met before a child is brought into existence, it may then be difficult for them to love and accept this child unconditionally. Indeed, any parent who agrees to the investment of selection already reflects a predisposition towards conditionality. Willingness to select on the basis of certain characteristics may suggest an equal readiness to practise conditional acceptance.

But of course, the mere possibility of parental disappointment may not, in itself, represent an ethical argument against the selection procedures under discussion. Any decision to select cannot be ethically suspicious just because it may generate disappointment in the parents. However, when eugenic selection has taken place, the parents' disappointment may well express itself in a dissatisfaction with the child, resulting in a possible rejection of the child for who he or she is.

Moreover, from a Christian standpoint, and as already explained, the very act of procreating a child in *agapē*-love means that no conditions should be present, since *agapē*-love by its nature can never be conditional. This implies that no eugenic selection can ever be accepted since each procedure is dependent on certain conditions being fulfilled in the possible future child.

On the other hand, accepting a child unconditionally may also reflect a wish not to control or determine the way he or she should exist. As Pope Francis explained in 2016:

> Scientific advances today allow us to know beforehand what colour a child's hair will be or what illnesses they may one day suffer, because all the somatic traits of the person are written in his or her genetic code already in the embryonic stage.
>
> Yet only the Father, the Creator, fully knows the child; he alone knows his or her deepest identity and worth.
>
> Expectant mothers need to ask God for the wisdom fully to know their children and to accept them as they are ... It is important for that child to feel wanted. He or she is not an accessory or a solution to some personal need. A child is a human being of immense worth and may never be used for one's own benefit. So it matters little ... whether it has features that please you, or whether it fits into your plans and aspirations. For ... [e]ach one is unique and irreplaceable ...
>
> We love our children because they are children, not because they are beautiful, or look or think as we do, or embody our dreams. We

> love them because they are children . . . The love of parents is the means by which God our Father shows his own love. He awaits the birth of each child, accepts that child unconditionally, and welcomes him or her freely.[91]

Thus, parents who bring a child into existence without the use of selection procedures may already be indicating by this that they will follow God's example and accept this child unconditionally. At the same time, the possibility of regret for the child's very existence is much reduced since he or she will simply be seen as the consequence of God's providence. Such children may then find it easier to believe they have a common right to exist.

How should parents decide to have a child?

As already noted, most parents generally have different reasons for wanting a child, such as the companionship a child may provide in a family and/or for God to love the child. Others may have a number of reasons for not wanting a child, including because they believe they already have the right family size. Of course, such reasons may be completely acceptable. But other motives may be less legitimate, such as when parents aim to exploit or abuse their child in some way. In a similar manner, parents have many reasons for deciding not to have a child, including both ethical and unethical ones.

Generally, however, there are two stages in the decision process of parents. First, they must decide whether or not they actually want a child; and if they do, whether or not they want to select the child's traits. At each of these stages complex eugenic considerations may be involved, so it is important that they are examined successively in order to explain the decision-making process.

Deciding to have a child

To begin with, the couple need to decide whether or not they want a child. In this regard, some secular commentators believe that a couple's decision to have a child cannot only be out of interest for the child, since when the decision is made, no child yet exists. They argue that the only reason why a

91 Pope Francis, 'Post-Synodal Apostolic Exhortation: Amoris laetitia (English: The Joy of Love)', 19 March 2016, para. 170; retrieved 18 February 2020 from <https://w2.vatican.va/content/dam/francesco/pdf/apost_exhortations/documents/papa-francesco_esortazione-ap_20160319_amoris-laetitia_en.pdf>.

couple decide to bring a child into existence is that he or she is considered a means to furthering the parents' interests, whatever these may be.[92] But this perspective may represent only a limited understanding of the situation, especially from a Christian perspective. As already noted, children are not only procreated 'for' the parents but also 'for' the child's, others' and God's sakes. The very existence of the child can then be considered as something wonderfully meaningful and positive, in itself, something to be welcomed and celebrated even though it cannot, of course, be compared to non-existence. This means that it is impossible to state that a child should not exist because he or she is affected by some biological trait. Moreover, it is not feasible to compare a life associated with suffering with non-existence, since such a statement does not mean anything that can be understood in any reasonable manner. As the American philosopher Joel Feinberg (1926–2004) explains, 'to be harmed is to be put in a worse condition than one would otherwise be in (to be made "worse off"), but if the negligent act had not occurred . . . [the child] would not have existed at all'.[93]

The problem of non-existence is relevant because it is philosophically impossible to compare non-existence to existence, no matter how much this existence may be pleasurable or difficult. Indeed, non-existence is neither good nor bad nor neutral to anyone, since good and bad can only be ascribed to individuals who can be identified. Thus, no rational comparison is ever possible between a person who already exists and a possible future person who does not. As a result, a parent can never harm a child merely by bringing him or her into existence even if the parents were aware that the child would have a serious genetic disorder.

In contrast, however, the *initial reasons* for bringing a child into existence and the manner in which this is undertaken can be evaluated from an ethical perspective. For example, it may be seen as irresponsible and immoral for parents to bring a child into existence if they have no intention of caring for him or her. In addition, once the child does exist, his or her future life may be considered in a positive or negative light. For instance, the child may encounter significant abuse or exploitation. But the mere act of bringing a child into existence cannot be

---

92 D. S. Davids, 'Genetic Dilemmas and the Child's Right to an Open Future', *Hastings Center Report* 27.2 (1997), pp. 7–15.

93 J. Feinberg, *The Moral Limits of the Criminal Law*, vol. 1: *Harm to Others* (Oxford: Oxford University Press, 1984), p. 102.

criticized or condemned. This means that it is impossible ever to argue that a possible future child should not have been brought into existence. As soon as a human life exists, regardless of his or her biological characteristics and the amount of pleasure or suffering he or she may experience, that life should always be welcomed by society and be recognized as having the same inherent value and worth as any other human person.

Non-identity dilemma. As already argued, as soon as a person exists, even with a serious disorder, that life cannot be seen as being wronged in any way because of its mere existence, since the wrong could have been avoided only by also preventing the very existence of the person.[94] Indeed, the bringing into existence of a child without the disorder would be a completely different child with an entirely different life. As the British philosopher Jonathan Glover observes:

> The claim under consideration is that to be brought into existence with an extremely severe disability may not be in the best interest of a child. This entails a general problem of comparing existence with nonexistence. When medical techniques determine that some people rather than others come into existence, can those people be said to be better or worse off for the intervention?[95]

Another British philosopher, Derek Parfit (1942–2017), explains this argument with the example of a woman who decides to postpone coming off the contraceptive pill. She is informed that if she stops taking the pill and conceives immediately, her child will have a disorder. On the other hand, if she waits another three months to conceive, the causes of the disorder in the child will have vanished and she can have a child without disability.[96] Parfit indicates, 'It seems clear that it would be wrong for this . . . woman, by not waiting, to deliberately have a handicapped rather than a normal child.' However, he then begins to query his statement, since waiting three months would bring into existence a totally different

94 D. Parfit, *Reasons and Persons* (Oxford: Oxford University Press, 1986), pp. 351–380.

95 J. Glover, 'Future People: Disability, and Screening', in J. Harris (ed.), *Bioethics* (Oxford: Oxford University Press, 2001), pp. 429–444 (p. 439).

96 It should be noted that in this example the genetic heritage of the child is not affected. However, the dilemma of the woman may be similar to cases where a genetic disorder may affect a possible future child.

child from the one who would have been born had she not waited. In this way, it is a choice between two completely different possible children, which reflects what is called the 'non-identity' concept. The first child would have been born with a disorder and the second one, who would have been entirely different from the first, would have been born without a disorder. But in both cases the disabled and non-disabled children come into existence with their own specific bodies, which are intrinsically part of who they are in reflecting their particular identities.[97]

Thus, the non-identity dilemma is a philosophical puzzle which recognizes that had the child not been born with the disability, he or she would not have existed. Instead, a very different child, with a different identity to the one affected by the disability, would have been born. It would have been a different child with another life and existence. This also means that bringing a child into existence with a disorder (in other words: from the very beginning) means that this child's very existence is related to the disorder. Moreover, in the previous scenario of the woman deciding when to have a child, it is worth noting that the woman's dilemma is entirely different from deciding whether to treat a disorder in an already existing child – something she should always be prepared to do. There is thus an important difference here (which will be developed below) between preventing a future person with a disability from existing and seeking to treat a person who exists with the same disability.

In addition, it is worth emphasizing that if every existing individual is valued by society in exactly the same way as any other individual, independently of whether he or she is disabled, then the value and worth of the two possible future children, who might be born three months apart, are completely the same. In other words, it does not depend on whether they are affected by a disorder and how much pleasure or suffering they will experience throughout their lives. This means that there is no reason, based on the inherent value of life, to select between a disabled and a non-disabled possible future child, because both are exactly equal in worth.

Nonetheless, the British ethicist Stephen Wilkinson, among others, resists making this conclusion by suggesting that the message 'It would be better if you did not exist' may be acceptable. Accordingly, he believes that

---

[97] D. Parfit, 'Rights, Interests and Possible People', in S. Gorovitz, A. L. Jameton, R. Macklin, J. M. O'Connor, E. V. Perrin, B. P. St. Clair and S. Sherwin (eds), *Moral Problems in Medicine* (Englewood Cliffs: Prentice Hall, 1976), pp. 369–375.

'selecting higher over lower probable future welfare is permissible and rational (other things being equal)'.[98] Similarly, the American bioethicist Dan Brock indicates:

> Individuals are morally required not to let any possible child . . . for whose welfare they are responsible experience serious suffering or limited opportunity if they can act so that, without imposing substantial burdens or costs on themselves or others, any alternative possible child . . . for whose welfare they would be responsible will not experience serious suffering or limited opportunity.[99]

Both these arguments imply that it is ethically preferable for a healthy and happy child to be brought into existence rather than one who is not healthy and happy. But again, if it is believed that all individuals are absolutely equal in worth and value, there is no basis to select between possible future children or to assert that any life is unworthy of life.

Deciding to have no child

In many cases the decision by individuals not to bring a child into existence has no ethical implications for the new eugenics if they believe that they would be inappropriate parents because of, say, age, finances or limited societal support. In such a situation the decision is not related to any selection *between* possible future children. Had the individuals been able to bring a child into existence they would have been ready to have *any* child – the child's biological characteristics and quality of life would not, as such, be an issue.

But if a couple decide to bring a child into existence but then change their minds solely because of some anxiety relating to the biological quality of the child (while acknowledging that they have the ability to look after him or her), then this could be seen as reflecting eugenic considerations. Such a change of heart could take place in a number of ways, and the following examples may help to explain the similarities between the different situations:

98 S. Wilkinson, *Choosing Tomorrow's Children: The Ethics of Selective Reproduction* (Oxford: Oxford University Press, 2010), p. 175.

99 D. Brock, 'The Non-Identity Problem and Genetic Harms', *Bioethics* 9.3–4 (1995), pp. 269–275 (pp. 272–273).

1 Prospective parents may decide to bring their own child into existence but then give the child up for adoption because of the child's disability.
2 Prospective adoptive parents may decide to adopt a child but then reject the one being proposed by the adoption agency because he or she has a disability.
3 Prospective parents may decide to have their own child but then change their minds because they are informed of the risks that he or she may have a disability.

In each of these scenarios different consequences exist, but the ethical elements are comparable. In each situation an initial decision to welcome a child was made by the couple but was then changed because of considerations based on the biological quality of their prospective child. In this situation every decision not eventually to have a child may be seen as reflecting a eugenic element. To be sure, in the third case it may be impossible for someone other than the couple wanting a child to determine whether their decision not to welcome a child was based on his or her possible disability and the previously mentioned general decision not to have a child. In other words, it would only be the prospective parents, themselves, who would know whether their decision was based on eugenic considerations, such as the biological quality of the child, or on non-eugenic factors, such as their inability to welcome a disabled child.

A comparable situation would exist if prospective parents first agreed to bring a child into existence and then decided (in a later decision) to take certain drugs or implement other measures to affect the biological quality of their possible future child (before conception) that are unconnected to any ability to cope on the part of the future parents. Indeed, this second decision would also be seen as reflecting a eugenic element. It would mean making a choice between what kind of child the prospective parents preferred, based on quality of life considerations, as any child conceived with or without the prior use of drugs would be a completely different child because of the already mentioned non-identity principle. This also means that a decision based on the value and worth of the possible future children would be taken – a decision based on whether one child should exist instead of another because of quality of life preferences.

To be sure, prospective parents have a responsibility to be healthy for their own sakes, which implies making sure they behave in a certain manner such as taking, if required, certain dietary or other supplements or avoiding toxic substances. Future parents who seek to live in a healthy way may then directly influence the health of their prospective child in a positive manner. For example, a woman who stops smoking or takes health supplements before conception may do so as much for herself as for her possible future child. But the fact that different future children may be brought into existence because of her *pre-conceptual* behaviour is a sort of secondary-effect situation to her principal goal (becoming healthier), which she cannot avoid, and is generally seen as ethically acceptable. Similarly, a woman may choose to take folic acid supplements primarily because she wants to be as healthy as possible for when an embryo, *already* created inside her body, implants into her uterus. She would seek to do this to reduce the risk of spina bifida in her *existing* embryonic child in the same way that most mothers would consider any other form of treatment for a prenatal child with a disorder who already exists. However, if a woman behaves in a certain way *before conception* with the specific aim of bringing a certain kind of child into existence (one with a particular biological trait or even a disorder), then this situation would be comparable to the one previously mentioned, where a drug is specifically being taken for selective purposes.

This means that in the previous cases of individuals thinking about bringing a child into existence, they might initially have made a non-eugenic choice to welcome a child but might then have made a second decision that does reflect a eugenic element – a decision grounded in the biological quality or traits of the possible future child.

Certainly, such decisions are understandable and justifiable if the basis of all ethical assessment in society is limited to the avoidance or reduction of suffering. But when a deeper meaning and purpose to life exists, as in the Christian understanding of life, even when suffering is present such decisions become controversial. This is because every human life has an inherent equal worth and value since it reflects the same image of God which is independent of how much happiness or suffering it experiences.

Of course, it may be difficult for individuals, once they have decided to bring a child into existence, then to find ways of having a child without making a choice based on his or her biological quality. For example, should a woman who agreed to bring a child into existence and is aware of the risks of conceiving a child with a disorder because she is temporarily affected by a sickness wait until she is better again? If she wants to steer clear of any eugenic aspects relating to the kinds of individuals who should exist, she should perhaps seek (as far as possible) to avoid making a decision. In other words, she should not try to prefer the possible future disabled child over the possible non-disabled one, or the reverse.

In this regard, it may be difficult not to make any decisions at all since deciding not to choose may also be seen as a choice. It could for example be argued that because all possible future children have the same worth, then deciding to do nothing, with the knowledge that a disabled possible future child will be born, may also be a choice – a choice of having a disabled instead of a healthy child. As the British scientist Kevin Smith and others suggest:

> Every decision that we take may have some impact on future generations and some . . . are likely to have a very profound one. Whereas these decisions may be made for better or worse, we if anything have a duty to make them for better, but we cannot refrain from making them.[100]

In response, however, it should be recognized that if anything is deliberately undertaken, a eugenic choice is being made. Moreover, it is worth emphasizing that the nature of the choices may be different. Choosing between two different possible future persons (a eugenic decision) is entirely different from choosing not to choose (which is not a eugenic decision).

This all means that if all persons are equal in value and worth, it is impossible to decide between them from a Christian and ethical perspective. Put another way, if parents want to avoid any eugenic factors in bringing a child into existence, they should not even think about the possible genetic heritage of their possible future child. They can then just unconditionally love and accept him or her for who he or she is when born with or without a disability. But this also means that parents may need to examine carefully their own ethical value systems as well as how this decision may be received by others before even deciding to have a child. This is important if they do not want to be confronted, afterwards, with a decision that may be considered eugenic in character.

---

100 K. R. Smith, S. Chan and J. Harris, 'Human Germline Genetic Modification: Scientific and Bioethical Perspectives', *Archives of Medical Research* 43.7 (2012), pp. 491–513 (p. 504).

Deciding to have only a certain kind of child

Finally, if certain individuals do indeed believe they would be appropriate parents, while having access to relevant support, and then decide to bring a child into existence while making sure their possible future child has only certain biological characteristics, they clearly have eugenic motives. As already indicated, some may then see such a course of action as a form of discrimination between prospective children.

The child's longing for unconditional love and acceptance

The ethical challenges arising from setting eugenic preconditions in bringing a child into existence can also be considered from the child's perspective. In this regard, it is worth remembering that all children want reassurance that they are unconditionally loved and accepted by their parents. They want to know that their parents see them as important, with inherent value and worth, irrespective of disability or health. They want to know this even if they are considered by society as being genetically weak and not attaining a certain standard of performance. Indeed, if a child becomes aware that he or she is accepted only for a specific reason, and not because he or she merely exists, he or she is likely to experience existential questions a child should never have to face.

In seeking unconditional love and acceptance, children experience similar needs to most adults. All humans, irrespective of age, want to know that their very existence matters. Both children and adults need to know that they have an unconditional place in society and that their lives have inherent worth and value irrespective of having to fulfil any arbitrary criteria. Knowing that one has a right to exist and a rightful place in society is central to a person's flourishing. Moreover, experiencing a sense of belonging to a community is essential to human identity. This is because every human being seeks meaningful relationships with others.

Regrettably, such an experience of belonging is not experienced by many individuals. As a result, a relentless search for acceptance is a common feature of human beings longing for recognition, who may even try to impress their peers in different ways. In this context, if children discover that they were brought into existence only because they fulfilled certain characteristics, they may then question their purpose in life. Such children may even ask whether they have an unconditional place in society. As Andorno says:

> This individual will live with the awareness that he only deserved to be born because he possessed the characteristics that *others wanted, and not because his life had any intrinsic value*. This clearly contradicts the very idea of human dignity, which implies that every individual has an inherent worth as part of humankind and that, as a result, all human beings *have the same worth*.[101]

When individuals are at their weakest and most vulnerable stages of life, such as when they are infants, an affirmation of unconditional love and acceptance is crucial for their psychological well-being and, fortunately, most infants are cared for in a way that expresses this acceptance.

Children are brought into existence for many different reasons. Some children are planned and others are surprises; some are wanted and others are not. But, significantly, it is the children who are not really desired who may ask the most penetrating questions about their identity. In examining the reasons why many adopted individuals eventually search for their birth parents, the social care researchers David Howe and Julia Feast note, 'The experience of adopted people who search for birth relatives follows . . . a story which throws light on not only adopted people's search for identity but on the universal themes of who we are and where we belong.'[102] Howe and Feast also note that the desire to feel 'whole' and 'connected' is unrelated to the adoption's success. However, the question why the concept of identity is so important to adopted persons still needs to be fully explained. They write, 'Issues around identity and the desire to establish a full personal history appear to crop up in most findings, but beyond that the picture remains blurred.'[103] The longing of persons to find a meaning for their identity and their desire for a reason for their very existence is a universal and timeless experience.

In 1817 the English author Mary Shelley (1797–1851), in her classic novel *Frankenstein*, which may be considered a parable of what may happen in the future, developed this search for identity and the reasons persons generally seek to understand why they exist. The book refers to a scientist, Victor Frankenstein, who brings into existence a new living being made from the body parts of human corpses. But this individual

---

[101] Andorno, 'Fondements philosophiques et culturels', pp. 131–132 (emphases original).

[102] D. Howe and J. Feast, *Adoption, Search & Reunion: The Long Term Experience of Adopted Adults* (London: The Children's Society, 2000), p. 11.

[103] Ibid., p. 157.

ends up being more of a monster than a man and Frankenstein eventually regrets what he has achieved in his experiment and runs away in panic. However, the monster (who has no name) hunts him down in pursuit of meaning as well as identity and because he experiences a strong sense of rejection and abandonment. He does not understand why he was brought into existence or why his creator has rejected him. The cry of the monster reveals his anguish: 'My person was hideous and my stature gigantic. What did this mean? Who was I? What was I? Whence did I come? What was my destination? These questions continually recurred, but I was unable to solve them.'[104] Of course, this story is fiction, but the very fact that readers understand the monster's predicament is significant. It raises the question whether similar existential dilemmas are present in individuals who know that they were brought into existence only because they met certain preconditions. The psychological balance, well-being and integrity of children may, in this way, be intimately associated with their knowledge of the reasons for their very existence.

In this respect, an imbalance is also beginning to develop in the parent–child relationship. Until the end of the twentieth century parents did not really have any choice about the kinds of children they could bring into existence and children have never been able to decide what kind of parents they are given. But this is now changing, and parents are now being offered an ever-increasing choice about the kinds of offspring they want, though the children, themselves, will still be unable to decide what kind of parents they are given. In other words, this imbalance in choice that is developing may undermine the unconditional parent–child relationship, which may have significant consequences for the child. Indeed, the mutual unconditional acceptance between the child and the parents may be transformed into one where the parents no longer unconditionally accept the child, whereas the child is expected to continue to accept unconditionally his or her parents.

Though modern human bioethics may not understand the importance of this unconditional acceptance of children, this has long been recognized in other disciplines such as in psychology, which began to highlight the concept in the 1960s.[105] Counsellors and therapists now recognize that

---

104 M. Shelley, *Frankenstein* (London: Penguin, 1994), p. 124.

105 The most robust exposition of the concept occurs throughout C. Rogers, *On Becoming a Person* (Boston: Houghton Mifflin, 1961).

if unconditional love from the parents to the child is not present, this affects the child's overall self-acceptance. This means that if parents set preconditions or do not accept their child for the mere sake of his or her existence, then the child may fail to experience a full and balanced life in which he or she recognizes that he or she has an unconditionally accepted place. The child will always be aware that his or her very life was related to the selection procedure and the associated preconditions, instead of being appreciated for the mere fact of existing. Worse still, the child will be aware that had he or she not satisfied the prerequisites, then he or she would not even have existed. As a result, the child's sense of self-acceptance may be undermined, especially in the challenging years of childhood, including in the transition to maturity. Moreover, since the parents were already prepared to consider preconditions before the child was accepted into existence, further dangers may be present in that their conditional acceptance of the child may continue to characterize the parent–child relationship.[106]

The resulting children may also question the value systems of their parents in (1) the selection process itself and (2) the particular preconditions put into place. When they realize how they were brought into existence, these children may, for example, disagree with the possibility of making selection procedures – they may see them as undermining a relationship of unconditional love and acceptance which should exist with their parents. In addition, if children are selected for certain traits, they may end up very much disliking these traits and preferring others, though they will again be confronted with the non-identity problem. Then again, some may welcome the selected characteristics given to them by their parents, recognizing them as a positive contribution.

It may even be possible for some children to feel especially wanted by virtue of the very fact that they were chosen. For instance, they may feel a sense of value when they realize that they outcompeted all their possible future siblings for the right to be born because of their biological superiority. Though this sense of superiority may, unfortunately, once more lead to a view that certain kinds of persons are less valuable than others. Yet again some children may feel that an injustice was done to them if they were not brought into existence with a genetic heritage that reached an expected standard (but in such a case the non-identity dilemma returns).

---

106 Waters, *This Mortal Flesh*, p. 74.

At this stage it is worth noting that many of those who support selection for positive traits generally have only certain kinds of physical characteristics in mind, such as sporting abilities, good looks or intelligence. There is little mention of enhancing a person's humility, compassion or sense of justice, which some may see as far more important though maybe less dependent on biology.

The Scottish philosopher Alasdair MacIntyre published a short article in 1979 entitled *Seven Traits for the Future*, in which he examined the kinds of traits some parents may choose for their future children. He suggested that positive traits, such as an ability to live with uncertainties, an acceptance of one's mortality and a spirit of hope may be far more relevant and useful than the physical traits generally suggested as desirable. However, MacIntyre also predicted that if commendable moral qualities were ever selected in future children, then '[w]hat we would have done is to design descendants whose virtues would be such that they would be quite unwilling in turn to design *their* descendants' (emphasis in the original). He then concluded that such a selection process should not be contemplated in the first place, '[o]therwise we shall risk producing descendants who will be deeply ungrateful and aghast at the people – ourselves – who brought them into existence'.[107]

Should parents choose to have only healthy children?

The aim of most selection procedures is to ensure that only a healthy child is brought into existence – parents want a guarantee that their child will not be affected by a disability. Some commentators have even suggested that future parents may have a responsibility to avoid bringing children into existence who will be affected by significant suffering or a severely diminished quality of life.[108]

Meaning in life

From this perspective, however, it is important to come back again to the reasons why parents have children and why so many do not want to have

---

107 A. MacIntyre, 'Seven Traits for the Future', *The Hastings Center Report* 9.1 (1979), pp. 5–7 (p. 7).

108 The literature from this perspective is increasingly voluminous. Representatively, see J. Savulescu and G. Kahane, 'The Moral Obligation to Create Children with the Best Chance of the Best Life', *Bioethics* 23.5 (2009), pp. 274–290.

a disabled child. What these parents may be looking for is a good and successful life of meaning and comfort for themselves. The ethical expert on disability Hans Reinders, from the Netherlands, explains, 'Given the modern view of "meaning" as the object of choice and decision it is not surprising that the lives of profoundly disabled people appear to be meaningless in the eyes of those who are committed to this view.'[109] But he then questions this modern perspective, arguing that a disabled life can bring real meaning. Reinders argues that to be able to live with a disabled person and to see this as meaningful, it is important to care about the person. He indicates, 'Without being personally involved, very little meaning can be found. Being engaged in their lives is where it all begins. Whatever meaning can be found will only be found in the contact of that relationship.'[110]

Thus, when a deliberate decision is made relating to the concept of 'meaning' in prospective parents' lives, this may have implications for their wish to have children: they may decide to have a child so that he or she may become a part of the meaningful and successful lives they planned for themselves. But, as Reinders explains, such a plan is unlikely to succeed:

> Children, whether handicapped or not, are not a means to a meaningful life. Not only because it is morally questionable to regard one's children as instrumental to one's happiness, but also because it's rather short-sighted. Parenthood is a bad idea for people who want to be in control of their own lives. The more we tend to regard children as instrumental to fulfilling our expectations in life, the greater the chance that we will fail. The reason is that parenting is one of those activities that can confer meaning upon our lives only if we give ourselves to that activity in a noninstrumental way.[111]

Thus, if children are seen as a means to the parents' own fulfilment of a meaningful life, the birth of a seriously disabled child may cause a significant amount of disappointment and resentment. Such a child may even

[109] H. S. Reinders, *The Future of the Disabled in Liberal Society: An Ethical Analysis* (Notre Dame: University of Notre Dame Press, 2000), p. 203.
[110] Ibid., p. 203.
[111] Ibid., p. 204.

be considered the cause of profound unhappiness and frustration, because he or she may be seen as limiting the parents' ability to control their own lives.[112] The child, in a way, would have ruined the parents' right to successful and meaningful lives.

From this perspective prospective parents who decide to select a healthy child may be prioritizing their own interests. Moreover, selection would not only express what the future parents might consider to be acceptable but would also encourage a revolution of the parents' approach towards parenthood. Children brought into existence as a result of such expectations might come under significant pressure to fulfil their parents' desires and ambitions in order to feel accepted.

The value and worth of a disabled child in the eyes of the parents

When parents decide to avoid bringing into existence a disabled child, the reasons for such a choice generally relate to how parents, or even society, see the consequences of such a life for the child itself, for the child's parents, for other family members or for the whole community. For instance, when parents select one embryo instead of another based solely on genetic traits, this is clearly a value judgment concerning one possible life over another on the basis of predetermined values and perceptions. Thus, from the perspective of the parents or the healthcare professionals who undertake the selection, a possible future child *with* a disability is considered to be less desirable or valuable than a child *without* a disability. As Reinders indicates, when discussing the challenges that parents of mentally disabled children may experience:

> From an objective point of view there are facts about their children that makes these parents regard their lives as burdensome rather than attractive. Presumably, some of these facts are that these children are incapable of living an independent life, they will never be self-supporting, pursue a career of their own, build a family, and so on. From this point of view, the state of their lives is such that the resulting picture does not unambiguously appear attractive.[113]

112 Ibid.
113 Ibid., p. 180.

But at the same time some parents may have happy memories of being with their disabled children and of learning how to live together. Thus, a certain amount of conflict may exist in the parents and their perceptions of their disabled child.[114] Moreover, when rejection and disappointment are replaced with acceptance, the lives of both the parents and the child can move on more positively.[115] Reinders states with respect to the relationship of parents with disabled children, '[T]here are those for whom acceptance marks the change of being able to concentrate upon what is rather than upon what could have been. Only then are they capable of learning to love their child as it is.'[116] Similarly, as one parent of a disabled child recalls:

> You know, I bargained with God. I could handle all this for the next year if he just smiled or if he learned how to walk or talk. A year later he hadn't changed at all. And I remember being hit on this birthday thinking I made this deal and he hasn't changed . . . And I look back at that point and realized that nothing had changed, except that I'd learned to love him for what he is.[117]

For some parents there may also be a moment when they finally give up their dream concerning the child they wanted to have and just get down to the business of accepting and raising the child they have.[118] But in this regard the concept of parental acceptance may be somewhat inappropriate here because this may suggest some kind of resignation or defeat, which is not what many parents with disabled children experience. Instead, a kind of 'embracement' may be a more accurate depiction of what happens, since this does not deny the moments of sadness that may return. 'Embracement' marks a change that enables parents to express their emotions while being open to the possibility of seeing their disabled child as being lovable and wonderful for who he or she is.[119] As Emily

[114] Ibid.

[115] K. I. Scorgie, 'From Devastation to Transformation: Managing Life When a Child Is Disabled', PhD dissertation, University of Alberta, 1996, pp. 104–105; quoted in Reinders, *Future of the Disabled*, pp. 184–185.

[116] Ibid., p. 184.

[117] Ibid., pp. 184–185.

[118] Ibid., p. 185.

[119] Reinders, *Future of the Disabled*, pp. 184–185.

Rapp, the mother of a child dying from the terminal Tay-Sachs disease, movingly writes:

> I would walk through a tunnel of fire if it would save my son. I would take my chances on a stripped battlefield with a sling and a rock à la David and Goliath if it would make a difference. But it won't. I can roar all I want about the unfairness of this ridiculous disease, but the facts remain. What I can do is protect my son from as much pain as possible, and then finally do the hardest thing of all, a thing most parents will thankfully never have to do. I will love him to the end of his life, and then I will let him go.[120]

Of course, every experience is different, and some parents may sincerely regret the very existence of their disabled child. When this has happened, the ensuing suffering for them and their child does not appear to have been compensated for by the very existence and inherent value and worth of their child. Indeed, had they had a choice, such parents would have decided only to bring a non-disabled child into existence.

But this cannot be accepted as an appropriate way forward. Indeed, if a meaningful life for the parents can be considered only from the context of having a healthy child, then questions can be asked concerning their value systems. This is because rejecting possible future children because they do not meet certain standards may contradict the principle of the universal equality of all human beings, which is the basis of civilized society. Moreover, by using selection procedures, future parents may be indicating that they do not accept and appreciate their children just because they exist. On this account, accepting a child only because he or she is healthy is as difficult to support ethically as rejecting a child because he or she is disabled.

The value and worth of a disabled child in the eyes of God

As already noted, in a Christian understanding of procreation, the unconditional and sacrificial love of the parents towards each other and towards God should expand onto the child. This means that every child

120 E. Rapp, 'Notes from a Dragon Mom', *The New York Times*, 15 October 2011. See also the book by A.-D. Julliand, *Deux petits pas sur le sable mouillé* (Paris: Les Arènes, 2011).

brought into existence from this love should, in the same way, be unconditionally loved and accepted by his or her parents. Thus, if certain genetic preconditions are laid down relating to the procreation of a possible future child, thereby excluding persons with certain conditions, this can no longer reflect the Christian basis of unconditional procreative love.

This means that although suffering will always remain a mystery, its avoidance should never be seen as having priority over the inherent as well as equal value and worth of every human life. In this regard, it may be worth emphasizing how positively amazing it would be for a disabled child to learn that his or her parents could have decided to bring into existence a healthy child through selection but chose not to make such a decision because they wanted him or her *just as much*. This means that it is only when parents unconditionally love and accept their children for who they are, as reflecting God's image (and being loved by him), that their children can experience a healthy sense of emotional development and acceptance.

The new eugenics and the equality of all

One of the highly significant concerns relating to new eugenic procedures is their effect on the equality in value and worth of all persons, which is based on the reality that all individuals reflect the same image of God. In other words, that discrimination against certain kinds of persons may arise. John Paul II explains that accepting selective objectives, such as an abortion when a foetus is discovered to have a serious disorder, can be considered '[G]enuine eugenics that leads to a sort of anaesthesia of consciences, gravely wounding, in addition, persons with congenital handicaps and those who accept them.'[121] He adds that such procedures may constitute 'grave assaults against the absolute respect for every life and against the grandeur of every human being, which does not depend on his external aspect or the ties he has with other members of society'.[122]

[121] John Paul II, mentioned in 'Ethics-Free Genetics Is a Threat to Man's Dignity, Pope Warns', *Zenit*, 26 November 2001; retrieved 7 February 2020 from <https://zenit.org/articles/ethics-free-genetics-is-a-threat-to-man-s-dignity-pope-warns>.

[122] Ibid.

But in order to understand this argument based on the risks of discrimination in the context of reproductive eugenics, two different kinds of reproductive rights should first be presented. These are (1) the fundamental rights relating to the possibility of procreating a child, which are usually respected in international law, and (2) the substantive rights that relate to the possibility of intentionally selecting characteristics in a child. Indeed, it is generally accepted that regulations may legitimately restrict substantive reproductive decisions without endangering the more important and legally protected fundamental reproductive rights, which are considered to be negative rights. In other words, a freedom exists for a person to express these rights without any interference by the state. Thus, the freedom to procreate a child is qualitatively different from the freedom to select between possible future children.

In this regard, Stephen Wilkinson defines selective reproduction as 'the attempt to create one possible future child rather than a different possible future child'.[123] In other words, this would be a decision only between different future children. But any selective decision in reproduction is not just a selection against a disorder or for a positive characteristic in a future child: it is making a very real choice between different possible future persons, even if they are sometimes only imaginary and thus do not actually exist when the decision is being made.

Disorders are always embodied

Some of those supporting the new eugenics emphasize that it is important to differentiate between a genetic disorder and the person with the illness. They argue that a disorder may be seen as negative, but that the person affected by the ailment may be considered in a positive way. As a result, they suggest that there is no conflict in making sure a disorder does not come into existence while, at the same time, supporting those affected by this disorder. As Wilkinson says:

> There is nothing wrong with assigning a negative value to the functional impairment aspects of disability and this negative valuation of impairment does not entail and need not be accompanied by any negative valuation of the *person* with the impairment.[124]

123 Wilkinson, *Choosing Tomorrow's Children*, p. 2.
124 Ibid., p. 166 (emphasis original).

Similarly, the British philosopher Baroness Mary Warnock (1924–2019) said in 2018:

> The one thing I do deplore is the attitude of what I think of as the disability lobby who think it's wrong to try and eliminate hereditary diseases because it is suggesting that they are unworthy of life. That is an absolutely terrible argument. The disability lobby is very vocal on this subject and it does form a real obstacle on progress.[125]

But though well intentioned, these arguments are difficult to receive, since making sure that certain disorders are not brought into existence through eugenic deselection really does mean making sure certain persons with these disorders are also not brought into existence. Indeed, it is difficult to affirm that a certain disorder should not come into existence while maintaining that such a statement would not be detrimental to the way persons *born* with the same disorder are perceived. As the American scientist and social commentator Richard Lewontin, who has a Jewish heritage, indicates:

> To conflate . . . the prevention of *disease* with the prevention of *lives* that will involve disease, is to traduce completely the meaning of preventive medicine. It would lead to the grotesque claim that the National Socialists did more to 'prevent' future generations of Tay-Sachs [a lethal genetic disease found most commonly among Jews] sufferers than all the efforts of science to date.[126]

In other words, it is crucial not just to equate a person with a disorder. For example, it is important to note that a person has haemophilia or diabetes instead of just reducing this person to being a 'haemophiliac' or 'diabetic'. Indeed, it is impossible (1) for disorders to exist on their own without being embodied in persons, and (2) for persons just to be considered as disorders. Thus, a person is never just a disorder that should not exist.

---

125 M. Warnock, *BioNews* 947 (30 April 2018); retrieved 7 February 2020 from <www.bionews.org.uk/page_135644>.

126 R. C. Lewontin, 'Science & "The Demon-Haunted World": An Exchange', *New York Review of Books*, 6 March 1997, pp. 51–52; quoted in A. Buchanan, D. W. Brock, N. Daniels and D. Wikler, *From Chance to Choice: Genetics and Justice* (Cambridge: Cambridge University Press, 2000), p. 46 (emphases original).

Personal identity factors

Interestingly, individuals who are *brought into existence* with a disorder (as opposed to those who are afflicted later in life) may recognize that their disability is part of their very identity and who they are as persons, since the disorder correlates to their origin of existence. This implies that any suggestion of eliminating hereditary disease does not consider the intimate relationship between a person's identity, the origins of his or her existence and his or her disorder.[127] For example, the Chief Executive of the UK Cystic Fibrosis Trust indicated in 2003 that information relating to prenatal tests among families at risk of bringing into existence children with this serious disorder was difficult to obtain. She indicated that this was because 'Families obviously feel that a child already born affected by Cystic Fibrosis may feel unwanted if they know their parents have made a decision of this nature in relation to a subsequent pregnancy'.[128] On the other hand, the German Ethics Council stated in 2012:

> Parents with a genetic risk who already have a child with a disability . . . cannot be accused, if they express a wish that their second child may not have a disability, that they wish to reject or humiliate the first child. It is argued that prenatal practice and postnatal reality must be distinguished in principle.[129]

Some scholars, moreover, suggest that prohibiting eugenic selection because of a possible discriminatory risk towards persons affected by a disorder who already exist is a weak argument. They argue that if it were discriminatory to seek to prevent disability, then it would be discriminatory to seek to cure disability (such as blindness or deafness) in persons who already exist, which is something that most in society welcome. They suggest that it would be comparable to preventing children at risk of being affected by Polio from being vaccinated to prevent

127 Stephen Wilkinson also notes (unpublished paper) that though it is possible to harm someone who already exists by afflicting him or her with a disorder, it is impossible to harm someone who is brought into existence with a disorder since without the disorder he or she would not have existed. Someone else would have existed instead.

128 R. Barnes (Chief Executive: Cystic Fibrosis Trust), *Letter to the Scottish Council on Human Bioethics*, 22 July 2003.

129 German Ethics Council, *Preimplantation Genetic Diagnosis: Opinion* (Berlin: German Ethics Council, 2012), p. 60.

paralysis just because existing adults, who already have a dysfunctional limb from a previous infection, may feel discriminated against and undervalued.[130]

But this argument does not take into account the reality that persons brought into existence, *from the very beginning*, with a specific trait or a disorder may consider this condition an existential part of their very identity. As one parent of a disabled child, David, indicated:

> Any artificial attempt to split my child from his disability is dishonest, dissociatively psychotic, or without any knowledge of my child. It is like saying, 'I like your child; its just his body, mind, and spirit that I don't like.' David's disability is global. It is part of him just as much as his species or gender. It affects every aspect of his existence. It is not like a pair of shoes that he can take off. Without it, he would be a total stranger to me.[131]

It is worth noting that some individuals are very proud of the traits with which they were brought into existence and may even seek to value themselves through their inborn characteristics, such as intelligence, sporting abilities or good looks. They see these traits as a part of who they really are in their very identities. In a similar way, persons brought into existence with a disorder may consider it a part of who they are, even though they recognize that challenges may exist. For example, Rebecca Cokley, who has achondroplasia (the most common form of dwarfism) and served in US President Obama's administration from 2009 to 2017, writes:

> I am who I am because I have dwarfism. Dwarfs share a rich culture, as do most disability groups. We have traditions, common language and histories rich in charismatic ancestors. I can honestly say that I may not have been able to work in the White House doing diversity recruitment for President Barack Obama had I not been born a little person. It allowed me to understand discrimination, isolation and society's lowered expectations.

130 D. J. Galton, *Eugenics: The Future of the Human Life in the 21st Century* (London: Abacus 2002), p. 46.
131 D. Sobsey, quoted in Reinders, *Future of the Disabled*, p. 51.

> While non-disabled people fear a prenatal diagnosis of disability, disabled people think of the possibilities. How rich would our society be if we all did this? . . .
>
> Now think about the message that society's fear of the deviant – that boogeyman of imperfection – says to disabled people: 'We don't want you here. We're actively working to make sure that people like you don't exist because we think we know what's best for you.' . . . It's denying us our personhood and our right to exist because we don't fit society's ideals.[132]

Significantly, this sense of identity of persons born with a disability is often different from that of individuals who may have become disabled later in life who may not associate their very existence with this condition. But the important concept of identity is difficult to define because this may, for example, change with circumstances and with time, such as when a person becomes sick or healthy. However, this does not affect their very existence as persons in time and space. This also means that any decision to modify an existing person's identity over time is completely different from deciding which person should exist in the first place.

The equality of all possible future and existing children

Making a selective decision between future children based on their quality of life may also mean that all human beings are no longer equal in value and worth no matter how healthy or disabled they are. In addition, it implies that there may be such a thing as a 'life unworthy of life' in society.[133] As Andorno explains:

> In reality eugenic ideology presupposes stepping from a 'worthiness of life' culture to a 'quality of life' culture, in other words, to the idea that not every life is worthy of being lived, or to put it more bluntly, that there are some lives that do not have any worth.[134]

132 R. Cokley, 'Please Don't Edit Me Out', *The Washington Post*, 10 August 2017.

133 The term 'life unworthy of life' (in German *Lebensunwertes Leben*) first occurred in the title of a book by German psychiatrist Alfred Hoche and lawyer Karl Binding, *Die Freigabe der Vernichtung Lebensunwerten Lebens* (Leipzig: Felix Meiner, 1920).

134 R. Andorno, 'Fondements philosophiques et culturels', pp. 129–141 (p. 137).

Certainly, the advancement of autonomy, the reduction of suffering and the increase in flourishing of human persons are important goals in any Christian ethical appraisal. But these aims do not give any true value or worth to human life, at least not the kind that is equal to all. If only autonomy or quality of life, including the lack of suffering, were the basis of the value or worth of an existing or possible future person, then every human being could be classified on a scale – classified as having a different value or worth.

It is thus imperative for Christians always to value equally, without selection and preconditions, every human individual. This is why a Christian civilized society must welcome into existence all possible future persons independently of their biological or other characteristics, such as genetic qualities or disorders. If human beings are to believe that every person who exists has exactly the same value and worth, then they must also believe that every possible future person has the same inherent value and worth.

It is difficult to see how an individual with the same value system can, in any rational and consistent way, agree that (1) it is acceptable to discriminate between possible future persons but that (2) it is unacceptable to discriminate between existing persons. For example, he or she cannot prioritize the concept of quality of life over the equal worth of life in order to discriminate between possible future persons, while at the same time indicating that all existing persons have the same inherent and equal worth irrespective of their quality of life. And this is as true for the value system of a person in a society as for parliaments in a democracy. As the international Christian Medical & Dental Association indicated in 2006:

> Society, while advocating tolerance, has become increasingly intolerant of any 'defective' human life. Our society exerts increasing pressure on parents to neither accept nor bring to birth a child perceived as defective. This intolerance violates the sanctity of human life . . .
>
> We must not deem inferior anyone with a 'defective' genetic heritage . . . Any efforts to create or eliminate perceived superior or inferior individuals are to be condemned . . . There are no 'lives unworthy of life'.[135]

[135] Christian Medical & Dental Association, Position Statements: Beginning of Human Life (2006).

From a Christian perspective it is not possible to reduce human worth to scientific principles. Instead, the equal value and worth of all persons must be considered as being more important than quality of life. Without this equality there is no rational argument for the very basis of a civilized society. Thus, since all possible future persons reflect the same image of God and have exactly the same worth and value, no choice between them can ever be made. This is because any choice would be based on the wrong reasons. In this regard, the ominous eugenic slogan of a 'life unworthy of life' undermines the equality of all persons created with the same image of God.

It is also worth remembering that in contemporary philosophy there is no logical justification for basic equality. Instead, this is usually just presumed without any supporting arguments.[136] Members of a society may believe (and it is only a belief) that all persons have equal value and worth, or they may believe (and it is only a belief) that they do not. But what society believes is crucial. For instance, a society which believes that a life is meaningful only if it has a certain quality is based on dangerous foundations. For instance, it would be possible to ask whether the seriousness of the murder of a person would be dependent on that person's worth as an expression of his or her quality of life.

Thus, if society intends to retain the values it sought to protect in the second half of the twentieth century, then every child's existence should be seen as inherently valuable and meaningful. Every child should be recognized as reflecting the same moral status as those who brought him or her into existence, while also deserving to be treated in a way that reflects these deepest realities. Some may seek to argue that wrongful lives do in fact exist, meaning that society may have a responsibility to bring into existence only children not affected by physical or mental disorders. But, from this perspective, protecting the interests of the possible future child merely focuses on enabling the best overall outcome from a biological perspective, rather than focusing on the inherent value and worth of a particular child.

Selecting means inequality and discrimination

Clearly, being able to choose between potential future children reflects an individual's right to autonomy. Moreover, there are no ethical implications

136 R. Song, 'Knowing There Is No God, Still We Should Not Play God? Habermas on the Future of Human Nature', *Ecotheology* 11.2 (2006), pp. 191–211.

for future parents to imagine or desire different possible future children who do not actually exist. Most prospective parents wish to have healthy and not disabled children. But when future parents decide to select between possible future children, they then make a very real discriminatory decision. Indeed, the decision would be meaningless if the future children were considered to be absolutely equal in value and worth. To be sure, while the parents may not be discriminating against existing children, as such, if the future children remain imaginary in the minds of the prospective parents, the choice is real and remains a discriminatory decision.

Such decisions would be comparable to what future adoptive parents could express if an irresponsible adoption agency were used, which did not put the needs and interests of a child first. Future adoptive parents could insist on the fulfilment of certain preconditions for their possible future child, such as the child being physically healthy or having other characteristics. Of course, when future adoptive parents desire such characteristics for the possible future child they want to adopt, this child may exist only in their imagination. In other words, they are not discriminating against any existing child. But their decision in an adoption process to select children with certain biological characteristics may be seen as a very real discriminatory decision if no other extenuating circumstances are present.[137] This means that it is the very possibility of *choosing* that is at the centre of the problem in any kind of selection procedure of real or imagined children, since most choices reflect, to some extent, a preference between children, which implies that they are unequal in worth in the eyes of the person making the choice. In addition, a selective decision is likely to reflect or even express the core values of prospective parents; and a decision to select and even discriminate between children reveals a prospective parent's preparedness to compare the meaningfulness and worth of one child's life and existence over another based on the child's quality of life or other biological traits.

The possibility of choosing between children may also betray the future parent's moral values. Moreover, the decision is one that would generally become public and might even become publicly acceptable, with serious

[137] Obviously, prospective parents may sometimes have legitimate reasons for wanting to make some restrictions to the kind of child they wish to adopt. For example, they may decide to have a healthy child only because they are not wealthy and would not obtain the necessary social support to look after an unhealthy child in an appropriate manner.

consequences for the persons who already exist with the unwanted traits and for the whole of society. As Reinders says:

> In any given case, the only reasonable answer to the question of why a disabled child should not be born is by reference to what one thinks about the lives of people actually living with the same disorder ... One may certainly refrain from making this judgement explicit, but the evaluation as such must be implicit in one's reasoning. This suggests that the lives of existing people with disabilities are at least indirectly implicated in strategies of prevention, because without such evaluations these strategies could not make sense.[138]

The US bioethicist Scott Kim develops this argument with the example of a man with Parkinson's disease observing and describing a fellow patient in a more advanced state. In so doing, he gives a frightening perspective of the pitiful appearance of this person while expressing disgust at the manner in which he eats and lives. At first, it may seem that the man is expressing only his own private views without giving any value judgments about the patient with advanced Parkinson's, but Kim then goes on to say:

> Although the writer may have intended to illustrate why he himself does not want to live like the man portrayed, that illustration works by way of evoking in us a reaction about the man portrayed ... The writer is judging the life before him as not worth living; that judgment is logically prior to and serves to justify why he does not want that life. Judgments about whether a life is worth living, even if it is ostensibly only about one's own life, is not a private judgment. What this author shows the reader is his belief that any life such as the one he sees is not worth living.[139]

This argument is important since it implies that those who are prepared to deselect possible future persons because of disability are revealing and

---

138 Reinders, *Future of the Disabled*, pp. 8–9.

139 S. Y. H. Kim, 'Lives Not Worth Living in Modern Euthanasia Regimes', *Journal of Policy and Practice in Intellectual Disabilities* 16.2 (2019), pp. 134–136 (p. 135).

disclosing their real views and core beliefs concerning those who already exist with disability.

In addition, not all discriminatory decisions need to involve reproductive procedures, as such. For example, a couple may refuse to procreate their own children because they know that they are both carriers of a serious genetic disorder. But applying this right not to have a child could still convey a message that certain existing persons should not have existed – a message that may be difficult to receive by those already born with a similar disorder. As Reinders again explains:

> Reasons for avoiding the birth of a handicapped child will refer primarily to what we think such a life will entail for the child or for its parents and other siblings. In either case a rational justification involves passing negative judgements on lives characterized by similar handicaps.[140]

To be sure, a decision by parents not to bring a child into existence is essentially different from a decision to select a child with certain characteristics, but each decision may still express similar values and ways of thinking. A couple may, for example, decide not to have their own biological child because he or she may be at a significant risk of developing a certain disability, and choose instead to adopt a child. But what would then happen if the adoption agency enabled them to choose between a healthy child and another one affected by the same disorder? Would not their decision to select between the two possible adoptive children become, once more, very real? Moreover, would not this decision express, yet again, their set of core values, which influenced them not to have a child in the first place?

In such a case, if the couple agreed not to decide between any children and left the choice to the adoption agency, the parental decision to select between different kinds of children would not exist. However, if the couple had the financial and psychological means to adopt any child but decided to select between possible children, then this would clearly and openly express their belief that some children can be preferred over others and are unequal in value and worth. It would also be a decision, if it was shared in society, that would be of interest and importance to people already

140 Reinders, *Future of the Disabled*, p. 67.

affected with the disorder in question. For example, if someone faced the decision whether or not to accept a child with Down syndrome, Reinders says:

> Clearly, anybody who faces this decision needs some basis for arguing for or against having . . . such [a] child. Obviously, the required basis is provided by a judgement about what one believes life with Down syndrome or with a child with this syndrome to be. It seems that the only way to arrive at this judgement is to look and see what such a life is like. In other words, one needs to be informed about what one can expect from living such a life or from living with a child with Down syndrome. The question then is: What source provides the required information and how can that source be established as adequate? The answer to this question must be that – unless one is satisfied in relying on myth and prejudice – there is no other way than to look at the lives of actual people with Down syndrome and then ask oneself whether or not one would want to live that kind of life or be involved in it . . .
>
> The question is on what basis do we decide to prevent a life with a particular genetic disorder if not on the basis of information about the lives of actual people with the same disorder? In that sense it must be true that a decision to prevent a life with that disorder exemplifies a negative view of the lives of people who are actually living with it. Without such a view this decision would fail to make sense.[141]

As a result, one important argument against eugenic procedures relates to how individuals with disabilities may be indirectly affected by a societal acceptance of selection. The basic concern in this objection is that eugenic selection may, arguably, encourage society to see possible future as well as existing persons as unequal in worth and value.

Indirect expression of discrimination

As already mentioned, making sure that persons with a certain disorder are not brought into life gives a clear message to individuals who already exist with the same disorder that they should not have come into existence.

141 Ibid., p. 57.

As Didier Sicard, past president of the French National Consultative Ethics Committee, explained in 2009, 'Concern for the other may first mean recognising his or her right to exist.'[142] A similar argument related to the very existence of a child affected by a disorder is given by the British Protestant theologian Oliver O'Donovan, while discussing abortion:

> But that the interests of a fetus which might achieve life outside the womb, though under a disadvantage, could be served by destruction, is a most obscure claim. And the obscurity is deepened when the argument from compassion is combined with the insistence that the fetus is not a person, and so, presumably, not a suitable object for compassion. It is a strange conclusion indeed, that one may render a service of kindness to a Nobody which it would be immoral to render to a Somebody![143]

Many disabled individuals intuitively realize that children unaffected by disabilities are usually more desirable than children with disabilities.[144] This may then lead disabled individuals to consider themselves as different from those who are not disabled, not only because of their different abilities but also on the basis of who they are as individuals. This is not surprising since non-disabled individuals are clearly fashioned by what they understand as their positive traits. For example, international sports champions who achieve significant success may think of themselves in terms of being better at this sport than the rest. Their value and worth as persons may be based on their success, and a failure to succeed may lead some to believe that they are failures.

With respect to court cases in which some individuals may seek damages for the simple fact of being born with a disability (wrongful life cases), the philosopher Tim Bayne states:

---

[142] D. Sicard, 'La science médicale, la naissance et le risque d'eugénisme', in J. Laffitte and I. Carrasco de Paula (eds.), *The New Frontiers of Genetics and the Risk of Eugenics, Proceedings of the 15th Assembly of the Pontifical Academy for Life* (20–21 February 2009); retrieved 17 June 2012 from <www.academiavita.org/index.php?option=com_content&view=article&id=349%3Ad-sicard-la-science-medicale-la-naissance-et-le-risque-deugenisme&catid=60%3Aatti-della-xv-assemblea-della-pav-2009&Itemid=66&lang=en>.

[143] O. O'Donovan, *The Christian and the Unborn Child* (Bramcote: Grove, 1980), p. 19.

[144] A. Fletcher, 'Making It Better: Disability and Genetic Choice', in Institute of Ideas (compiled E. Lee), *Designer Babies: Where Should We Draw the Line?* (London: Hodder & Stoughton, 2002), p. 21.

> One of the many worries that courts have expressed about wrongful life cases is that a positive verdict would commit the court to the view that the plaintiff not only ought not to have been brought into existence, but would now be better off dead. Although the worry as stated is groundless, there is something both true and important to it . . . the kinds of conditions that prevent life from being worth starting are just those that prevent it from being worth continuing.[145]

Interestingly, there also seems to be an element of discrimination in the discrimination process itself, with some forms of selection seen as acceptable and others not. For example, the American social commentator Elizabeth Kristol says:

> There is a curious double standard at work here. Virtually everyone writing on medical ethics condemns abortion for the purpose of sex selection, on the grounds that it makes a powerful statement about the relative value of the female gender . . . But when it comes to the disabled, no such concern is apparent, since society has already sanctioned abortion for virtually any disability that the testing uncovers . . .
>
> The landmark [US] President's Commission on Bioethics in the 1980s illustrates this double standard. The commission gives approval for genetic testing but also condemns use of such testing for sex selection: '[Sex selection] is incompatible with the attitude of virtually unconditional acceptance that developmental psychologists have found to be essential to successful parenting. For the good of all children, society's efforts should go into promoting the acceptance of each individual – with his or her particular strengths and weaknesses – rather than reinforcing the negative attitudes that lead to rejection.'[146]

Similarly, Wyatt makes the point that:

> There is widespread condemnation of the abortion of female fetuses for 'social' reasons in some Asian countries. This practice is seen as

145 T. Bayne, 'In Defence of Genethical Parity', in D. Archard and D. Benatar (eds), *Procreation & Parenthood* (Oxford: Oxford University Press, 2015), pp. 31–56 (p. 56).

146 Quoted in E. Kristol, 'Picture Perfect: The Politics of Prenatal Testing', *First Things* (April 1993), pp. 17–24 (p. 23); mentioned in Rae, *Brave New Families*, pp. 208–209.

> enshrining widespread social discrimination against women in these countries. In the same way social approval of abortion of fetuses with Down's syndrome could even be seen as 'chromosomalism', enshrining social discrimination against certain forms of DNA.[147]

As a result of eugenic selection, therefore, some individuals affected by disabilities may receive the message that they are less able or even less valuable than those society considers as 'able-bodied'. This is because they may be incapable of achieving a performance or accomplishment considered to be normal in certain fields. But, as disability rights campaigners indicate, such a way of thinking may be inappropriate since it may reflect a tacit assumption that disabled people are inferior in value and worth in some way. The term 'ableism' was coined in the 1970s to emphasize the negative experiences of persons who do not fulfil species-typical physical, mental, neurological or cognitive ability expectations.[148] Ableism thus includes a number of beliefs, processes, presumptions and practices that project the normal human standard while devaluing those who do not fulfil these characteristics. In other words, an ableist perspective indicates that able-bodied are the norm in society, and that those who are affected by disabilities must either strive to become part of the norm or should distance themselves from normal individuals through marginalization. In many ways, therefore, ableism seeks to express similar concerns to those who experience other forms of discrimination, such as in racism, sexism and ageism. As disability scholar Ivan Brown, in Canada, and others indicate:

> New eugenics practices, unfortunately, perpetuate the status quo by using numerous and sometimes insidious methods to devalue the human experience of disability. They act against full social acceptance and inclusion, and in this sense, they are at odds with the current philosophy of the worldwide disability community . . .
>
> For example, treating disability as something that requires support and accommodation only functions to continue to pathologize it . . . ,

[147] J. Wyatt, 'Medical Paternalism and the Fetus', *Journal of Medical Ethics* 27 (2001), suppl. II ii15–ii20 (p. ii17).

[148] G. Wolbring, 'Expanding Ableism: Taking down the Ghettoization of Impact of Disability Studies Scholars', *Societies* 2.3 (2012), pp. 75–83.

> while changing the lens to providing environments that enhance quality of life for every citizen and to value the experience and contribution of every citizen functions to expand empowerment, equality, and emancipation. These objectives go beyond merely accepting and tolerating disability, and rather see disability as a positive contributor to human diversity that merits celebration.[149]

Thus, it is suggested that the negative perception of disability may be the result of a lack of understanding of a disabled person's actual life experience as well as the existing social and material barriers that make disability difficult.[150]

How is disability perceived?

One of the most important concerns relating to reproductive eugenic selection is the manner in which those with disability may begin to be perceived. This is because, even at present, society has not been able to uphold fully the needs and rights of disabled persons, and selection procedures may only further increase the feelings of discrimination that persons born with a disability may experience. As indicated by Wyatt, when commenting on the message prenatal tests give to the disability community:

> In fact many in the disabled rights movement regard antenatal testing for fetal abnormalities as a form of social discrimination against disabled people. They argue that it is disingenuous for scientists and clinicians to claim that the development of antenatal screening is neutral and value free. The option of abortion for a range of genetic and other disorders places a negative value on people with the condition, and implies that it is socially desirable to prevent the birth of certain fetuses.[151]

Of course, it is not easy to interpret unintentional and indirect messages that may be received by persons. But the deliberate selection of individuals with 'normal', or deselection of those with 'abnormal', traits, or even the

---

149 I. Brown, R. Brown and A. Schippers, 'A Quality of Life Perspective on the New Eugenics', *Journal of Policy and Practice in Intellectual Disabilities* 16.2 (2019), pp. 121–126 (p. 122).

150 Ibid., pp. 121–126.

151 Wyatt, 'Medical Paternalism and the Fetus', p. ii17.

availability of such selective tests, can be interpreted as an unintentional rejection of individuals with a disorder. For instance, the UK's prohibition on prospective parents specifically selecting, through new reproductive procedures, a deaf child may give the message that such deaf persons should not be born – a position that many in the deaf community would find unacceptable. This may be one of the reasons why many members of the disability community are sometimes so outspoken in arguing that their lives should be considered of equal value to those of everyone else. They believe that society should learn to accept and integrate them as they are and not seek to make sure they are not brought into existence. Moreover, they recognize that society is far readier to work with non-disabled individuals than with those who have a disorder.[152] This means that new selective reproduction procedures, ensuring that persons with a disorder do not come into existence, may make it even more difficult for society to affirm the equal worth and value of individuals with disability. A curious confrontation seems to exist, therefore, between two very different worlds relating to disability. The first considers persons with disability as normal individuals, equal to everyone else, who have been unjustly cast out of ordinary life and thus deserve redress. The second, however, is a world in which having a disability is seen as being quite horrific and which thereby offers a number of deselection strategies, such as abortion, in the case of a severe disorder. It is a world in which the message given is that it would be preferable for everyone if disabled people did not exist.[153]

Societal acceptance of the new eugenics may then undermine the very concept of the inherent as well as equal value and worth of all persons in society – an equality based on the reality that all reflect the same image of God. With time, and as the number of persons affected by a disorder becomes ever smaller, financial challenges may also serve to damage the fragile equality that disabled people experience. For example, the cost of caring for persons with disabilities may increase as the number of persons with such traits decreases. This is because the cost of providing assistance will grow if fewer people eventually need them. Moreover, as eugenic selection reduces the number of persons brought into existence with

[152] The first-person account of M. J. Deegan illustrates this well in '"Feeling Normal" and "Feeling Disabled"', in S. Barnartt (ed.), *Disability as a Fluid State* (Bingley: Emerald, 2010), pp. 25–48.

[153] Reinders, *Future of the Disabled*, pp. 3–4.

special needs, their voices and protests may become increasingly difficult to hear among the many other demands of interest groups in society.

All this implies that persons living with disability are unlikely to consider selection procedures in a positive way, either for them or for society at large. Indeed, there is a risk that they will increasingly be seen as an unfortunate minority. In fact, eugenic selection may make matters worse for them since such procedures may reinforce the view that disabled persons are undesirable and should not come into existence. The International League of Societies for Persons with Mental Handicaps indicated in 1994:

> Modern scientific practices such as selection by prevention cannot help but be informed by paradigms about disability and the human ideal. Certain commonly held assumptions put people with disabilities at risk in relation to genetic and reproductive technology. These include such questionable assumptions as people with disabilities suffer because of their disability; human value is judged according to intellectual or physical qualities of the individual; the human race can and should be improved; and we need only consider genetic factors to comprehend human difference. If the application of genetic research is driven by these sorts of spurious assumptions, the lives and rights of people with disabilities may be at risk.[154]

Thus, serious concerns exist for disabled people and the way they see the value and worth of their lives.[155] As Ian Macrae, the editor of the magazine *Disability Now*, who is himself affected by a congenital condition, indicated in 2011, the screening of embryos 're-enforces the stereotypical notion that . . . disabled lives are intrinsically less valuable'. Macrae would prefer to see a society that can address the different requirements of persons with a disability, rather than making sure that they are not brought into existence.[156]

---

154 The International League of Societies for Persons with Mental Handicaps, *Just Technology? From Principles to Practice in Bioethical Issues* (North York: L'Institut Roeher, 1994), p. 11; quoted in Reinders, *Future of the Disabled*, p. 9.

155 German National Ethics Council, 'Position in Favour of the Retention and More Precise Specification of the Ban on PGD', in *Opinion: Genetic Diagnosis Before and During Pregnancy* (Berlin: Nationaler Ethikrat, 2003), pp. 68–94 (p. 86).

156 Quoted in V. Barford, 'Should My Hereditary Disability Stop Me Having a Baby?', *BBC News*, 18 April 2011; retrieved 28 April 2011 from <www.bbc.co.uk/news/magazine-12987504>.

Finally, another important argument for opposing such selecting-out procedures is the message which may be received by a number of individuals with disability and the deep distress this is causing to their self-perception. Moreover, just telling them that they should not react in such a way is simply unacceptable.

Discrimination in the context of disability and suffering

Making sure persons with disability do not come into existence is also inconsistent with crucial societal values, including (as already noted) Article 1 of the UN Universal Declaration on Human Rights, which states, 'All human beings are born free and equal in dignity and rights.' Accordingly, a person with disability, regardless of its severity, is of equal worth and value to a person without a disability. This implies that no matter how much suffering a person experiences in his or her life, it has absolutely no effect on his or her inherent value and worth as a person.[157] Indeed, any change in this position undermines the basic principles enacted in the UN Declaration and challenges the very existence of contemporary civilized societies. On this account, the value and worth of a person (whether or not he or she is disabled) cannot depend, in any way, on the suffering or contentment he or she experiences. God values and loves his created human beings in an absolutely equal manner.

Of course, parents are often torn between the joy of having a child and the suffering he or she is experiencing if a disability is present. On the one hand, they indicate how much they appreciate their child for all that he or she brings to them. But they also admit that, had they been able to choose before the birth of their child, they would have most likely decided against bringing him or her into existence. Thus, parents of children affected by disability face the dilemma of not wanting to miss the very existence of their child which they would not have chosen.[158]

More specifically most parents who have welcomed a child with a serious disability into existence – a child who may even experience a significant amount of suffering during a short life – do not regret the very existence of their child. Instead, it is the resulting suffering, not the life of

---

[157] It is worth noting here that the aim of many utilitarian commentators is the demise of the capacity to suffer in individuals. However, this also implies the demise of any meaningful free will since all human beings are then reduced to 'happy' automatons.

[158] Reinders, *Future of the Disabled*, p. 60.

the child, that the parents want to end. Though overwhelmed by the distress of their child (and their own distress), most parents remain grateful for the very existence of their child – a child who is extremely important to them. They would never want to exchange this child for another, healthier, one.

This does not mean that the parents welcome the child's suffering. But, as already indicated, in philosophy and medicine it is important to distinguish between disorders and the existence of individuals with those disorders. A father of two children with serious genetic disorders writes:

> There is one other essential observation regarding the human side of the suffering that comes with genetic disease. I hate what this disease has done to our sons and our family through their suffering (and ours, with them). So if the genetic disorder could be dealt with for future generations through genetic therapy, I would rejoice. Had I known ahead of time the agony that genetic illness would bring us, I would have preferred to avoid it. So I understand why people who approach this issue on a purely human level using secular values and reasoning may choose to kill unborn, genetically different children in an effort to avoid the kind of pain I have just described.
>
> But there is more than a purely human dimension to life. Spiritually speaking, when I ask myself would I rather that Jonathan and Christopher had never been born, the answer is: absolutely not. Though it broke my heart twice to share their sufferings, through them I know a lot more about love and faithfulness, kindness, gentleness, and humility than I could possibly otherwise have known.[159]

Accordingly, most parents agree that the life of their child is inherently valuable and worthy even though it may be affected by substantial suffering.

How are persons with disability supported?

As already noted, the effect of a disorder in a person may be significantly lessened by a caring society. Every person is part of a community that has a tremendous influence over the well-being of its members. This implies

159 D. M. Biebel, 'The Riddle of Suffering', in J. F. Kilner, R. D. Pentz and F. E. Young (eds), *Genetic Ethics: Do the Ends Justify the Genes?* (Grand Rapids: Eerdmans, 1997), pp. 3–6 (p. 4), quoted in Reinders, *Future of the Disabled*, pp. 176–177.

that a more communal approach to disability may well alleviate a prospective parent's perceived need to pursue selection, and that a society should never ostracize one of its members. Disability advocates indicate that many disorders become more bearable if supportive provisions exist.

However, the difficulties associated with disability cannot always be seen as the result of social discrimination. This is because the disorder itself may restrict certain functions that a community cannot fully address for a variety of reasons. But as a society seeks to attend to all the needs of its disabled and non-disabled individuals, selection procedures may begin to be seen as superfluous and meaningless.

Moreover, eugenic selection procedures are often supported by those who want to avoid any suffering in possible future children – a motivation that can, of course, be seen as laudable. But at the same time such an aim may offend, if not harm, many in the disability community and the very basis of equality in a civilized society. This means that if the needs of persons with a disability are to be respected, then the eugenic procedures currently under consideration cannot be accepted.

Again, and as already emphasized, this conclusion does not support the increase of suffering. But it does recognize that suffering and the value and worth of a life are completely different concepts.

Choosing possible traits and discrimination

Fears concerning discrimination may also arise if possible future persons with superior abilities are accepted for selection, since, as already noted, it may be difficult to draw a line between selecting-out and selecting-in certain biological characteristics. As a result, it may be easier to choose possible future children with positive traits, such as sporting or musical abilities, and not just for the absence of disability. This would be a development that might also polarize societal perspectives concerning disability and ability. An individual with what might be perceived as a normal ability might then be seen as second-rate and a greater number of persons might subsequently experience discrimination merely for lacking superior abilities.

Of course, selecting for positive traits is quite different from actively discriminating against individuals with disorders. But every living person has abilities and disabilities. Thus, enabling such selections to take place may eventually give the message that society prefers these enhancements and even requires them. Parents may then be under pressure to take part in a never-ending eugenic race for ever better abilities for their children.

The importance of a compassionate society

If a society begins to accept eugenic procedures, it may then slowly become impossible for it to escape the manner in which it considers disabled persons. Being influenced by selective models, it may start to consider those with disabilities as pathetic and worthy of stigmatization or discrimination, rather than considering them as meaningful and full participants. Society may then become more demanding and intolerant, rather than compassionate and supportive, which are fundamental Christian values.

The development of eugenic procedures may then limit the amount of acceptance and compassion for the 'abnormal', especially for individuals brought into existence with disorders who could have been selected-out. With a diminished acceptance of persons born with a disability and who need support, their existence may progressively be considered in a negative way. For instance, parents with a child with Down syndrome may increasingly be asked why they did not terminate their child before birth. In other words, with genetic testing becoming ever more common, it is possible that society may eventually hold responsible and blame prospective parents for the birth of a disabled child. As a result, political considerations for their special requirements may diminish.[160]

Thus the predominant message in such a situation may well be that a disabled child is an undesired member of society. Questions may then be asked about the way such a society will be seen in the future and whether compassion and empathy may be undermined.

Other arguments relevant to the new eugenics

Not surprisingly a number of other arguments have been developed both supporting and opposing a return of eugenic procedures, thus creating a heated debate. These will now be examined in turn.

160 Reinders, *Future of the Disabled*, p. 14.

The need to protect embryos and foetuses

One significant challenge to many forms of eugenic practices stems from the belief that all living human beings have inherent value and worth because they reflect the same image of God and thus deserve protection from the moment of their creation.[161] Yet some forms of selection between embryos and foetuses result in some being destroyed.

Of course, any discussion concerning the inherent value and worth of human life is deeply theological in nature, meaning that science alone cannot provide adequate answers. From a purely scientific perspective, all human life (including all adult life) can just be reduced to biochemical molecules that do not have any inherent value and worth or reason, whatsoever, to survive. This means that any position concerning the value and worth of human life is essentially based on unprovable assumptions, such as that God exists and that all of humanity reflects his image.

Consequently, secular society as a whole is unable to reach a consensus about the moral status of an embryo or foetus. Moreover, if it were honest with itself, society would recognize that it is unable to give any scientific reason for the worth and value of any human being, embryonic or adult. This means that the worth of all human life in society can only be considered as a belief – a belief which everyone in civilized society should have.

In addition, if the inherent value and worth of human life is to be rejected as an ethical foundation because it is not based on science, it is for its detractors to suggest an equally effective and meaningful overriding principle that would enable a civilized society to survive. Until this happens the belief in the inherent value and worth of all human life must remain. A belief which is also supported by Christianity, which accepts the reality that God created and therefore loves all human life. This remains the most important bulwark against any proposition that would construct a hierarchical evaluation of the value and worth of embryonic, foetal or adult human beings.

Does the new eugenics involve 'playing God'?

Another objection to eugenic selection relates to concerns about intervening in the natural way human life comes into existence, which may include both religious and secular perspectives.

---

161 MacKellar, *Image of God.*

From a religious perspective, concerns about playing God through deciding what kinds of children should exist are related to the belief that such a choice contradicts a divine prerogative, which only God should exercise. In other words, this argument seeks to respond to the order of God's creative love in which human parents are recognized as only participating in God's creation of his human beings and it is God who is in control. However, some Christians may question this reticence in 'playing God'. As Ted Peters explains:

> After trying to discern whatever theological content the phrase playing God might have, it appears that it has very little. Its primary function is to serve as a protective shield against a technological threat to an assumed sacredness . . . of nature in general. Having relatively little cognitive content, 'Thou shalt not play God' comes from the voice of panic amidst the overwhelming flood of new knowledge and new opportunities and new vested interest groups and new potentials for injustice. As a warning against foolish prometheanism, we should heed it.
>
> This prompts a serious theological and ethical question: How should we play human? How should we understand our human relationship to God and to nature and to future generations of God's creatures?[162]

In response to this position, it may be suggested that God always intended human beings to 'play God' when he created the possibility for human beings to procreate. God could easily have created billions of human beings, all at once, right from the beginning, if he were only seeking to bring into existence many individuals whom he could love. This means that God may have wanted to share his joy in creating his human creatures with the parents' joy in procreating their own. Moreover, as already indicated, playing God may mean that rules for the game exist. For example, that unconditional love and acceptance must exist in bringing children into existence. This may then mean that it is in the possibility of cheating in the game of 'playing God' that serious ethical problems may arise.

The secular concern about 'playing God' has a similar emphasis but without including a deity and is usually related to the wielding of power

162 Peters, *Playing God?*, p. 213.

over life and death. It acknowledges that humanity may be affected by a certain amount of pride, arrogance and false belief in its own abilities while insisting on its right to use eugenic selection without understanding the possible consequences. Peters indicates that 'when we humans make life-and-death decisions we exhibit hubris or pride – that is, we overreach ourselves and transgress divinely imposed limits'.[163] In this respect, Leon Kass explains relating to the concept of playing God:

> By it is meant one or more of the following: man, or *some* men, are becoming creators of life, and indeed, of individual living human beings . . . ; they stand in judgment of each being's worthiness to live or die . . . – not on moral grounds, as is said of God's judgement, but on somatic and genetic ones; they also hold out the promise of salvation from our genetic sins and defects . . .
>
> Never mind the exaggeration that lurks in this conceit of man's playing God . . . Consider only that if scientists are seen in this godlike role of creator, judge and savior, the rest of us must stand before them as supplicating, tainted creatures.[164]

Thus, the secular argument against playing God states that parents have not, until now, sought to control the biological characteristics of their children but have humbly accepted, instead, as the result of a kind of natural lottery. In this manner, resisting the desire to interfere with the natural way of bringing children into existence would reflect a willingness not to seek any control over the child, while encouraging parents to accept their children unconditionally. This way of thinking would also accept that the way of nature should be respected, not least because any divergence from this might result in unforeseen and potentially irreversible negative consequences.

Broadening the definition of a disorder

Serious concerns relating to eugenic selective procedures exist because such procedures are seen to contribute to a broadening of the definition of what may be considered a serious physical disorder. For example, this

163 Ibid., pp. 11–12.

164 L. R. Kass, *Life, Liberty and the Defense of Dignity: The Challenge for Bioethics* (San Francisco: Encounter, 2002), p. 129.

becomes relevant when disability provisions already permit abortions to be carried out until birth for disability in some countries, such as the UK. Thus, because of the uncertainty of what may be considered a 'serious' condition worthy of termination, individuals with disorders such as Down syndrome have expressed concern about how they are considered. Already in 2006 the UK newspaper *The Telegraph* reported that the number of abortions for this condition had reached record levels, with more than 90 per cent of all foetuses diagnosed with Down syndrome being terminated.[165] One of the reasons for this sad outcome is that many consenting adults and medical professionals now consider Down syndrome to be sufficiently serious to justify an abortion. This is happening even though a 2011 study indicated that when parents kept their child with Down syndrome, 79 per cent agreed that their view of life was more positive as a result of the child.[166]

Another UK newspaper, *The Sunday Times*, published an article in 2006 which indicated that between 1996 and 2004 more than twenty foetuses in the UK had been terminated after 20 weeks because scans indicated they had club feet. A further four were aborted because they had webbed fingers or extra digits. This resulted in some concern when the figures were published, since these conditions can all be addressed through surgery or physiotherapy. This same *Sunday Times* article interviewed the father of a boy born with club feet. Prior to the boy's birth, and when the club feet were detected, he was asked to consider aborting the foetus. Discussing the incident for the interview, the father was quoted as being 'appalled'.[167] These examples show that the concept of the seriousness of disorders needs to be carefully examined and explained.

What constitutes a serious disorder?

What actually constitutes the 'seriousness' of a disorder is usually difficult to define. As the UK House of Lords remarked in 2002, '[I]t is uncertain whether it means serious for the individual or serious for society'.[168]

165 Anonymous, 'Harrison's Parents Chose His Name'.

166 B. G. Skotko, S. P. Levine and R. Goldstein, 'Having a Son or Daughter with Down Syndrome: Perspectives from Mothers and Fathers', *American Journal of Medical Genetics Part A* 155 (2011), pp. 2335–2347.

167 L. Rogers, 'Babies with Club Feet Aborted', *The Sunday Times*, 28 May 2006; retrieved 10 August 2011 from <www.timesonline.co.uk/tol/news/uk/article669212.ece>.

168 House of Lords, *Stem Cell Research, Report from the Select Committee* (London: The Stationery Office, 2002), p. 39.

Similarly, in 2003 the US President's Council on Bioethics noted that, with advances in selective technology, it is likely to prove impossible to draw a clear line between identifiable serious disorders and those disorders that parents might (or should) be able to find acceptable.[169] Further difficulties may also result from the ambiguity surrounding the resources society can access to help parents in making important reproductive decisions.

Moreover, if a eugenic selection is made that is considered to be acceptable based on the seriousness of a disorder, it may then be possible to ask on what basis healthcare professionals differentiate the serious from the non-serious. But it is unlikely that an exhaustive list of serious disorders could ever be prepared in a satisfactory manner. There are at least two reasons for this difficulty.

Perceptions are different

Defining the seriousness of a disorder is first dependent on the way individuals and families perceive disorders and suffering. For example, individuals with genetic disorders, as well as their families and medical professionals, often have different views about what may be considered to be a poor quality of life. Those who are themselves affected by a genetic disorder often rate the quality of their lives more highly than do medical professionals.[170] Defining what is considered to be a serious disorder, therefore, is likely to be subjective. For instance, if a scale could be prepared for biological disorders, one individual whose condition measured a 5 out of 10 might find the associated discomforts acceptable, while another might find the same condition unbearable.

Two related challenges are the way the seriousness of a child's disorder is determined and who should decide. Should it be the future parents, the healthcare professionals or society in general – or should it be a combination of all these parties? Persons who already have experience of a disorder within a family, including the parents of a disabled child, will undoubtedly have different views. First-hand experience of a disorder will certainly include factors that an essentially clinical approach is not able to determine. The difference between professional and personal perceptions of a disorder may then vary quite significantly. As a result, a

---

[169] The President's Council on Bioethics, *Beyond Therapy: Biotechnology and the Pursuit of Happiness* (Washington, D.C.: The President's Council on Bioethics, 2003), pp. 56–57.
[170] House of Lords, *Stem Cell Research*, p. 39.

eugenic procedure may be seen as acceptable in one setting but not in another.

But defining disability becomes even more difficult in the context of reproductive technology. This is because as soon as any person asks a third party, such as the state, for assistance in bringing a child into existence, this actor has a responsibility to examine whether it should take part in the process. Thus, if a party, such as a government which represents the views of society, objects to a procedure, it does not have a duty to address the wishes of the individuals seeking the assistance. This means that even though the views of those directly affected by a medical condition should be carefully considered, they may not always be best placed to judge a condition, including its seriousness. For example, individuals confronted with decisions about a person with a disorder will generally consider their own interests rather than the wider implications for the whole of society. As a result, the parties seeking assistance should understand that they cannot be exclusively responsible for deciding the seriousness of a condition.

But determining the level of input from people who may be seeking eugenic selection is difficult. This means that, regardless of a procedure for determining seriousness, listening to the voice of individuals with disabilities is vital. It is worth noting again that some of the most passionate objectors to the use of selection procedures, such as embryo selection, are disabled persons.

Definitions are different

A second challenge in understanding the seriousness of a disorder is that precise definitions may be seen as discriminatory by some interest groups who have their own values or concerns. Developments in genetic testing have already given rise to significant anxiety among disability rights organizations, when such testing is used to deselect an embryo or foetus considered to have a serious disorder.[171] As the Council of Europe recognizes, screening against disability may 'undermine the equal value of human beings' and may be prone to occur under the pretence of objectivity rather than recognizing 'that notions like "severe genetic diseases" are social constructions reflecting the misperceptions of those "temporarily

171 For a discussion, see e.g. E. Parens and A. Asch, 'The Disability Rights Critique of Prenatal Testing: Reflections and Recommendations', *The Hastings Center Report* 29 (1999), S1–S22.

able"'.[172] As an alternative to selective procedures, disability rights groups suggest developing societal and familial support that will eventually challenge what they consider to be false and dangerous definitions.[173]

Moreover, if under a restrictive definition of 'disability' selection procedures eventually give rise to stigmatization of and/or discrimination against certain categories of people, it is likely that a broader definition may bring even further difficulties for individuals with disability. But at the same time refusing to define 'disability' in any way may bring its own problems.

How is it possible to consider the burden of a disorder?

A final difficulty in establishing an exhaustive list of serious disorders recognizes the challenges of defining what 'seriousness' means, since even the burden of a condition may vary in the light of social, financial, cultural and psychological settings. On the other hand, the very fact that such a list of severe disorders may not exist creates a highly subjective framework for decisions and practices that will vary wildly, leading to confusion and even abuse.

Moreover, a nuanced evaluation of what counts as disability or severity requires awareness of social norms. For example, disorders that society now considers as minor may have been seen as severe in past generations. In other words, criteria for what is 'serious' or 'severe' should be examined carefully and be reviewed frequently, since medical progress will continue to address concerns about the restrictive power of certain disorders.

In short, eugenic selections may make ethical matters more complicated by expanding the highly subjective definition of 'serious' to include conditions for which treatments may already be available or for conditions that do not necessarily meet accepted standards for seriousness.

The influence of society

Societal pressures have always featured as a real concern with eugenic procedures. Moreover, the widespread availability and practice of such

---

[172] Council of Europe Steering Committee on Bioethics, *The Protection of the Human Embryo in Vitro* (Strasbourg: Council of Europe, 2003), p. 32; retrieved 15 June 2010 from <www.coe.int/t/dg3/healthbioethic/texts_and_documents/CDBI-CO-GT3(2003)13E.pdf>.

[173] M. Saxton helpfully states the goal of disability rights groups in this regard as lobbying for 'the right *not to have to have* an abortion' when informed that a foetus may have a 'serious' condition, 'Disability Rights and Selective Abortion', in R. Solinger (ed.), *Abortion Wars: A Half-Century of Struggle, 1950–2000* (Berkeley: University of California Press, 1997), pp. 374–394 (p. 375; emphasis original).

procedures may eventually change what is considered to be 'normal'. As a result, even though more opportunities may become available to prospective parents, this may not necessarily mean that they are given greater freedom to act. This is because there is a risk that future parents, in order to meet cultural expectations, may feel an indirect influence from society to consider the selection of possible future children.

This would happen, for example, if parents decided to take a course of action because of peer pressure, with which they might be uncomfortable, rather than following what they believe is right. As the British legal ethicist Shaun Pattinson observes:

> The empirical evidence does indeed suggest that gradually increasing social pressure is a realistic consequence of widespread trait selection. This social pressure is also likely to be directed towards children with the undesired genes, rather than being restricted to the parents of such children.[174]

In this respect, such a situation would be especially serious if the prospective parents were Christians, since this might erode their conscience.

These pressures may then give rise to unfortunate consequences for the whole of society. For example, society may (directly or indirectly) find itself passing judgment on parents if their children do not meet certain quality of life criteria. Such a concern may reflect the common practice of individuals praising parents for their children's appearance or innate skills, such as intellectual or athletic abilities. This may suggest that they may also be held responsible for failing to bring into existence healthy children.

All this implies that the freedom to choose, so treasured by supporters of selection procedures, would actually be limited to those who choose to select, while the choice not to select would be undermined. As the British bioethicist David King argues, 'It will be seen as irresponsible and cruel to even consider bringing a disabled child into the world. We may soon start to hear that every child has the "right" to a healthy genetic endowment.'[175] In short, once different eugenic procedures become more

---

[174] S. D. Pattinson, *Influencing Traits Before Birth* (Farnham: Ashgate, 2002), p. 149.

[175] D. King, 'Eugenic Tendencies in Modern Genetics', *Ethics and Medicine* 14.3 (1998), pp. 84–89 (p. 87).

common in a society, parents may eventually be compelled to use them if they seek the best for their child in an increasingly competitive society. In other words, if a certain amount of choice is given to parents, then decisions may still be driven in a certain direction that, if not controlled by the state, will still be restrained by public opinion.

Fairness and eugenic selection

Another difficulty with selecting the kinds of children who should exist relates to the issue of fairness: the treatment of persons without favouritism or prejudice.

However, from the very beginning these arguments have been met with a number of counterarguments, since fairness is a complex topic open to a number of challenges. Thus, while noting possible problems with the concept of fairness, the following section will simply focus on discussing two of the strongest strands of the argument.

Equality and fairness in the light of the open future argument

Making a decision concerning another person is not always easy, especially when it relates to a possible future child. Of course, parents often make decisions for their children once they are born and until they reach maturity. This generally happens with the best of intentions for the child and is usually accepted by society. Moreover, because both the child and his or her parents are members of society, legislation may indicate what is in the best interest of the child. In other words, society can intervene in order to protect a child from something that it believes is dangerous. For example, one of the factors that may be considered is the way an intervention may affect a child's future capacity to choose. This indicates that, though it may be necessary to restrict a child's freedom in certain cases, it may also be important to support this child's freedom to decide as he or she matures.

Thus, the first strand of the fairness argument relates to the future of the prospective child. It suggests that eugenic selection procedures seeking to favour certain biological characteristics in a child may determine his or her future in an unacceptable manner. Such procedures would prevent the child from being able to define his or her own freedom to choose when he or she grows up. This means that the selection may have a narrowing effect on the child's future options, thereby hindering him or her from maximizing his or her chances of self-fulfilment. According to this line of argument, when prospective parents impose their own eugenic preferences on their future child, they inappropriately control their child's freedom. In other words, the parents limit their child's 'open future' because they prevent him or her from choosing the kind of life he or she may want. Instead, the child is restricted and constrained to the bio-design of his or her parents and to an inappropriate form of genetic control of one generation over the next.

In addition, the German ethicist Jürgen Habermas suggests that when a child is designed by his or her parents, this establishes an asymmetrical relationship. He explains:

> Our principal concern with programming here is not whether it will restrict another person's ethical freedom and capacity of being himself, but whether, and how, it might eventually preclude a symmetrical relationship between the programmer and the product thus 'designed'.[176]

Similarly, Leon Kass is concerned about the level of control parents may have over their future children in the context of selecting for a certain kind of child, such as with cloning:

> The child is given ... [the genetic heritage of a person who] has already lived, with full expectation that this blueprint of a past life ought to be controlling of the life that is to come. Cloning is inherently despotic, for it seeks to make one's children (or someone else's children) after one's own image (or an image of one's choosing) and their future according to one's will. In some cases, the despotism may be mild and benevolent. In other cases, it will be mischievous and downright tyrannical. But despotism – the control of another through one's will – it inevitably will be.[177]

In other words, the designer of life and the designed who received this life can never be on an equal footing in their relationship with one another.

---

176 J. Habermas, *The Future of Human Nature* (Cambridge: Polity, 2003), p. 65.

177 L. R. Kass, 'The Wisdom of Repugnance: Why We Should Ban the Cloning of Humans', *Valparaiso University Law Review* 32.2 (1998), pp. 679–705 (p. 698).

One will be in a superior or inferior position. This is also the power relationship discussed by C. S. Lewis, who argued that 'if any age really attains by eugenics and scientific education, the power to make its descendants what it pleases, all men who live after it are the patients of their power'.[178]

In this situation the child may have valid grounds for complaint. For example, if parents select for a son who will likely turn out to be very tall, the child may protest that his trait, and thus his likely possibilities in the future, were predetermined by his parents. It would also be possible for some children, who were selected for a certain trait, to complain since they might resent the fact that they were not given the same genetic traits that their peers received. In this case there is a risk that a selected child might take the position of being a judge over the biological decisions and values of his or her parents. An apt summary of the key issue is given by Habermas:

> Exercising the power to dispose over the genetic predisposition of a future person means that from that point on, each person, whether she has been genetically programmed or not, can regard her own genome as the consequence of a criticizable action or omission. The young person can call his designer to account, and demand a justification for why, in deciding on this or that genetic inheritance, the designer failed to choose athletic ability or musical talent, which would have been vastly more useful for the career that she had actually chosen to pursue.[179]

In other words, Habermas is suggesting that selection procedures violate the natural order of parent–child relationships by enabling children to question their parents' choices. Moreover, the sense of security that naturally arises from children's trust in their parents' moral stance may be undermined. This may give rise to children questioning their relationships with their parents, resulting in the disappearance of the innocence and safety of early years.

However, the 'open future' argument gives rise to a number of criticisms. One problem is that it is unclear what actually constitutes an 'open future'. In addition, it is difficult to state at what stage of development a

---

[178] C. S. Lewis, *The Abolition of Man* (New York: HarperSanFrancisco, 2001), p. 57.
[179] J. Habermas, *The Future of Human Nature* (Cambridge: Polity, 2003), pp. 82–83.

child may no longer be entitled to this openness and may be considered responsible for the direction of his or her life. Moreover, it may be argued that future children may have a far greater potential for self-fulfilment and an 'open future' if they are brought into existence free from a debilitating disorder that will significantly limit their life possibilities.

Another difficulty with the 'open future' argument is the recognition that no child ever comes into existence with a free 'open future'. Instead, from the earliest stages of embryonic development every member of the human species has a number of limiting genetic traits. As the British bioethicist John Harris explains, 'we are all in the position of having had "the way we are" determined by a combination of the acts and omissions of our parents and others with whom we have interacted since conception'.[180]

In addition, 'open future' arguments may need to address the 'non-identity' dilemma mentioned in the earlier discussion. This philosophical argument indicates that it is impossible to draw any ethical conclusions about a person's genetic constitution if any changes to this composition would result in another person coming into existence. For instance, a girl cannot complain about her parents' decision to select her sex since, had they chosen to have a boy, she would not have existed. In short, the non-identity dilemma may suggest that the 'open future' argument is unsuitable against the new eugenics. This is because the different biological characteristics with which all individuals are brought into existence are part of who they are in their personal identity and in their very existence. Children cannot then complain about not having an 'open future' since, had they not been born with their own set of biological characteristics (whether these were given by their parents or by chance), they would not have existed in order to make such a complaint.

It may also be suggested that controlling a child's development before birth may be no different from controlling his or her development after birth. For instance, a moral upbringing usually encourages a child to accept certain ethical principles, and this kind of control by parents of their child does not generally initiate much opposition. Critics of the 'open future' argument thus question why any control of the child's biological traits in eugenic selection should be seen as different. They indicate that children may end up trying to refute and defy, in their very conduct, any genetic or behavioural design and expectations their parents might have

180 J. Harris, *Enhancing Evolution* (Princeton: Princeton University Press, 2007), p. 140.

planned for them. In response, it should be recognized that there is a qualitative difference between biological pre-determination and social determination. This is because the former relates to controlling an individual's very existence, whereas the latter affects only the characteristics of an individual who already exists.

This all means that the 'open future' argument may still, to some extent, be useful if seen in the light of the parent–child relationship. From this perspective, the difficulty with selection is not that it directs a child's future in an inappropriate way but that, from the very beginning, it introduces elements of control by the parent that fundamentally change the child's life and may affect the parent–child relationship. As such, the 'open future' argument supports the previous section of this book, which suggests that parents should unconditionally love and accept their children, which is a far stronger argument against the new eugenics.

Would everybody have equal access to eugenic selection?

The second way of examining the fairness argument focuses on the future of society. This argument acknowledges that financial resources are generally not shared evenly across a population, meaning that it may only be the rich who are able to access expensive eugenic procedures for their children because of the extraordinary cost involved. As a result, the challenges experienced by the poor may be accentuated since they have to address not only their economic plight but also the inequality arising from their genetic heritage.

However, it may be emphasized that many forms of unfairness are already present in other arenas of society. Thus, any person who agrees with the right of parents to send their child to an expensive private school will not be able to use the fairness argument as a reason for refusing to use biological selection. Still, the main element of the fairness argument stresses that inequalities should not be heightened or supported in any way. Members of society should not seek to further separate themselves into what the American legal ethicist Maxwell Mehlman called the 'genobility' and the rest.[181] Interestingly, the possibility for a society to have a biological elite with superior intelligence and other biological characteristics, who would rule over a biological underclass, was proposed by

[181] M. Mehlman, *Wondergenes: Genetic Enhancement and the Future of Society* (Bloomington: Indiana University Press, 2003), pp. 116–117.

the Greek philosopher Plato (who lived between 428 and 347 BC) in his book *Republic*. He suggested that an elite class of 'Guardians' should be created through selection who would themselves not be allowed to have children with ordinary individuals.[182] In a way, such a society is comparable to what existed in countries such as the UK, where, until recently, the aristocratic upper classes were generally able to marry only among themselves in order to preserve their 'blue' or noble blood. This was because this biological aristocracy were considered superior in some way, making it necessary for them to reproduce among themselves to keep their superiority while enjoying the wealth and other advantages that usually came with their status.

In response to this unfairness argument it may also be noted that inequality is not always detrimental to society. For example, in the same way that philanthropic organizations assist the poor, a 'genobility' could behave beneficently towards the genetically poor, in a yet unforeseen manner. In other words, a certain amount of genetic inequality may not be the basis for alarm.[183]

But suggesting a form of acceptable inequality may mean limiting selection procedures to only a privileged few, which should in fact be available to all, making the whole set-up seem less than attractive. For example, if selection procedures eventually gave rise to a restricted subgroup of elite and privileged individuals who flaunted and enjoyed their superiority, while disregarding the rest of society, then it is likely that the non-elite majority would see the situation negatively. In addition, such a form of unfairness would be accentuated if the eugenic resources devoted to the enhanced elite were diverted from helping those with limited means. Furthermore, as the British philosopher Philip Kitcher indicates:

> [T]he genetic conditions the affluent are concerned to avoid will be far more common among the poor – they will become 'lower-class' diseases, other people's problems. Interest in finding methods of treatment or for providing supportive environments for those born with the diseases may well wane.[184]

---

182 D. J. Galton, 'Greek Theories on Eugenics', *Journal of Medical Ethics* 25 (1998), pp. 263–267.

183 R. M. Green, *Babies by Design: The Ethics of Genetic Choice* (New Haven: Yale University Press, 2007), pp. 147–153.

184 P. Kitcher, *The Lives to Come* (New York: Simon & Schuster, 1996), p. 198; quoted in L. M. Silver, *Remaking Eden* (London: Phoenix [Orion], 1999), p. 260.

In order to address this unfairness, society may then agree to limit selective eugenic selection for the elite, though implementing and justifying such restrictions may create significant challenges. Moreover, if the state then sought to intervene to address the financial costs of selection for possible future children, this could become a serious financial drain on its resources. On the other hand, if the financial support of healthcare providers were used, this would mean further interference of parties in an already complex network of actors with an interest in selection. Thus, the involvement of these actors might represent an unfortunate intrusion into a private matter.

The American philosopher Michael Sandel also highlighted the principle of equality and solidarity through sharing in society, suggesting that any positive genetic trait in a person should be available to all. For him, society should be a place where inequality should be addressed by individuals working together to use their different biological gifts for the benefit of the whole community. He writes:

> If our genetic endowments are gifts, rather than achievements for which we can claim credit, it is a mistake and a conceit to assume that we are entitled to the full measure of the bounty they reap in a market economy. We therefore have an obligation to share this bounty with those who, through no fault of their own, lack comparable gifts.
>
> Here, then, is the connection between solidarity and giftedness: A lively sense of the contingency of our gifts – an awareness that none of us is wholly responsible for his or her success – saves a meritocratic society from sliding into the smug assumption that success is the crown of virtue, that the rich are rich because they are more deserving than the poor.[185]

Another element in the fairness argument notes that society is already divided, with, for example, richer patients often having access to drugs or treatment that others cannot afford. Because of this it is difficult to object to assisting the sick unless treatment can also be given to all those in need. As a result of such a position, the fairness argument is weakened because

---

[185] M. J. Sandel, *The Case Against Perfection: Ethics in the Age of Genetic Engineering* (Cambridge, Mass.: Harvard University Press, 2007), p. 91.

it may be suggested that helping some individuals through selection procedures may be better than helping no one at all. As the New Zealand ethicist Nicholas Agar recognizes with respect to the costs of eugenic procedures, 'To insist on universal access would be, in effect, to ban all but the most rudimentary enhancement technologies.'[186]

In short, it is true that new eugenic procedures may exacerbate the differences between those persons who can afford to acquire a biological advantage for their children in a competitive society and those who cannot afford such procedures. But, as already mentioned, such a situation is not entirely new since the wealthy are already providing advantages for their offspring such as private healthcare and superior education. However, a lot depends on the social and political contexts.

Healthier children

One of the strongest perceived advantages of the new eugenics is the possibility for couples or individuals to ensure that their children do not have certain disabilities. For instance, prenatal screening can now enable disorders to be detected, giving parents the option of terminating the pregnancy in order to prevent the child from being born. Such eugenic procedures are sometimes considered to be a form of empathy towards the possible future suffering child. In other words, by making sure certain persons with debilitating conditions are not brought into existence, the new eugenics would aim at reducing suffering.

In many way, this manner of thinking reflects the Golden Rule presented by Jesus Christ in Matthew 7:12, 'So in everything, do to others what you would have them do to you' (see also Luke 6:31). This means that a person should seek to stop others experiencing what he or she would want to avoid. For example, it suggests that nobody should want to see another person suffer. But on the basis of compassion those supporting the new eugenics may also go beyond the mere alleviation of suffering and take a eugenic step towards desirable characteristics. For instance, it may be possible to argue that since parents have a right to seek the best for their future child by selecting only embryos without genetic disorders, they may also have a right to select embryos with superior biological traits. In other words, parents should always be entitled to pursue the best possible life for their future children. This argument is all the more relevant since,

---

186 Agar, *Liberal Eugenics*, p. 141.

as already noted, it is often difficult to distinguish between paired terms such as 'healing' and 'enhancement' or 'ability' and 'disability'.[187]

It is also recognized that many parents are already seeking to improve their children's capabilities by providing coaching in sport or sending them to the right schools. Those supporting the new eugenics thus emphasize the difficulty of defining a meaningful difference between using such activities to give a child specific abilities and genetically improving a child with the aim of developing the same abilities. This is because most parents seek to have not only healthy children but also highly gifted ones who are able to live successful and fulfilling lives in an extremely competitive world.

The Australian medical ethicist Julian Savulescu uses a principle he calls Procreative Beneficence to argue that 'couples (or single reproducers) should select the child, of the possible children they could have, who is expected to have the best life, or at least as good a life as the others, based on the relevant, available information'.[188] Of course, he recognizes that this child may not be perfect, but the aim is optimization not perfection. This argument is all the more relevant because eugenic procedures are already available in developed countries, enabling prospective parents to select future children with the best lives possible. Consequently, parents who do not select for such children may be ignoring their duty. The argument is thus similar to the one for education in that parents have a responsibility to educate their children, with parents who do not do so being seen as irresponsible.

However, the problem with this position is the subjective nature of what a successful and flourishing life represents. Does this reflect a life which is recognized and respected in society while the person experiences a lot of physical and emotional pleasures? Or is it a life that seeks to help and support others even in the midst of difficulty and suffering? Indeed, the concept of a 'good life' varies significantly according to each person's world view and his or her understanding of what is important in life. In addition, parents may not have the same world views as their future children and significant disagreement may then arise. It is worth noting,

---

187 A. Grunwald, 'Human Enhancement – What Does "Enhancement" Mean Here?', *Europäische Akademie zur Erforschung von Folgen wissenschaftlich-technischer Entwicklungen Newsletter* 88 (2009), pp. 1–3.

188 J. Savulescu, 'Procreative Beneficence: Why We Should Select the Best Children', *Bioethics* 15 (2001), pp. 413–426 (p. 415).

as well, that one of the pillars of the Christian world view of life is that all human beings are absolutely equal in value and worth because they reflect the same image of God. This means that if parents select only for healthy children, they are undermining this equality since they are indicating that some children are preferable to or more valuable than others. Moreover, from God's perspective it is not only the life of a person on earth that matters but also his or her whole existence in all of eternity. This means that if an infant is very sick and lives only a few months on earth before going to be with God, the actual length of his or her life is of little significance to God. For him, immeasurable joy already exists in looking forward to spending all of eternity with this child. Thus, it should be remembered that parents procreate a child not only for their or society's sake but also for God's.

Protecting reproductive freedom and autonomy

Another reason given for supporting reproductive eugenic procedures engages the concept of parental procreative freedom, which may be defined as a person's right to decide what kind of child to have.

In this regard the new eugenics is seen as different from earlier practices of selection, such as in Nazi Germany and the USA, which as noted earlier disregarded parental reproductive autonomy through the authoritative rule of the state.[189] In addition, past eugenic programmes had very specific understandings of what constituted the ideal human, to the detriment of any other characteristics. For example, persons with high intelligence were believed to be more valuable to society just because of their intellectual abilities.[190] Some early eugenicists even indicated that antisocial behaviour, such as a living a life of crime, could be associated directly with intellectual incompetence.[191]

With the new eugenics, however, it is suggested that new selective procedures would seek to promote diversity, permitting and not coercing individuals to pursue their eugenic choices according to their own desires

189 D. B. Paul, *Controlling Human Heredity: 1865 to the Present* (Amherst: Humanity, 1998), p. 133.

190 A. Buchanan, D. W. Brock, N. Daniels and D. Wikler, *From Chance to Choice: Genetics and Justice* (Cambridge: Cambridge University Press, 2000), p. 49.

191 A. C. Carey, 'Beyond the Medical Model: A Reconsideration of "Feeblemindedness", Citizenship, and Eugenic Restrictions', *Disability & Society* 18 (2003), pp. 411–430.

and aspirations. In other words, in preserving reproductive freedoms, it is proposed that a libertarian society would be committed to supporting a pluralism of values. Moreover, it is intimated that this would not result in any abuse of selfish individualism since a permissive society presumes that individuals are free to act in any way they wish as long as this does not impinge on the autonomy of others to act with equal freedom. This means that procreative liberty, including choosing whether or not to have a child, is considered to be a fundamental right relating to the most basic meaning that people may give to their lives.

It has even been implied that unless the new eugenics is allowed to flourish, a form of compulsion may return. That without access to liberal eugenic procedures, many future parents may experience the difficult challenges of being burdened with a disabled child whom they would be obliged to endure and look after. This means that if libertarian freedoms are not protected, some individuals may risk a form of oppression comparable to previous compulsory eugenic activities.[192]

This assertion, however, is difficult to accept in the light of the widely acknowledged ethical difference between acts and omissions. A society that deliberately imposes suffering on its members is completely different from one that recognizes that unintended and unwanted suffering may result from a natural procedure. In addition, future parents should be reminded that any selection cannot guarantee a child with a desired outcome since the eugenic procedures work only in the context of increased or decreased probabilities and cannot be used to provide certainties.

The effects of a biologically degenerate society

Collective responsibility has always been a significant argument for those supporting eugenic ideology. It has been suggested that all individuals have a responsibility to participate in the goal of doing what is best for society, including in seeking to rescue it from those considered to be a burden on others and who undermine the overarching aim of progress. This argument was one of the main reasons for the development of eugenic policies in Europe and North America in the early twentieth century. For example, Charles Darwin's son Leonard (1850–1943), who was secretary

[192] E.g. J. Glover, *What Sort of People Should There Be?* (Harmondsworth: Penguin, 1984), pp. 84–89.

of the British Eugenics Education Society, shared his father's concern about the future prospects of his country. In 1928 he expressed his fears for society when feeble-minded individuals 'have large families and many descendants because they have little power of looking into the future, or of foreseeing the consequence of their own acts'.[193] Similarly, in her book *The Pivot of Civilization*, originally published in 1922, the American commentator on human reproduction Margaret Sanger (1879–1966) dedicates a whole chapter to birth control and her concern that governments are not doing enough to restrain the reproduction of those she considers to be undesirable. She states:

> There is but one practical and feasible program in handling the great problem of the feeble-minded. That is, as the best authorities are agreed, to prevent the birth of those who would transmit imbecility to their descendants. Feeble-mindedness as investigations and statistics from every country indicate, is invariably associated with an abnormally high rate of fertility. Modern conditions of civilization, as we are continually being reminded, furnish the most favorable breeding-ground for the mental defective, the moron, the imbecile.[194]

In this respect she criticized charity work for encouraging such a situation:

> The most serious charge that can be brought against modern 'benevolence' is that it encourages the perpetuation of defectives, delinquents and dependents. These are the most dangerous elements in the world community, the most devastating curse on human progress and expression.[195]

More recently, Glanville Williams indicated in 1957 that '[t]o allow the breeding of defectives is a horrible evil, far worse than any that may be found in abortion'.[196]

But yet again this reflects a strong discriminatory element based on inequality, which is completely unacceptable. As the American bioethicist

193 L. Darwin, *What Is Eugenics?* (London: Watts, 1928), pp. 46–47.

194 M. Sanger, *The Pivot of Civilization* (New York: Humanity, 2003 [originally published in New York in 1922 by Brentano's]), pp. 107–108.

195 Ibid., p. 138.

196 G. Williams, *The Sanctity of Life and the Criminal Law* (New York: Knopf, 1957), p. 234.

Osagie Obasogie explains, 'A troubling yet consistent theme for eugenics is that only certain types of people – the smart, the beautiful and those without disability – deserve to exist, as those who are less than ideal are simply too burdensome.'[197]

Of course, this kind of thinking also goes against any understanding of Christian compassion and empathy towards the weakest members of society, which is one of the main callings of the Christian church. This is again based on the immeasurable but also equal value and worth of all human beings created in the image of God.

The cost of disability

One final argument supporting the new eugenics is based on the reality that individuals affected by a disorder often consume more resources than others. Because of this, national governments are not impervious to the possibility of limiting, in some way, the ever-increasing healthcare costs of individuals born with a disorder. As David King observes, 'Politicians are looking for ways to cut healthcare budgets, and it is clear that preventing the birth of disabled children, with lifelong healthcare costs, is very cost effective.'[198] Billions of dollars could be saved, worldwide, on lifetime treatment costs if it were possible to ensure that persons with a disability were not brought into existence. Lady Warnock, one of the main architects of human reproduction legislation in the UK, has actually objected to the significant costs of care for high-needs patients. In 2008, during an interview on the topic of euthanasia, she claimed, 'If you're demented, you're wasting people's lives, your family's lives, and you're wasting the resources of the [UK National Health Service].'[199]

However, the cost of caring for individuals born with a disorder, as an argument for eugenic practices, is not generally promoted since it is far too close to the main message developed in Nazi Germany. Nevertheless, the high cost of healthcare is a reality. For example, the US philosopher Arthur Caplan indicated:

---

197 O. K. Obasogie, 'The Eugenics Legacy of the Nobelist Who Fathered IVF', *Scientific American*, 4 October 2013.

198 King, 'Eugenic Tendencies in Modern Genetics', p. 87.

199 M. Wade, 'You'll Kill Patient Trust if You Let Doctors Help Suicides', *The Times*, 10 October 2008; retrieved 31 May 2011 from <www.timesonline.co.uk/tol/news/uk/scotland/article4923128.ece>.

> When the state of California offers . . . [a test] to all pregnant women it does so in the hope that some of those who are found to have children with neural tube defects will choose not to bring them to term thereby preventing the state from having to bear the burden of their care.[200]

The argument thus emphasizes that the extra costs of caring for people with disabilities puts the already limited resources of society under pressure. As a result, and in order to balance these limited resources in an appropriate manner, some selection procedures may then be considered attractive or beneficial if not even essential. This means that a decision to deselect certain possible future children may not merely be seen as the preserve of the prospective parents' personal choice – it may eventually become the responsibility of society as a whole since disabled individuals may begin to be considered a financial burden to all.

But in addition to financial advantages, eugenic programmes may also be seen as useful in addressing social costs of care. As the French physician Farhan Yazdani notes:

> It is true that a severely handicapped child can be an unbearable strain to parents and endanger the development of other children in the family. Social institutions can compensate through a helping hand, but they lack necessary funds for doing so. Again, even though it is morally wrong to eliminate the handicapped before birth, it could be in some cases the least inappropriate solution in our present situation.[201]

But further consultation with persons affected by congenital conditions and their carers may be required before inappropriate assumptions are made.[202] As already noted, the manner in which the carers of a disabled person may consider what is expected of them may be very different from

---

200 A. L. Caplan, 'Neutrality Is Not Morality: The Ethics of Genetic Counselling', in D. Bartels, B. LeRoy and A. Caplan (eds), *Prescribing Our Future: Ethical Challenges in Genetic Counselling* (Hawthorne: Aldine de Gruyter, 1993), p. 159.

201 F. Yazdani, 'Ethical Decision-Making for in Vitro Fertilisation in a Multicultural Setting', in E. Hildt and D. Mieth (eds), *In Vitro Fertilisation in the 1990s* (Aldershot: Ashgate, 1998), p. 125.

202 P. Alderson, 'Down's Syndrome: Cost, Quality and Value of Life', *Social Science and Medicine* 53 (2001), pp. 627–638.

that of healthcare professionals. Moreover, the cost of looking after persons with disability should always be addressed from a perspective of radical solidarity and a sharing of resources. As the American politician Hubert Humphrey Jr (1911–78), vice president of the USA from 1965 to 1969, indicated:

> The moral test of government is how it treats those who are in the dawn of life, the children; those who are in the twilight of life, the aged; and those in the shadows of life, the sick, the needy and the handicapped.[203]

Thus, making sure that certain individuals considered costly are not brought into existence in a wealthy society cannot be seen as an ethical or responsible way forward.

[203] Remarks at the dedication of the Hubert H. Humphrey Building, 1 November 1977, *Congressional Record*, 4 November 1977, vol. 123, p. 37287.

4
Presentation of different eugenic procedures

Eugenic selection procedures enable prospective parents to control the genetic make-up of possible future children by selecting-in (positive eugenics) or selecting-out (negative eugenics) different kinds of children. However, it should be emphasized that even a successful genetic selection may not always give the desired results, since many of the characteristics sought by parents are heavily influenced by other factors such as the environment. Moreover, different eugenic procedures range from the already established to the highly speculative, with some likely never to become reality. But they all share a common theme in supporting the selection of biological traits, though a few may also raise their own ethical questions.

In the following section the different procedures so far suggested to affect the genetic heritage of future children are presented. Examples of each practice will also clarify what is at stake.

Reproductive eugenics through the selection of partners

Generally, human relationships that lead to procreation begin by mutual attraction that expresses a whole set of emotions and aspirations. Two persons do not usually just come together to have children, though it is likely that the selection of a partner may be based on some perceived biological suitability as a parent. For example, a woman may choose a healthy man whom she finds physically attractive, but this may also reflect her subconscious desire for similar characteristics in her children. This means that all decisions to have a child may involve some kind of selection of a reproductive partner; so natural conception is not entirely a random exercise. But such a choice of partner may be seen as an innocent form of unintentional eugenics or as a secondary outcome to physical attraction, which cannot be avoided and can be considered ethically acceptable.

An example of a deliberate non-voluntary form of selection for reproductive partners was developed in the Nazi party in Germany when the national leader of the SS (*Schutzstaffel*, 'Protection Squadron') Heinrich Himmler (1900–45) decreed that SS men could marry only 'if the necessary conditions of race and healthy stock were fulfilled'.[1] Moreover, before this could be considered both the SS member and his fiancée had to demonstrate the quality of their genetic heritage by passing a comprehensive physical examination administered by a doctor.[2] A further programme that existed in Germany at the time was the implementation of marriage restrictions which decreed that Jews and racially pure Germans were not permitted to engage in sexual relations, even in marriage. This had as its aim the creation and development of a pure master race.[3]

A more voluntary example of a selection programme for reproductive partners has been taking place since the 1980s in certain Jewish communities. These have used advances in human genetics to assist in making decisions about the selection of marriage partners with the aim of preventing the birth of children with certain serious genetic diseases.[4] The programme operates through representatives of a screening organization visiting Jewish high schools and inviting pupils to give a blood sample, whereby a number is then assigned to each student. The samples are later screened for genetic disease and the results stored for future use. When two past students subsequently become adults and express an interest in getting married, they then contact the screening organization, which retrieves the assigned numbers for each partner to check whether

---

[1] H. Höhne, *The Order of the Death's Head: The Story of Hitler's SS* (New York: Penguin, 2000), p. 148.

[2] J. M. Steiner, *Power Politics and Social Change in National Socialist Germany: A Process of Escalation into Mass Destruction* (The Hague: Mouton, 1975), pp. 78–79. Note that the term 'Aryan' as used in Nazi laws and regulations generally denoted a person of non-Jewish, European origin.

[3] M. Mouton, *From Nurturing the Nation to Purifying the Volk: Weimar and Nazi Family Policy, 1918–1945* (Cambridge: Cambridge University Press, 2007), p. 88.

[4] J. Ekstein and H. Katzenstein, 'The Dor Yeshorim Story: Community-Based Carrier Screening for Tay-Sachs Disease', in R. J. Desnick and M. K. Kaback, *Tay-Sachs Disease* (London: Academic, 2001), pp. 297–310.

they are carriers of certain genetic diseases. If both the man and the woman are positive for the same gene mutation, which may give rise to a disorder, the organization advises against the marriage.[5] Thus, because every person who eventually declines marriage on the basis of a genetic test makes a deliberate reproductive decision to prevent the bringing into existence of a child with a serious genetic disease, questions reflecting eugenic concerns may be asked. In addition, since ever more genetic disorders are being discovered among certain Jewish or other communities, the balance between the advantages and the risks of such a selection of reproductive partner needs to be considered carefully. This is especially the case since such a selection may be intrusive to the individuals who come together – they may at this stage not want to know the kinds of children they may procreate.

Also, in many Christian denominations it is impossible to marry a close blood relative. The prohibition is expressed in Leviticus 18:6, which indicates that no one is to have a sexual relationship with a close relative. As a result, in the Roman Catholic Church from 1550 to 1917 marriage was generally prohibited within the fourth degree of relationship (first cousins). However, it is unlikely that this prohibition of consanguinity arose from eugenic concerns. The condemnation of affinity, such as a parent marrying a stepdaughter (canon 1092) or adopted child, or even a child marrying an adopted sibling (canon 1094), implies that these codes were drafted on the basis of avoiding sexual relationships between people who were considered too similar or who had something overtly 'in common' or in which one partner had a position of power over the other that might be used inappropriately. In some Christian communities the prohibition against marriage went as far as even to include godparents and their godchildren, because such parents had a strong spiritual involvement with and influence over a child.

In the context of selecting a reproductive partner, it is also worth noting that there is no condemnation, at present, by society of couples who know that they have a high risk of bringing children into existence with serious disabilities but decide to have these children anyway. Perhaps society operates with an understanding that the child is the fruit and representation of the love that exists between the partners and that this child should, therefore, always be welcomed in that love.

---

5 C. Rosen, 'Eugenics – Sacred and Profane', *The New Atlantis* 2 (2003), pp. 79–89 (p. 80).

Reproductive eugenics through selecting to have many, few or no children

Reproductive eugenics may take place when some parents specifically decide to have many children because they believe that their genetic heritage is desirable. Some communities or even whole countries, in the past, have implemented eugenic policies that encouraged certain individuals to have many children with the aim of improving their communal corporate genetic heritage. This took place in Nazi Germany, where it was expected that its biological elite should have large families in order to build the master race. In the end, however, these efforts failed, as the birth rates of such individuals were little different from that of the overall population.[6]

Though some couples may decide to have many children for positive eugenic reasons, other couples may decide to have few children or none at all. As already mentioned, this may arise for a number of different reasons, but such a decision may be based on information that they are carriers of a serious genetic condition that could be passed on to a possible future child. Yet again, couples may have all sorts of non-eugenic reasons for not having children. For example, they may recognize that they would not receive any support and could not look after a severely disabled child. In this case, the decision not to have children would not be based on a selection decision *between* possible future children. Had the parents been able to do so, they would have been prepared to have *any* child. In other words, the emphasis here is on the parents and their situational background and not on the child's characteristics or quality of life.

But once parents capable of looking after a disabled child take a decision to have a child, but then decide to go back on their decision because of the biological quality of their prospective child, eugenic elements are certainly present. Indeed, there is a crucial ethical difference between (1) deciding whether or not to bring a child into existence based on eugenic values and whether he or she is affected by a disorder, and (2) welcoming him or her into existence, whoever he or she is, as an equal member of society. For example, if a couple have a high risk of passing on a serious genetic disorder to a possible future child and still decide to have the child without

---

[6] L. V. Thompson, '*Lebensborn* and the Eugenics Policy of the *Reichsführer-SS*', *Central European History* 4 (1971), pp. 54–77.

screening for the disease, then it can be argued that what they are doing is ethical. The parents will be prioritizing the mere existence of their child, whom they recognize as having the same value and worth as any other child, over other features of the child's life. In this manner they would demonstrate unconditional love and acceptance towards their child, and thereby acknowledge that all life is worth living for its own sake. For such parents a person's length of life or possible suffering does not make an impact, in any way, on his or her inherent worth and value.

In this regard, even if one or both partners is/are affected by a serious genetic disorder, they are under no obligation to refrain from having a child. Indeed, it is generally accepted that the couple have a right to have a child even if it has a high risk of disability or ill health. Therefore, there is a difference between couples deciding whether to have children in the first place and determining, once this decision has been taken, what kind of children to have (a decision that may be based on eugenic factors).

On the other hand, if the couple decide not to have a child because one, or both, of the partners carries a serious genetic disorder that may be passed on to their possible future child, even though they may be capable of looking after him or her, they are clearly making a eugenic decision. In this respect, they may also indirectly be communicating the message that persons born with similar serious disorders should not be born – an implicit message that individuals already born with such disorders may receive with consternation and concern about discrimination.

Eugenics through selective adoption

Adoption is often life-changing for both the child and the future parents, with significant emotional and psychological experiences taking place. If all goes well, an adoption procedure should go smoothly with the interest and welfare of the child being seen by the adoption agency as having priority over any other interests, including those of the future parents. That the child's interests should come first is crucial, since it is the responsibility of the state to look after such children in the best possible manner. Moreover, if the adoption process is carefully managed, the parents will also put the interests of their future child first and he or she will be valued and welcomed unconditionally.

Ethical challenges arise, however, when the child's welfare or best interests are not a priority in the adoption process. For example, this would happen when prospective adoptive parents put down certain conditions for their future adoptive child – when parental selection becomes central in the adoption process and the child's own interests become secondary.

In this respect, the manner in which the unregulated selection of children may take place can demonstrate some of the real risks of reproductive eugenic procedures. Indeed, if prospective parents are given a certain amount of *choice* between the kinds of children they adopt, such as in deciding only to have healthy children, this provides an illustration of some of the ethical challenges that may arise when a eugenic choice in reproduction is given to future parents. Thus, the feelings and experiences facing these prospective adoptive parents may be similar to what parents of the future may experience when new reproductive selective procedures are developed. For example, some of the choices facing prospective adoptive parents will probably include the sex or ethnic background of the child; but where such selection becomes especially relevant is when the health of the future child is considered. For instance, questions arise when possible adoptive parents are not willing to accept a disabled child who would require more support and thus would be significantly more demanding to them. This is in contrast to the present reproductive situation when parents bring into existence their own biological children since they generally have little choice about their child's characteristics.

Deciding whether or not to adopt children

As already mentioned, the adoption process is useful in examining some of the factors that may arise in some of the other reproductive procedures being examined, since adoption differentiates between (1) the parental decision whether or not to have a child and (2) a decision about what kind of child to adopt. Indeed, in both adoption and procreation future parents are under no obligation to have a child. They are entirely free to make this decision to have a child, which is usually dependent on a number of factors, including their willingness to be parents, the prospects of the possible future child and a recognition of their own abilities to look after a child.

Deciding to adopt

If parents decide to adopt a child and this takes place through a responsible adoption agency, then, as previously mentioned, it is the interests of the already existing child that are generally seen to have priority over the wishes of the future parents. In other words, it is the independent adoption agency, and not the prospective parents, that decides where the child is placed. The agency then plays a similar role to that of chance in natural procreation, though a few parental preferences may be considered, such as age and sex. Of course, the agency may also take some of the biological characteristics of the child into account, but these will always be seen as secondary to the child's best interests.

On this account, it is interesting to note that the unconditional acceptance of the child that adoption agencies demand from future parents may increasingly be at odds with the kind of eugenic quality control of children that is creeping into some of the new reproductive procedures. Indeed, the consequences of some of these new procedures would be similar to prospective parents going into an unregulated orphanage as if it were a supermarket in which different children are on offer. They would then visit the different rooms of this orphanage to choose which child they prefer. That is to say, they would be free to choose with full autonomy, while considering their own preferences and the kinds of children they wanted from a large number of options.

Deciding not to adopt

When a couple decide not to adopt a child, this may be based on a number of reasons, such as contentment with the number of children they already have or a conviction that they would be inadequate parents, which do not reflect any eugenic elements. In other words, these decisions relate to the prospective parents and not to any characteristics in the child as such. However, if a clear decision to adopt a child is made but subsequently retracted because of concerns relating to the health or other biological characteristics of the child, then the reasons behind this change of mind may need to be further examined from an ethical perspective. In such a situation the biological aspects of the child seem to have taken precedence over the decision to have a child. Eugenic concerns may be present, and the following two possibilities may be considered.[7]

In the first case, if the prospective parents are able to care for a child with serious health problems and are expected to receive sufficient support from the state, but still decide against adopting such a child because of health concerns, then the interests of the child would not be seen as having

[7] C. MacKellar and C. Bechtel, *The Ethics of the New Eugenics* (New York: Berghahn, 2014).

priority. In a way, the child's health difficulties would be the sole reason for the refusal to adopt, and the parents might be demonstrating ethically questionable values in their decision-making that might reflect a eugenic bias. But, as with other similar choices, the decision can be fully evaluated from an ethical perspective only by the parents themselves.

If, on the other hand, parents refuse to adopt a child with serious health problems because they believe they would not be able to care for the child, then the situation may be very different. In this case the parents would have been prepared to adopt *any* child regardless of his or her characteristics. But they refused because they did not have the means, including social support, to do so properly. This would reflect a failure by:

- the adoption agency to consider fully, or enquire about, all the different parental factors in addition to the best interests of the child and/or
- the parents to examine carefully all the possible outcomes before deciding to adopt.

The parents' decision not to adopt the child with serious disability would then not reflect any eugenic element since it would still prioritize the best interests of the child. The parents would have recognized their own inability to look after him or her in an appropriate way. The emphasis would not so much be on the characteristics of the child as on the parents' own limitations or inability to adopt. In other words, it may suggest that the child deserves a couple better able to welcome him or her.

Eugenics through sex selection

The possibility for parents to select the sex of a future child is a form of positive eugenics if the definition at the beginning of this book is used. Usually, however, choosing the sex of children is not considered a choice for a 'desired genetic heritage', since the only biological trait being decided is a child's sex and not, for example, his or her health. But at the same time sex selection may be seen as coming under the definition of eugenics in the limited but significant sense of selecting the sex chromosomes that one desires. In other words, sex selection may be one of the first cases in which parental preferences for the future child are the principal motivation. For example, such a situation may arise in societies where one sex (usually male) is preferred over the other. In other words, in choosing a child of a certain sex parents are expressing their own preferred outcome for their child.

The case for sex selection

Sex selection is sometimes considered for medical reasons in order to avoid bringing into existence children affected by severe sex-linked disorders. At present approximately 200 such ailments, of varying seriousness, have been identified, the majority of which affect only boys. Deselecting possible future children with such sex-linked disorders enables prospective parents to choose to avoid the challenges often associated with the more serious sex-linked conditions.

However, some prospective parents may wish to have a child of a certain sex for a number of non-medical reasons. For instance, when parents already have at least one child of a particular sex, some may believe that having another of the opposite sex would enable them to have a balanced family while increasing diversity. It has also been proposed that sex selection might benefit children since more children would then be of the preferred sex and far less likely to be unwanted by their parents. It may even be suggested that without sex selection parents may end up with a child of the undesired sex. Thus, it is proposed that parents should be able to exercise their autonomy by choosing to have a balanced family with their preferred sexes and that this would result in few (if any) risks to societal values.

The case against sex selection

But a number of reasons for opposing sex selection have been raised, including concerns relating to the equal treatment of future children resulting from such procedures. According to this objection, allowing parents to choose a certain sex for their children for non-medical reasons may foster a setting in which the opposite sex is treated negatively. For instance, this may happen when parents prefer to have a male offspring because he will then preserve the family's presence in society through factors such as the continuation of a name or business. However, such views may undermine the foundation of universal equality on which civilized society is built.[8] In this regard the Health Council of the Netherlands indicated in 1995:

[8] The first article of the Universal Declaration of Human Rights states unequivocally, 'All human beings are born free and equal in dignity and rights.'

> The possibility cannot be excluded that the actual availability of sex-selective insemination as a family-planning instrument will result in parents finding the sex of their children more important than they claim at present. Because choice involves making distinctions, the possibility of sex selection could result in the undermining of the idea of sexual equality and therefore of the struggle for emancipation. Making sex an object of choice could lead to the reinforcement of stereotypical ideas about sexual roles.[9]

In other words, one very real concern relating to sex selection is the claim that any support of such preferences is likely to reinforce discrimination and be contrary to the equality to which all human beings are entitled. In addition, it is suggested that the desire to select for sex will eventually lead to a broadening of choice for more trivial features, such as eye colour or complexion. Thus, sex selection could be seen as only the first step along a dangerous eugenic pathway to an unknown future that nobody can predict or control. Of course, there will always be a few hard cases for which a certain option will seem reasonable, but giving in to pressure in order to conform to the wishes of prospective parents in these hard cases opens the door to widespread future practice.

Eugenics through egg and sperm selection

This section considers the question of egg and sperm selection, which is becoming ever more widespread in society because of a number of factors. This includes medical reasons, for which future parents may decide to choose healthy sperm and egg cells from a provider that enable them to have children without heritable genetic disorders. Another motive exists when one of the partners in a couple is infertile. In such a situation, and in countries where donation is legal, fertility clinics are expected to provide eggs and sperm from a donor whose ethnic background and physical characteristics resemble, as far as possible, those of the infertile partner. The aim is to reduce the eventual social stigma that donor-conceived children may experience within their own family or in

---

[9] Health Council of the Netherlands, *Sex Selection for Non-Medical Reasons* (The Hague: Health Council of the Netherlands, 1995), p. 37.

society because of noticeable differences. For example, most fertility clinics in the USA now offer a wide range of sperm and a more limited number of eggs from donors who are selected for characteristics such as appearance and ethnic origin. Sometimes sperm or eggs are even selected for a non-genetic trait, such as a religious background, in order to support a sense of cohesion between a donor-conceived child, his or her family and society at large. Such efforts to connect donor-conceived children with their families suggests that sperm and egg selection raises concerns about the identity of the child conceived.

Another identity aspect in the resulting child may relate to his or her origins. Although the child will have a relationship with the parents that enabled his or her conception, it is recognized that the child may also want a significant relationship with his or her sperm or egg parent on account of the shared biological material that brought the child into existence. Undoubtedly, responsible (non-biological) parents will aim to develop a loving environment in which the donor-conceived child will consider them as parents in a similar way to how an adopted child considers his or her adoptive parents. Nevertheless, on account of the biological bond that exists through sperm and egg donation, the donor-conceived child may want to have a relationship with the donor (biological) parent.

Eugenics through sperm selection

At present, sperm is generally selected only on the basis of donor screening among relatively young men, who when donating sperm must share various details concerning genetic traits and disease history, as well as less determining qualities, such as education and career aspirations. When the samples are received, they are then usually classified on the basis of donor characteristics and frozen for storage in a sperm bank. This enables prospective parents to choose the desired donor sperm from the bank based on the biological qualities and other traits of the donor. The woman is, subsequently, artificially inseminated with the selected sperm at the most appropriate time and, if the procedure is successful, will give birth to a child.

On the presumption that individuals with supposedly desirable genetic characteristics can (to some extent) reproduce such traits in their biological children, those supporting eugenic policies have often endorsed this procedure as a potential means of improving the human genetic heritage.[10] In the past a number of interesting programmes were even suggested, including the proposal to send superior US sperm to solitary British women during the Second World War.[11] But another form of sperm selection began in 1981, when the US businessman Robert Graham (1906–97) established a sperm bank called the Repository for Germinal Choice.[12] Graham's aim was to provide superior sperm to women or couples who desired to have a child with a trait such as greater intelligence. The Repository only accepted sperm donations from Nobel Prize laureates or other similarly successful donors such as leading personalities in the academic and business worlds. But, despite its exciting aims, the Repository for Germinal Choice produced relatively few children. In 1999, when the sperm bank finally closed following Graham's death two years earlier, only 215 children had been born using its deposited sperm.[13]

Another procedure involving the selection of sperm cells is intracytoplasmic sperm injection (ICSI), which is used when a man's sperm is incapable of naturally fertilizing an egg. In this case a scientist in a laboratory selects the best sperm cell produced by the man and injects it directly into the egg of the woman. The resulting embryo is then implanted into the woman's uterus. Thus, because a form of selection is also present in this procedure, which is usually performed by a biomedical scientist, some eugenic elements may be present. But the scientist usually only chooses a sperm cell that seems more appropriate than others from a visual perspective without any knowledge of the cell's genetic heritage. In other words, the selection procedure is not really based on any genetic characteristics as such.

Eugenics through egg selection

The donation of eggs is physically far more demanding than sperm donation because of the risks associated with the medical procedure

---

[10] J. McMillan, 'The Return of the Inseminator: Eutelegenesis in Past and Contemporary Reproductive Ethics', *Studies in History and Philosophy of Biological and Biomedical Sciences* 38.2 (2007), pp. 393–410.

[11] M. Richards, 'Artificial Insemination and Eugenics: Celibate Motherhood, Eutelegenesis and Germinal Choice', *Studies in History and Philosophy of Biological and Biomedical Sciences* 39.2 (2008), pp. 211–221.

[12] D. M. Tober, 'Semen as Gift, Semen as Goods: Reproductive Workers and the Market in Altruism', in N. Scheper-Hughes and L. J. D. Wacquant (eds), *Commodifying Bodies* (London: Sage, 2002), pp. 137–160 (p. 149).

[13] R. M. Green, *Babies by Design: The Ethics of Genetic Choice* (New Haven: Yale University Press, 2007), p. 165. For the full story of the Repository, see D. Plotz, *The Genius Factory: The Curious Story of the Nobel Prize Sperm Bank* (New York: Random House, 2005).

required for retrieving the eggs, which is done in a clinic. Generally, women undergoing the procedure will be able to provide an average of ten to fifteen eggs in a single treatment cycle.[14] Moreover, because the preservation of eggs in storage is more difficult than with sperm, the removal of the donor's eggs often takes place just before they are fertilized in vitro and the resulting embryos are immediately implanted into the woman or stored for future use.

Some of the challenges relating to egg selection are similar to those of sperm selection. Again, future parents and fertility clinics generally select egg donors for various biological characteristics. In this regard, the financial compensation received by the donors may be significant, especially if they are physically attractive and intellectually superior. Buyers can even pay up to US$ 100,000 for eggs that match their desired requirements.[15]

Ethical challenges relating to the eugenic selection of sperm and eggs

Of course, in normal intercourse there is a natural form of competition between the large number of sperm cells seeking to fertilize the woman's egg(s), but this process is not linked to any ethical decision to choose between them. The vast numbers of sperm cells and (to some extent) eggs available for procreation originating in a couple allow natural selection to take place while also enabling the couple just to accept unconditionally whatever child is brought into existence through 'chance'. In other words, there is no element of selection of the sperm and egg cells.

But, as with most other eugenic procedures, real risks exist when sperm and egg selection takes place, including the risk of instrumentalizing the resulting child, who may be considered a means to an end. Moreover, despite the significant costs and emotional challenges involved in these (and other) programmes, aspiring parents are not promised success. This is because the outcome of every selective procedure involves an element of uncertainty, since science cannot predict with complete confidence which genetic traits will be present in the future child or that he or she

---

14 The possibility of even fifty eggs is reported in G. Sher, V. M. Davis and J. Stoess, *In Vitro Fertilization: The A.R.T. of Making Babies*, 3rd edn (New York: Facts on File, 2005), p. 63.

15 M. Enge, 'Ad Seeks Donor Eggs For $100,000, Possible New High', *Chicago Tribune*, 10 February 2000; retrieved 18 October 2010 from <http://articles.chicagotribune.com/2000-02-10/news/0002100320_1_egg-donor-program-infertile-ads>.

will meet parental expectations.[16] However, despite this uncertainty, a number of aspiring parents still believe that the advantages of sperm and egg selection outweigh the risks. Indeed, most parents still prefer to bring children 'of their own' or as much as possible 'of their own' into existence (and not adopt), even if this means using donated sperm and eggs.

At the same time, because of the availability of so much choice in sperm and egg donation, new ethical challenges may arise. For example, a controversial case of egg donation occurred in 1993 when a black South African woman, who was unable to produce her own eggs, decided to be implanted with an embryo created through the use of her white husband's sperm and the donated egg of a white woman. The woman's primary motivation was her conviction that a white child would have a better future than one of mixed race.[17] Such examples, however, raise questions about the extent to which future parents should be able to select donor characteristics. Is it ethical to select for race if it is believed that the chosen child will have a better future? And is the practice of selecting-out a trait that is widely seen as a genetic disorder acceptable? These questions raise genuine ethical challenges, especially since sperm and egg selection for eugenic purposes has already gone far beyond screening for physical disorders – sperm selection is already being used to select traits such as intelligence.

A final unrelated question that arises is whether each sperm and egg cell may be considered a kind of representative of the person from whom it originates when used to bring into existence a child. From this perspective each sperm cell, though somewhat different genetically from another, becomes a representative of the whole man; and each egg cell, though genetically different from another, becomes a representative of the whole woman. It can then be argued that because the partners in a couple should unconditionally accept each other, they should also unconditionally accept whichever representative sperm or egg cell from each other is used in procreation, without any selection or the use of donated eggs or sperm.[18]

---

16 E. N. Glenn, *Shades of Difference: Why Skin Color Matters* (Stanford: Stanford University Press, 2009), p. 136.

17 The Church of Scotland Board of Social Responsibility, *Pre-Conceived Ideas: A Christian Perspective of IVF and Embryology* (Edinburgh: Saint Andrew Press, 1996), p. 7.

18 C. MacKellar, 'Representative Aspects of Some Synthetic Gametes', *The New Bioethics* 21.2 (2015), pp. 105–116.

Eugenics through prenatal genetic selection

Most women expecting a child in developed countries will be offered some form of prenatal examination, which is intended, among other reasons, to identify those who have an increased risk of giving birth to a child with a disorder. These women, who include those over the age of thirty-five or who know that they are at risk of passing on a heritable disorder, are then offered a diagnostic test. Prenatal diagnosis is a procedure undertaken on a woman to test whether her foetus may have a genetic condition such as Down syndrome. Generally, these diagnostic tests include taking a biological sample by inserting a needle into either the amniotic sac (amniocentesis) or the outer membrane surrounding the foetus (chorionic villus sampling). The invasiveness of these tests varies, however, and may carry a small risk of miscarriage. But a more recent non-invasive prenatal test has been developed, which examines the very small amounts of foetal DNA found in samples of the pregnant mother's blood. In this way foetuses affected by disorders such as Down syndrome may be detected without any risks of miscarriage. In the future the test could also be developed into examining a broad genetic profile of the child to be born.

Because these tests may enable parents to make a form of prenatal genetic selection, a number of commentators suggest that attitudes towards prenatal genetic diagnosis may reflect how society considers the development of the new eugenics.[19] Such testing may then become a predictor of the ever-increasing choice now becoming available in selecting children. Experts expect that prenatal screening for a large number of disorders may even become relatively common in the future if the costs and risks of testing continue to decrease.

The case in favour of prenatal genetic selection

As already mentioned, prenatal diagnosis can enable individuals wanting a child to be informed about the health status of their foetus and thereby make an informed decision about terminating it if it is diagnosed as having a disorder. Thus, those who support prenatal diagnosis emphasize

---

[19] President's Council on Bioethics, *Beyond Therapy: Biotechnology and the Pursuit of Happiness. A Report of the President's Council on Bioethics* (Washington, D.C., 2003), p. 35.

that without the option of prenatal screening many individuals wanting a child may decide not to bear their own children, though some may also opt for adoption. Moreover, by testing for disorders prior to the birth of the child, prospective parents may obtain peace of mind if the child is found to be free from the difficult experiences associated with severe disorders. But the reverse may also happen if couples who have already decided not to have an abortion choose to test in order to address their worries concerning the health of the prenatal child. They may then become distressed if the results show that the embryo/foetus is affected by a disorder.

So far, prenatal testing for non-medical reasons does not usually take place because it is associated with a small risk of miscarriage as well as with very real anxiety in the parents when they wait for the test results. Therefore such a procedure is not used at present if there are no risks of serious medical disorders in the foetus.

The case against prenatal genetic selection

Arguments opposing prenatal diagnosis are significant, with the most important being the possibility of an abortion should the foetus be affected by a biological disorder. This happens even though many members of society, including Christians, are prepared to consider a foetus as having the same moral status as a human being who has been born, thus giving it the same rights to protection. From their perspective an abortion represents only the unacceptable elimination of an individual before he or she is born instead of seeking to provide treatment for him or her in the context of medical practice. It becomes a form of negative destructive eugenics though voluntarily undertaken by the woman.

In this regard, though non-directive counselling may enable the woman to make a decision in accordance with her values, it should be recognized that disability is generally considered by many as being negative and not neutral. Thus, while counselling may be well intentioned, there is still a latent bias against preserving a life that has a disability. Prenatal screening may therefore encourage the development of a new perspective which accepts that certain disabilities invalidate the continued life of an embryo or foetus. As John Paul II explained in 1995:

> Prenatal diagnosis, which presents no moral objections if carried out in order to identify the medical treatment which may be needed

> by the child in the womb, all too often becomes an opportunity for proposing and procuring an abortion. This is eugenic abortion, justified in public opinion on the basis of a mentality – mistakenly held to be consistent with the demands of 'therapeutic interventions' – which accepts life only under certain conditions and rejects it when it is affected by any limitation, handicap or illness.[20]

Similarly, Pope Francis indicated in 2019:

> [H]uman life is sacred and inviolable, and the use of prenatal diagnosis for selective purposes must be strongly discouraged. It is an expression of an inhumane eugenic mentality that deprives families of the chance to accept, embrace and love the weakest of their children.[21]

In this context Francis explained that:

> No human being can ever be unfit for life, whether due to age, state of health or quality of existence. Every child who appears in a woman's womb is a gift that changes a family's history . . . That child needs to be welcomed, loved and nurtured.[22]

But recent trends, both among healthcare professionals and among the general public, indicate that embryos and foetuses are often expected to meet a certain threshold of quality of life before they are accepted as worthy of postnatal life.[23] The French Jesuit priest Bruno Saintôt says, 'With this prospect of systematic sorting of embryos in utero, we begin to drift into a eugenic perspective.' He adds:

---

20 John Paul II, *Evangelium Vitae* (1995); retrieved 7 February 2020 from <http://w2.vatican.va/content/john-paul-ii/en/encyclicals/documents/hf_jp-ii_enc_25031995_evangelium-vitae.html>.

21 Address of Pope Francis to participants in the conference 'Yes to Life! – Caring for the Precious Gift of Life in Its Frailness', 25 May 2019; retrieved 24 September 2019 from <http://w2.vatican.va/content/francesco/en/speeches/2019/may/documents/papa-francesco_20190525_yes-to-life.html>.

22 Ibid.

23 Cf. President's Council on Bioethics, *Beyond Therapy: Biotechnology and the Pursuit of Happiness. A Report of the President's Council on Bioethics* (Washington, D.C.: President's Council, 2003), pp. 36–37.

> How far will the measure of seriousness be placed? Without medical supervision or discernment, the demands of individual freedom will prevail, . . . liberal eugenics will develop because the selection possibilities on offer through biotechnology will be at the service of the fulfillment of the social ideals of performance, effectiveness and security.[24]

On this account prenatal diagnosis may change societal attitudes from the long-entrenched position that all human beings are equal and unconditionally worthy of existence. This is because, with the procedure, some prenatal children in society are deliberately deselected on account of their biological make-up, meaning that the equal value and worth of all human life is put back into question. As Leon Kass notes:

> Practitioners of prenatal diagnosis . . . already screen for a long list of genetic diseases and abnormalities, from Down syndrome to dwarfism. Possession of any of these defects, they believe, renders a prospective child unworthy of life.
>
> Persons who happen still to be born with these conditions, having somehow escaped the spreading net of detection and eugenic abortion, are increasingly regarded as 'mistakes,' as inferior human beings who should not have been born.[25] . . . Determining who shall live and who shall die – on the basis of genetic merit – is a godlike power already wielded by genetic medicine. This power will only grow.[26]

In this context, the Holy See's Pontifical Academy for Life has indicated that it 'is opposed to strategies of interference with fetal anomalies with a view to deciding who should and should not be born on the basis of genetic criteria'.[27]

---

24 In M. Verdier, 'Développer le diagnostic préimplantatoire ?', *La Croix*, 20 March 2018 (tr. C. MacKellar).

25 Kass mentions here in a footnote, 'One of the most worrisome but least appreciated aspects of the godlike power of the new genetics is its tendency to "redefine" a human being in terms of his genes.'

26 L. R. Kass, *Life, Liberty and the Defense of Dignity: The Challenge for Bioethics* (San Francisco: Encounter, 2002), pp. 129–130.

27 Pontifical Academy for Life, *Observations on the Universal Declaration on the Human Genome and Human Rights 1997*, Vatican City; retrieved 18 September 2019 from <www.vatican.va/roman_curia/pontifical_academies/acdlife/documents/rc_pa_acdlife_doc_08111998_genoma_en.html>.

Eugenics and embryonic selection

A number of preimplantation embryonic selection procedures already exist enabling an embryo to be created, through IVF, in a laboratory before being screened and selected prior to implantation into the woman. Not all of these procedures will be presented in this study but one of the most important is called preimplantation genetic diagnosis. This is generally used for individuals or couples who suspect or are aware that they may be carriers of a genetic disorder.

The procedure begins with the creation of embryos through IVF, which are then left to develop in the laboratory until they are formed from at least eight cells. The embryologist then removes one or two of the cells from each embryo and tests them for any faulty genes under consideration. Embryos without the disordered genes can then be implanted in the hope that they will develop normally into a baby, with any remaining unaffected embryos being stored for future use. On the other hand, those embryos with faulty genes are usually destroyed.

Preimplantation embryonic selection is slowly becoming more common in reproductive clinics. In addition, with the anticipated development of genetic testing, an increasing number of individuals may become more aware of the genetic risks of passing on a genetic disorder through natural non-selective reproduction and may then choose preimplantation embryonic selection to reduce this risk. It is suggested, therefore, that the different choices of the future parents should be respected – choices that should be taken solely by them, without the intervention of a third party.

The case for preimplantation embryonic selection

For some individuals or couples a significant advantage of preimplantation embryonic selection is that it may avoid any consideration, or even the decision, of terminating a pregnancy. This is because with this procedure embryos affected by a genetic disorder can be eliminated even before gestation begins. Only healthy embryos are thus implanted into the uterus of the woman wanting a child. For individuals who do not believe that embryos have a meaningful moral status, preimplantation embryonic selection then gives the possibility of considering a pregnancy without the anxiety of transferring a disorder since any embryos with the disorder are selected-out. Many persons believe, therefore, that the ethical concerns regarding preimplantation embryonic selection do not apply in the same way as in the use of prenatal diagnosis.[28]

Preimplantation embryonic selection may also offer a number of significant advantages to future parents. For instance, the procedure may help a greater number of them to have a child 'of their own' while making sure he or she is physically healthy. In other words, preimplantation embryonic selection reflects the values generally found in families and, by extension, in society at large. These include the reality that similarities may give rise to social bonds including bond-creating factors such as when similar traits, such as intelligence, musicality or even athletic abilities, exist. Parents with multiple common traits in their children may then develop a stronger sense of solidarity and common interest, enabling them to become more intimate with one another. That is to say, it would enable children to grow up in a better environment while developing social skills that enable them to flourish.

Another advantage of preimplantation embryonic selection is that it may be possible to use the procedure to select for specific traits, instead of just selecting-out embryos with a disorder. In other words, new developments and more precise testing procedures may enable individuals to use preimplantation embryonic selection to select for what may be considered desirable genes. As a result, the possibility of positive eugenics through embryo selection cannot be ignored, though a number of significant practical issues still need to be addressed before the procedure is routinely used. For example, it is uncertain whether preimplantation embryonic selection could efficiently select embryos on the basis of physical characteristics even if testing for multiple genetic variants becomes possible. This is because of the limited availability of DNA from the cell(s) being tested by the procedure, the sensitivity of the genetic tests and the ability to perform multiple tests on the same sample. In addition, selecting for characteristics controlled by multiple genes would require screening a large number of embryos in order to find one with the desirable complement. However, most rounds of IVF create only about a dozen embryos, which is not enough to screen for multiple traits. Nonetheless, techniques may be developed in the future allowing the screening of embryos for multiple genetic variants. New procedures are also being considered

---

28 As e.g. Nuffield Council on Bioethics, *Genetics and Human Behaviour* (London: Nuffield Council on Bioethics, 2002), p. 152.

enabling a much larger number of eggs to be obtained from the woman that would, after they were all fertilized in the laboratory, give couples access to a large number of embryos from which to choose.

The case against preimplantation embryonic selection

A number of significant arguments exist, however, in opposition to the use of preimplantation embryonic selection. To begin with, by using preimplantation embryonic selection a number of embryos are usually created, with only a few being selected and implanted. This means that a significant number of embryos may be left over, with those considered to be substandard immediately being destroyed, while those judged to be healthy are frozen in storage for possible future use. The fate of these surplus frozen embryos, which in countries such as the UK are numbered in their hundreds of thousands, gives rise to serious concern. This is because a decision will eventually have to be taken about whether they should be discarded, stored for a longer period of time, adopted by other parents, given to scientists for destructive research or have another fate.

Most of the human embryos not chosen for implantation are eventually destroyed. This means that, for those who consider embryos as having full moral status with a right to life from the moment of creation (or who are willing to give them the benefit of the doubt), preimplantation embryonic selection is associated with a morally unacceptable action in the destruction of human life. Persons with such a view then see no difference between preimplantation embryonic selection and prenatal selection.

In addition, one particular eugenic concern in the use of preimplantation embryonic selection is the range of both present and future conditions for which the procedure may be considered. In other words, anxiety exists with preimplantation embryonic selection that it may develop a eugenic mindset.

Some concerns also exist that such embryonic selection may result in valuing people on the basis of increasingly trivial traits. This means that the current practice of only screening-out embryos who are affected by disorders could expand to screening-out embryos with less serious physical disorders. In this way preimplantation embryonic selection raises ethical issues relating to discrimination and stigmatization of certain types of people as well as to the difficult issue of defining the seriousness of a disorder. In the past the procedure was generally used only for severe disorders. But this is now changing since some countries, such as the UK, are increasingly considering preimplantation embryonic selection for late-onset diseases expressed only in the later life of the individual, or low-penetrance diseases that affect only a relatively low percentage of individuals with the genetic disorder. The fact that such testing occurs even when some form of treatment may be available suggests that preimplantation embryonic selection is becoming more common for less serious genetic traits.[29]

It should also be remembered that preimplantation embryonic selection cannot enable the selection of enhanced babies, since the procedure can only select genes already present in the genetic parents of the embryo. In other words, the procedure cannot create new biological traits that do not exist in the parents. This means that parents who seek to use preimplantation embryonic selection to provide them with the perfect child may be disappointed.

A further challenge associated with preimplantation embryonic selection is that the procedure may be used to select-in embryos affected by what many may consider to be a certain disorder rather than being used to select-out a genetic condition. For example, it could enable deaf parents to select embryos that carried a gene for deafness in order to fulfil their wish to have a deaf child in order to support family cohesion. This would happen even though deafness is generally considered a disorder.[30] In this case, there is a significant difference between using the procedure to select for what can be considered a genetic disorder and refusing to use preimplantation embryonic selection to test for any condition. The former intentionally selects for a condition, whereas the latter simply accepts the deficiencies of human existence in a spirit of natural humility and unconditional acceptance of the child, irrespective of his or her biological characteristics. Of course, it is sometimes difficult to determine the fine line between the two situations, but the deliberate selection of what could be considered a negative trait makes the action ethically suspect.

---

[29] J. Gunning, 'The Broadening Impact of Preimplantation Genetic Diagnosis: A Slide Down the Slippery Slope or Meeting Market Demand?', *Human Reproduction and Genetic Ethics* 14.1 (2008), pp. 29–37.

[30] J. Savulescu, 'Education and Debate: Deaf Lesbians, "Designer Disability," and the Future of Medicine', *British Medical Journal (Clinical Research Edition)* 325.7367 (2002), pp. 771–773.

The selection of saviour siblings

In recent years biomedical developments have enabled a new application for preimplantation embryonic selection, which gives rise to unique ethical questions. This is in the creation of 'saviour siblings', which uses the procedure to determine whether an embryo has the potential to provide a life-saving treatment for an older child who has the same biological parents as the embryo.[31] This happens if the older sibling suffers from a grave illness which could be treated with compatible stem cells.

In the procedure the parents would undergo IVF to create a number of embryos in a laboratory. Preimplantation embryonic selection would then be used to choose those that were healthy while also selecting from these healthy embryos those whose cells are immunologically compatible with the sick, older, child. These selected embryos would then be considered for implantation into the mother. All going well, this would eventually give rise to the birth of a healthy infant. Stem cells from the umbilical cord blood of the new child would subsequently be collected and used to treat the older sibling. Since these cells would be immunologically compatible with the older sick sibling, it is expected that no rejection problems would exist when transplanted. This means that although preimplantation embryonic selection may be used to ensure that only a healthy embryo is selected, it is also further being considered to select an embryo (and the resulting future child) as a source of treatment for the older sibling.

The first 'saviour sibling' procedure was undertaken in the USA in 2000 for a family whose daughter had a serious bone marrow disorder. After four attempts and the creation of about thirty embryos, the couple successfully used preimplantation embryonic selection to conceive a healthy son who could provide stem cells from his umbilical cord for transplantation into his older sister. The procedure was described as 'a complete success' and the sick daughter's health improved dramatically.[32]

However, very real ethical difficulties exist with the 'saviour sibling' procedure because when embryonic selection is used to create a selected

---

31 At present it is generally a sibling that is considered for the treatment, but it could also be a close relative such as a cousin. In this regard, a child could even, theoretically, be conceived to save his or her parent (saviour offspring).

32 For the whole story, see B. Whitehouse, *The Match: 'Savior Siblings' and One Family's Battle to Heal Their Daughter* (Boston: Beacon, 2010).

child, he or she is primarily brought into existence for the benefit of another person and not for his or her own sake, which is a form of instrumentalization of the child. Of course, future parents wanting to create a saviour sibling may claim that they also desired to have an additional healthy child. But parental motivations for wanting a child are notoriously difficult to establish. In the event that a couple obtain only healthy but immunologically incompatible embryos, and then refuse to implant any of them, it could be inferred that their original motivation was not simply based on having a healthy child but to use the embryos for another purpose. To all intents and purposes, the embryos were valuable only when they could be used to provide a service.

Fears relating to instrumentalization also exist if, at birth, not enough umbilical cord blood is obtained. The infant may then be considered for removal of bone marrow, in which stem cells are also present, which could be transplanted into his or her older sibling. But, if this was not successful, the selected saviour sibling child would effectively have failed to save his or her older sibling. It would then be possible to ask whether the child's very existence might be seen as a failure. So it is important to query on what basis the success of a person's life is measured. In the same way, questions may be raised whether it is right that a child's very existence is dependent on addressing the hopes of his or her parents towards a sibling.

Eugenic selection through human cloning

Cloning is defined as a procedure that enables one organism to be brought into existence as a genetic copy of another. This is usually achieved when all the genetic material in the chromosomes of a cell from the body of a donor person (there are usually forty-six chromosomes in such a cell) is removed and introduced into an unfertilized egg whose own chromosomes (there are usually twenty-three chromosomes in a reproductive cell) have been removed. The genes from the forty-six chromosomes of the new 'fertilized' egg cell are then identical to those of the donor, and if all goes well will develop into a child whose genetic heritage is similar to that of the person who donated the original chromosomes. Thus, in contrast to natural or assisted forms of procreation, reproductive cloning brings into existence a child with the same chromosomal genetic make-up as the person who donated the original cell.[33]

Reproductive cloning raises important ethical questions relating to the larger discussion of the new eugenics because it can be used to examine how the selection of offspring may be considered when other selective procedures are employed.

The case in favour of selection through cloning

One possible advantage of reproductive eugenic cloning is the ability to replicate the most talented human beings who have been demonstrated to be of 'high quality'. Parents or even society could then clone individuals with remarkable traits such as intellectual capacity or physical beauty, which were influenced to some degree by their genetic heritage. Not only would these superior individuals be extremely talented, but they might also be gifted with faculties of leadership, confidence and enterprise, enabling them to support others in their accomplishments. Moreover, these enhanced cloned individuals would be able to continue reproducing in a normal way, thereby spreading their superior genetic heritage to future generations.

Another proposed advantage of reproductive cloning is that couples would be able to have a child genetically related to at least one of them. In other words, a child that could be considered 'of their own'. This could happen when a couple are unable to have children, including for such reasons as homosexuality or fertility problems or because of the risks of giving birth to a child with a genetic disorder. Reproductive cloning could then be used to bring into existence a child using genetic material from one of the future parents. In this way they could avoid the possible psychological concerns in the resulting child that might arise from the use of donor sperm, eggs or embryos. Moreover, the possibility for parents to raise a child biologically similar to one of them might be seen as an advantage, since they would already be aware of the biological features of the cloned child.

On account of these future possibilities society may then accept that reproductive cloning is a viable means for improving the whole of human society. But because many more children with superior biological traits

---

33 The donor is termed the 'somatic cell donor' since he or she has given a somatic cell, the type of cell that makes up the majority of human cells.

might be brought into existence, a competitive situation could develop, pushing for ever more enhancement and selection. However, the cloned child may not always turn out as expected and significant behavioural or even physical differences may develop between the cell donor and the resulting cloned child. For example, personality differences are not uncommon between identical twins, who can also be considered as genetic clones.

The case against selection through cloning

Scientific objections to reproductive cloning are quite substantial. Dolly the Scottish cloned sheep required 277 attempts to be born, meaning that cloning a human being would be very difficult.[34] Moreover, scientists have demonstrated a high rate of malformations (including extraordinary size) and premature deaths in certain cloned animals.[35]

However, in addition to the biological problems, a number of psychological consequences may result in cloned individuals. These could arise, for example, from overdemanding expectations and a sense of control by the parents. As Leon Kass indicated:

> [W]e don't recognize or admit the degree to which cloned children would fit perfectly into the postmoral ambience in which we now live. Thanks to our belief that all children should be *wanted* children . . . , sooner or later only those children who fulfil our wants will be fully acceptable.[36]

Of course, without really asking cloned individuals how they feel, there may be no way of determining how they would consider their own identity, their genetic parents or the scientists who helped bring them into existence. The resulting cloned persons would not only be indebted to their progenitors for their existence but might be expected to live particular and preconditioned lives in order to fulfil the expectations of those

---

[34] I. Wilmut, K. Campbell and C. Tudge, *The Second Creation: Dolly and the Age of Biological Control* (Cambridge, Mass.: Harvard University Press, 2001), p. 216.

[35] Similar risks are likely to be present in human cloning, though the successful cloning of non-human primates was announced in 2018 by Zhen Liu, Yijun Cai, Yan Wang, Yanhong Nie, Chenchen Zhang, Yuting Xu, Xiaotong Zhang, Yong Lu, Zhanyang Wang, Muming Poo, and Qiang Sun, 'Cloning of Macaque Monkeys by Somatic Cell Nuclear Transfer', *Cell* 172.4 (2018), pp. 881–887.e7.

[36] Kass, *Life*, p. 144 (emphasis original).

who brought them into being. Cloning may thus threaten to instrumentalize the human person, and in so doing undermines the respect due to his or her inherent value and worth. As Kass explained:

> Human cloning would ... represent a giant step towards the transformation of begetting into making, of procreation into manufacture ... [–] manufacture is further degraded by commodification, a virtual inescapable result of allowing baby-making to proceed under the banner of commerce.[37]

With reproductive cloning, parents may also be able to choose the exact genetic constitution of their children, making it possible for one generation to have a considerable amount of control over the next.[38] Kass indicates, 'Through cloning, we can work our wants and wills on the very identity of our children, exercising control as never before.'[39] This is also something the Holy See's Pontifical Academy for Life mentioned concerning cloning in 1997:

> Contrary to what may appear at first sight, the principle of parity and equality among human beings is violated by this possible form of man's domination over man, and the discrimination comes about through the whole selective-eugenic dimension inherent in the logic of cloning.[40]

Thus, any acceptance of reproductive cloning could lead to the selection of children as a means simply to satisfy the demands of their future parents or the expectations of the human society at the time. In other words, the real eugenic concern relates to the risk that a child could be valued for a reason other than his or her mere existence. Any reproductive cloning intent on bringing into existence a more perfect human being should, therefore, be considered with alarm and apprehension.

---

37 L. R. Kass, 'The Wisdom of Repugnance', *New Republic* 216.22 (1997), pp. 17–26 (pp. 23–24).

38 President's Council on Bioethics, *Human Cloning and Human Dignity: An Ethical Inquiry* (Washington, D.C.: President's Council, 2002), pp. 104–105.

39 L. R. Kass, 'The Wisdom of Repugnance: Why We Should Ban the Cloning of Humans', *Valparaiso University Law Review* 32.2 (1998), pp. 679–705 (p. 682).

40 Pontifical Academy for Life, *Reflections on Cloning* (1997), para. 4; retrieved 13 February 2020 from <www.vatican.va/roman_curia/pontifical_academies/acdlife/documents/rc_pa_acdlife_doc_30091997_clon_en.html>.

Eugenic selection through infanticide

Eugenic selection could also take place by deselecting newly born children by killing them through a direct act or through the intentional withholding or withdrawing of ordinary care necessary for the children's survival. Fortunately, to most members of society, infanticide is deeply offensive since an infant is accepted to be a human person with the same moral status as any other person. However, in some countries, guidelines have already been developed to terminate the lives of infants who are born with severe disability. For example, in the Netherlands the 'Groningen Protocol' was developed in 2004 at the University Medical Center of Groningen. This provides criteria under which physicians can end the life of infants (child euthanasia) without fear of prosecution. Among a number of reasons, the Protocol was prepared because it was believed that some infants would be limited to a life of poor quality that might represent, for them, unbearable suffering. But as Reinders explains concerning this Protocol:

> The conclusion presents itself that the prospect of a 'poor' quality of life for disabled infants necessarily depends on representations of what other people believe to be true about their lives. But accepting such representations as decisive is seriously flawed . . . In particular, children with congenital disabilities have never known themselves other than with these conditions. The assumption that the child's projected response to this condition will amount to 'unbearable suffering' is unwarranted. To them living with a disability is the 'normal' state of being, in which they experience the world around them.
>
> No doubt 'parents and medical experts' may regard living with their condition unbearable, but it does not follow that the children will experience the same. If suffering occurs in the life of these children, it is most likely the effect of beliefs held in their social and cultural environment assuming that their lives must be unbearable to the point of not being worth living.[41]

---

[41] J. Reinders, T. Stainton and T. R. Parmenter, 'The Quiet Progress of the New Eugenics. Ending the Lives of Persons with Intellectual and Developmental Disabilities for Reasons of Presumed Poor Quality of Life: The Quiet Progress of the New Eugenics', *Journal of Policy and Practice in Intellectual Disabilities* 16.2 (2019), pp. 99–112 (p. 102).

In other words, it may be the parents, healthcare professionals and society in general who may find the lives of these persons with disability to be unbearable and not the individuals themselves.

The case in favour of selection through infanticide

Some reasons have always been proposed in society for supporting infanticide, such as when a child's very existence is seen as being incompatible with a meaningful life from the perspective of his or her family and/or society. In ancient Greece, for example, Plato presented his view of the ideal state in his book *Republic*, in which infanticide was presented as being essential to maintain the quality of its citizens. He wrote, '[T]he children of inferior parents, or any child of the others born defective, they will hide [properly dispose], as is fitting, in a secret and unknown place.'[42] Similarly, Aristotle maintained that no deformed child should be allowed to live. In his *Politics* he wrote, 'As to exposing or rearing the children born let there be a law that no deformed child shall be reared.'[43] Thus, if a child was considered to have an inferior quality of life, or even a seemingly pointless life, while being a crushing burden on others, it was suggested at the time that a family might have an acceptable reason to kill the child, who did not have a guarantee to live.

Surprisingly, however, this position is also presented in contemporary society. For example, in 1978 Francis Crick was quoted as saying, 'no newborn infant should be declared human until it has passed certain tests regarding its genetic endowment and that if it fails these tests it forfeits the right to live'.[44] But Crick was by no means the only person with such a position. In 1973 James Watson had suggested:

> If a child were not declared alive until three days after birth, then all parents could be allowed the choice that only a few are given under

---

[42] Plato, *Republic*, Book 5, in A. Bailey, S. Brennan, W. Kymlicka, J. Levy and A. Sager (eds), *The Broadview Anthology of Social and Political Thought: From Plato to Nietzsche*, vol. 1. (Peterborough, Ont.: Broadview, 2008), p. 88.

[43] Aristotle, *Politics*, Book 7; retrieved 7 February 2020 from <www.perseus.tufts.edu/hopper/text?doc=Perseus:abo:tlg,0086,035:7:1335b>.

[44] Quoted in F. A. Schaeffer and C. E. Koop, *Whatever Happened to the Human Race?* (London: Marshall, Morgan & Scott, 1982), p. 38.

> the present system. The doctor could allow the child to die if the parents so choose and save a lot of misery and suffering.[45]

Although Watson himself denounced this future, he accepted that it was a logical conclusion. The same kind of thinking returned in the UK when John Harris in 2004 expressed what could be considered a limited acceptance of infanticide if, for instance, a genetic disorder in a foetus is undetected during pregnancy. He said, 'I don't think infanticide is always unjustifiable. I don't think it is plausible to think that there is any moral change that occurs during the journey down the birth canal.'[46]

Of course, any discussion of abortion and infanticide is a complex matter, with the underlying debate about the different stages at which a living being should be recognized as having full moral status. If the beginning of biological life is the same as the beginning of human personhood, then abortion cannot be supported. On the other hand, if to be a person one must have reached a certain stage of development, then the acts of abortion, and also infanticide, become more intellectually acceptable.[47] As the Australian moral philosopher Peter Singer made clear in 1993:

> Regarding newborn infants as replaceable, as we now regard fetuses, would . . . [result in] considerable advantages . . . Prenatal diagnosis still cannot detect major disabilities . . . At present, parents can choose to keep or destroy their disabled offspring only if the disability happens to be detected during pregnancy . . . If disabled newborn infants were not regarded as having a right to life until, say, a week or a month after birth it would allow parents, in consultation with their doctors, to choose on the basis of far greater knowledge of the infant's condition than is possible before birth.[48]

---

[45] Quoted in 'Medicine: Endorsing Infanticide', *TIME*, 28 May 1973; retrieved 10 August 2011 from <www.time.com/time/magazine/article/0,9171,910661,00.html>.

[46] E. Day, 'Infanticide Is Justifiable in Some Cases, Says Ethics Professor', *The Telegraph*, 25 January 2004; retrieved 10 August 2011 from <http://tinyurl.com/telegraph-harris-interview>.

[47] J. McMahan, *The Ethics of Killing* (Oxford: Oxford University Press, 2002), p. 6.

[48] P. Singer, *Practical Ethics*, 2nd edn (Cambridge: Cambridge University Press, 1993), p. 190.

It can also be argued that controlled infanticide, just like controlled late abortions, on the grounds of quality of life, could support societal progress by enabling yet another means of deselecting genetically defective human beings. In this way infanticide would merely be a further development towards a certain form of negative eugenics. These examples indicate that a resurgence may be taking place for proposals to reconsider infanticide as an acceptable option for deselecting the life of a child born with a serious physical disorder.

The case against selection through infanticide

Despite a number of reasons being proposed in favour of infanticide, which are generally based on quality of life arguments, contemporary society has, so far, completely rejected such a possibility. However, with ever more questions being asked as to the moral difference between late-term foetuses and newborn babies as well as the prioritization of the concept of a good life, the situation may be starting to change. As John Paul II indicated in 1995:

> [T]he point has been reached where the most basic care, even nourishment, is denied to babies born with serious handicaps or illnesses. The contemporary scene, moreover, is becoming even more alarming by reason of the proposals, advanced here and there, to justify even infanticide, following the same arguments used to justify the right to abortion. In this way, we revert to a state of barbarism which one hoped had been left behind forever.[49]

This means that even the apparent logic of an argument cannot reflect its acceptability. As numerous present legal and ethical codes indicate, the prohibition of infanticide is based on the belief that it is a form of murder, since the human being whose life is ended is a human person with an inherent value and worth. This is also the Christian position in which any killing of a born child is contrary to the inviolable worth of every human life created by God and reflecting his image.

49 John Paul II, *Evangelium Vitae* (1995), para. 43; retrieved 3 December 2007 from <www.vatican.va/holy_father/john_paul_ii/encyclicals/documents/hf_jp-ii_enc_25031995_evangelium-vitae_en.html>.

Eugenics through genome and germline modifications

One reason for questioning the legitimacy of eugenic genetic modifications arises from the kinds of characteristics parents may desire for their children, such as athleticism or intelligence, which may be the result of a large number of genes and be influenced by other non-genetic factors. In other words, they may result from a multifaceted relationship between biology and the environment. But a small number of genetic traits are also influenced by only a few genes, making it possible to use the new procedure of genome editing to influence the relevant biological characteristics in a human being.

Genome editing

The possibility of editing the genome (the complete genetic make-up) of living beings is set to revolutionize many areas of biological research. For the first time scientists can now precisely modify parts of these genomes by removing or inserting genetic material. This is especially the case with what is called the CRISPR-Cas9[50] editing system, which is relatively easy and inexpensive to use while only requiring two components to work. These are a guide ribonucleic acid (RNA) genetic coding sequence (a kind of genetic homing mechanism) and a Cas enzyme (a protein working as a kind of molecular scissors), with Cas9 being the enzyme that is most used to cut the DNA strands. In this way, the guide RNA with a certain genetic code seeks out the specific genetic target of the DNA strand of the genome and then forms a complex (a large molecular structure) with the Cas9 enzyme. This cleaves the DNA strand and enables a specific genetic sequence to be taken out. The strand can then either be rejoined or a new genetic sequence inserted.

Genome editing can be used in research, such as when specific gene sequences are disabled or replaced in early animal embryos in order to better understand embryonic development. It is also suggested that it will be possible in the future to inactivate disordered genes that may be responsible for a disease and replace them with healthy ones. The prevention of genetic disorders and even new treatments could then be considered.

---

[50] Clustered, regularly interspaced short palindromic repeats with the Cas9 protein; i.e. the CRISPR/Cas9 system.

Biomedical trials using genome editing on human cells are already under way, such as in the use of edited immune cells to treat cancer.[51] But two important milestones were achieved when Chinese scientists became the first to edit the genome of a human embryo in 2015[52] and bring to birth twin girls who were genetically modified as single cell fertilized eggs in 2018.[53] Other studies have been reported or suggested either using existing human embryos and genetically editing them after fertilization (post-conception) or injecting the genome editing system at the same time as fertilization.[54] A third possibility would be to edit the genes of the sperm or egg cell before conception (pre-conception). In these last two procedures it is expected that the embryo would develop in such a way that every cell and subsequent organ would contain the edited DNA, including the reproductive cells, enabling a more efficient, uniform genome editing to take place in the individual. In the UK all these different kinds of genome editing procedures in human embryos were approved in 2016 by the Human Fertilisation and Embryology Authority, but only for research embryos not intended to be used for reproductive purposes.[55]

Ethical perspective

From an ethical perspective a number of arguments have been presented relating to the advantages to humankind arising from the possibility of manipulating the genes of possible future or existing persons. But risks also exist, such as with the safety of the procedures. For example, inserting or deleting genes in the correct location of the genome of a developing embryo without upsetting the biological equilibrium of the cell(s) is a

---

51 N. Winblad and F. Lanner, 'Biotechnology: At the Heart of Gene Edits in Human Embryos', *Nature* 548.7668 (2017), pp. 398–400.

52 Puping Liang, Yanwen Xu, Xiya Zhang, Chenhui Ding, Rui Huang, Zhen Zhang, Jie Lv, Xiaowei Xie, Yuxi Chen, Yujing Li, Ying Sun, Yaofu Bai, Zhou Songyang, Wenbin Ma, Canquan Zhou and Junjiu Huang, 'CRISPR/Cas9-Mediated Gene Editing in Human Tripronuclear Zygotes', *Protein Cell* 6.5 (2015), pp. 363–372.

53 D. Cyranoski and H. Ledford, 'Genome-Edited Baby Claim Provokes International Outcry', *Nature News*, 26 November 2018.

54 Ibid.; Xiangjin Kang, Wenyin He, Yuling Huang, Qian Yu, Yaoyong Chen, Xingcheng Gao, Xiaofang Sun and Yong Fan, 'Introducing Precise Genetic Modifications into Human 3PN Embryos by CRISPR/Cas-Mediated Genome Editing', *Journal of Assisted Reproduction and Genetics* 33.5 (2016), pp. 581–588; Lichun Tang, Yanting Zeng, Hongzi Du, Mengmeng Gong, Jin Peng, Buxi Zhang, Ming Lei, Fang Zhao, Weihua Wang, Xiaowei Li and Jianqiao Liu, 'CRISPR/Cas9-Mediated Gene Editing in Human Zygotes Using Cas9 Protein', *Molecular Genetics and Genomics* 292.3 (2017), pp. 525–533.

55 J. Gallagher, 'Scientists Get "Gene Editing" Go-Ahead', *BBC News*, 1 February 2016; retrieved 29 October 2018 from <http://www.bbc.co.uk/news/health-35459054>.

difficult operation. A particular gene may influence a number of different characteristics, which means that even if a gene were modified to influence a specific dysfunction, this could give rise to unexpected consequences. The overall result would be a modification that might be less than beneficial. There is also a fear of creating new genetic changes in the wrong place, since examples of gene therapy treatments exist in which genetic modifications have been inserted into patients that have resulted in serious side effects.[56]

Because of these risks, gene therapy has so far been considered only for serious disorders when no other treatment is available. This means that making such genetic modifications for the sole purpose of enhancing certain traits may be seen as reckless and unethical. This is especially the case since any possible negative genetic mutation may be passed on to future generations. In addition, during the research and development stages of human embryonic gene therapy it is unavoidable that a significant number of embryos will be destroyed in the process. Since such embryos may be considered as having the same moral status as any other person made in the image of God, their destruction can be seen as being just as offensive and immoral as the destruction of any other person.[57]

With respect to the genetic modification of human beings it is also important to distinguish between two kinds of changes. The first usually involves the genetic treatment of a person who already exists and affects only him or her (so-called somatic gene therapy), which is generally seen as being acceptable by most Christians as long as safety concerns are addressed. The second kind of change involves a human germline genetic modification, which intentionally alters the genes of descendants – a possibility which gives rise to significant ethical questioning relating to its alluring eugenic implications. As Leon Kass indicates:

> [W]hy should we not effect precise genetic alteration in disease-carrying sperm or eggs or early embryos, in order to prevent in advance the emergence of disease that otherwise will later require expensive and burdensome treatment? And why should not parents

---

[56] M. Cavazzana-Calvo, A. Thrasher and F. Mavilio, 'The Future of Gene Therapy', *Nature* 427 (2004), pp. 779–781.

[57] M. Kirtley, 'CRISPR Update: Considerations for a Rapidly Evolving and Transformative Technology', *Dignitas* 23.1 (2016), pp. 4–8 (pp. 1, 4–8).

> eager to avoid either the birth of afflicted children or trauma of eugenic abortion be able to avail themselves of germ-line alterations?
>
> In short, even before we have had more than trivial experience with gene therapy for existing individuals . . . sober people have called for overturning the current (self-imposed) taboo on germ-line modification.[58]

Indeed, the heritable nature of germline procedures is so appealing that Kass concludes, 'The line between somatic and germ-line modification cannot hold.'[59]

In this context, and because of the very real eugenic risks arising from accepting germline modifications, it is unfortunate that very little has been written on this topic from a Christian perspective, especially in the Protestant and Orthodox Christian denominations. What little does exist relating to germline procedures generally comes from the Roman Catholic tradition, including its 'Magisterium', which usually provides the definitive and settled limits of orthodox doctrine given by all its bishops in communion with the bishop of Rome (the Pope). But even in this tradition, the Roman Catholic bioethicist David Jones explained in 2012:

> On matters that are not as yet defined doctrine (de fide) the current teaching of the Magisterium remains weighty and worthy of respect. However, it may be mistaken in some respects and may need to develop through internal theological criticism.
>
> The ethics of germ-line genetic engineering . . . is a case in point. This is a very new issue and the Church has little definitive teaching on it.[60]

From a Christian perspective, therefore, a lot more still needs to be developed and clarified relating to germline procedures and which genome editing proposals may give cause for concern. This is because there may be distinct factors dependent on the developmental stages at which the genetic modification is being considered and whether a germ-line or a somatic procedure is in fact taking place.

---

58 Kass, *Life*, pp. 122–123.

59 Ibid., p. 123.

60 D. A. Jones, 'Germ-Line Genetic Engineering: A Critical Look at Magisterial Catholic Teaching', *Christian Bioethics* 18.2 (2012), pp. 126–144 (pp. 126–127).

Can certain gene manipulation procedures be considered therapy?

However, before more specific ethical issues concerning genome editing are examined relating to the extent of the changes being contemplated, it is necessary to study the different kinds of personal identities that may exist. This is important in order to establish a difference between procedures that are therapeutic in nature and those that actually bring a new individual into existence who is different from the one who would otherwise have existed.

Different kinds of identities

In discussing the concept of personal identities it is important first to emphasize the various ways in which these can be distinguished. Though a degree of overlap may exist, and there is no consensus in literature, it is possible to differentiate between the following:[61]

1 Numerical identity, which reflects what is necessary for a relationship that a being has to himself or herself to remain over time. In other words, if it were possible to number different individuals (as individual number 1, 2, 3, etc.), numerical identity would mean that 'individual number 1' remains 'individual number 1' (and does not become, for example, a different 'individual number 2'). Thus, numerical identity considers whether an individual at a certain time is identical to the one existing at a later time. In this way, it examines the number of individuals who exist and whether they are distinct. For example, numerical identity considers whether the continuous sense of a living being remains one and the same being throughout his or her life trajectory (from creation to death) in the three dimensions of space and over time. In this case two perspectives are generally presented.

- A biological perspective that reflects the continuous biological being remaining one and the same whole being over time as a biological entity in space despite some qualitative changes such

[61] C. MacKellar, 'Genome Modifying Reproductive Procedures and Their Effects on Numerical Identity', *The New Bioethics* 25.2 (2019), pp. 121–136.

as those arising from the replication and division of cells making up this being.

- A psychological or biographical perspective that reflects the relationship a living being has to itself as remaining one and the same whole individual over time despite some qualitative changes. This generally includes continuity of consciousness, experiential contents or the maintaining of psychological connections or capacities. For example, a psychological connection is present when a memory exists at a certain time and continues to exist at a later time in an individual.

These two numerical identity perspectives can, moreover, be considered separately or together, as when a psychosomatic unity is seen as important.

2 Qualitative identity, which examines similarities in qualities or properties in the same individual in different settings (such as at two different times) or between distinct individuals. For example, two beings may be similar from a biological perspective but exist in different settings of space and/or time. In this way, identical twins are qualitatively identical (for the most part) but numerically distinct, since both individuals can be numbered as 'twin number 1' and 'twin number 2'. Each twin exists in a different setting of the three dimensions of space, though they generally live at the same time.[62]

This means that if a procedure results in numerical identity changes, a new individual is brought into existence who will not, otherwise, have existed. On the other hand, if a procedure results in qualitative identity changes, then the original individual continues to exist.

Somatic genome editing

Having clarified the important difference between procedures that may affect numerical and qualitative identity, it is now possible to examine the case of somatic genome editing. In this regard, if the genetic modification takes place with the aim of addressing a specific genetic disorder in a mature embryo, foetus, child or adult, this could be considered in a similar

62 Even conjoined twins can be considered distinct if each experiences a specific identity.

manner to already existing gene therapy procedures on individuals who already exist. In other words, such treatments would not be intended to affect descendants and have generally been accepted by society. This form of therapy would then correspond to the aims of classical medicine in the restoration of health to the patient. As John Wyatt indicates (from a Christian perspective), '[T]he task of the health professionals is to protect and restore the masterpieces [of human bodies] entrusted to . . . [their] care, in line with the original creator's intentions'.[63]

As already noted, this means that in the case of an individual suffering from a disorder who is seeking to have a genetic treatment, somatic genetic modifications are seen as acceptable for most Christians. The Council of Europe has also recognized this possibility in Article 13 of its *Convention on Human Rights and Biomedicine*. Here the Council states that such a procedure may be supported if it is for 'preventive, diagnostic or therapeutic purposes and only if its aim is not to introduce any modification in the genome of any descendants'. In other words, there is no prohibition on modifying the genetic composition of sperm and egg cells that may affect future generations, but this is possible only if the modification takes place as an unwanted side effect of the somatic genetic treatment of an existing person. This is similar to what happens in radiation therapy, where an existing person is treated even though his or her sperm or egg cells may be affected by the radiation being used and thus result in genetic changes in future descendants. This implies that using a powerful treatment on existing persons with the aim of saving their lives, while being aware that genetic mutations in their sperm and egg cells may take place as an unwanted side effect, may be acceptable. In other words, the balance between the possible risks and benefits is seen as being justified.

Such applications of genome editing for therapeutic purposes, therefore, would not raise many new significant ethical problems, apart from safety and efficacy. The numerical identity of the patient would not be changed; only a modification of the qualitative identity would be taking place.

Germline genome editing

On the other hand, using genome editing with the aim of deliberately changing the genes of children and descendants, defined as germline gene

[63] J. Wyatt, *Matters of Life and Death: Human Dilemmas in the Light of the Christian Faith*, 2nd edn (Nottingham: Inter-Varsity Press, 2009), p. 100.

modification, raises significant ethical concerns. This is because, as will be discussed later, proposed deliberate germline modifications are generally eugenic in nature and it is often in this context that so-called 'designer babies' are mentioned.[64]

A number of international legal texts have already condemned intentional germline modifications. These include the United Nations Educational, Scientific and Cultural Organization (UNESCO) 1997 *Universal Declaration on the Human Genome and Human Rights*, which indicates in Article 24 that germline interventions could be considered a practice 'contrary to human dignity'.[65] Additionally, as already noted, the Council of Europe's *Convention on Human Rights and Biomedicine* indicates, in Article 13, that interventions on the human genome are prohibited if their principal aim is to introduce a modification in the genome of descendants.[66] This means, according to paragraph 91 of the *Explanatory Report* to this Convention, that 'interventions seeking to introduce any modification in the genome of any descendants are prohibited. Consequently, in particular genetic modifications of spermatozoa or ova for fertilisation are not allowed.'[67]

A 2015 UNESCO International Bioethics Committee report also highlighted the eugenic dangers of germline procedures. This indicated that if any intentional germline selection was accepted (such as with genome editing), this would 'jeopardize the inherent and therefore equal dignity of all human beings and renew eugenics, disguised as the fulfilment of the wish for a better, *improved* life'.[68] Actually, it was in order to address such a danger that Article 3 of the EU *Charter of Fundamental Rights*

---

64 K. R. Smith, S. Chan and J. Harris, 'Human Germline Genetic Modification: Scientific and Bioethical Perspectives', *Archives of Medical Research* 43.7 (2012), pp. 491–513 (p. 509).

65 United Nations Educational, Scientific, and Cultural Organization, *The Universal Declaration on the Human Genome and Human Rights*, which was adopted unanimously and by acclamation at UNESCO's 29th General Conference on 11 November 1997. The following year the United Nations General Assembly endorsed the Declaration.

66 Council of Europe, 'Convention for the Protection of Human Rights and Dignity of the Human Being with Regard to the Application of Biology and Medicine', *European Treaty Series* 164, 4.IV (Oviedo, 1997), Article 13.

67 Council of Europe, 'Explanatory Report to the Convention for the Protection of Human Rights and Dignity of the Human Being with Regard to the Application of Biology and Medicine: Convention on Human Rights and Biomedicine', *European Treaty Series* 164, 4.IV (Oviedo, 1997), para. 91.

68 UNESCO International Bioethics Committee, 'Report of the IBC on Updating Its Reflection on the Human Genome and Human Rights', SHS/YES/IBC-22/15/2 REV.2, 2 October 2015; retrieved 7 February 2020 from <http://unesdoc.unesco.org/images/0023/002332/233258E.pdf> (emphasis original).

was drafted in 2000, which states that 'in the fields of medicine and biology . . . the prohibition of eugenic practices, in particular those aiming at the selection of persons' must be respected.[69]

The reason such texts rejected germline modifications, and thereby eugenic procedures, was that unacceptable discrimination is inevitably associated with selection strategies. The procedures were seen as unacceptable because they undermined the very basis of equality between all existing or possible future persons.

Changes in the biology of creation conditions affecting numerical identity

At this stage it is again important to note that a crucial (though complex) philosophical difference exists between therapeutic procedures, which seek to help individuals who already exist, and germline selective procedures, which are not therapeutic, and aim to bring into existence only certain kinds of individuals. As Kass observes:

> Correction of a genetically abnormal egg or sperm (that is, of the 'germ cells'), however worthy an activity, stretches the meaning of 'therapy' beyond all normal uses. Just who is the 'patient' being 'treated'? The potential child-to-be that might be formed out of such egg or sperm is, at the time of the [genetic correction] . . . , at best no more than a hope and a hypothesis. There is no medical analogue for treatment of non-existent patients.[70]

The philosophical difference between (therapeutic) somatic and (non-therapeutic) germline procedures gives rise to significant ethical consequences that are not always recognized by commentators, some of whom further argue that germline procedures will not affect the way society considers those born with a disorder. For example, the US National Academies of Sciences, Engineering, and Medicine 2017 report *Human Genome Editing* states that 'unconditional love for a disabled child once born and respect for all people who are born with or who develop disabilities are not incompatible with intervening to avert disease and disability prior

---

[69] European Union, 'Charter of Fundamental Rights of the European Union, *Official Journal of the European Communities*, C 364/1, 18 December 2000; retrieved 7 February 2020 from <www.europarl.europa.eu/charter/pdf/text_en.pdf>.

[70] Kass, *Life*, p. 122 (footnote).

to birth or conception'.[71] Unfortunately, however, this report does not explain how or why any deliberate discrimination can be seen as acceptable before birth while suddenly becoming unacceptable after birth. Indeed, as already mentioned, making sure that a possible future person with a disability does not come into existence is completely different from treating a person with the same disorder who already exists. This is because in the latter case one is just indicating that he or she should get better, which is different from saying that persons with the disorder should not exist.

For example, if a deaf person decides to have a treatment that would take away his deafness, it is possible to suggest that other deaf people (who may not want to be treated) may protest that such a course of action may discriminate against their very identity of being deaf. In response, however, it should be noted that people are, of course, being changed in their qualitative identity when they get better. But these persons remain in existence and only their traits are being changed. In creating a person, on the other hand, the whole philosophical situation is different. A person is being brought into existence and the manner in which this happens is inherently part of who he or she is. The individual is born with his or her specific genome (all his or her genetic heritage). If another genome had been used, then the resulting individual would be a completely (numerically) different individual from the one with the first genome. In a way, anything that changes the setting of the creation condition of a person results in a different person.

At this stage, it is also important to note that independent sperm and egg cells as well as early embryos, foetuses and human beings who have been born are all essentially whole and complete biological entities which/who are considered to be living when:

- a capacity to regulate and coordinate the various life processes is present and
- biological continuity regulates and coordinates the various life processes.[72]

[71] National Academies of Sciences, Engineering, and Medicine, *Human Genome Editing: Science, Ethics, and Governance* (Washington, D.C.: The National Academies Press, 2017), p. 97.

[72] S. M. Liao, 'The Organism View Defended', *The Monist* 89.3 (2006), pp. 334–350; S. M. Liao, 'Twinning, Inorganic Replacement, and the Organism View', *Ratio* 23.1 (2010), pp. 59–72; S. M. Liao, 'Do Mitochondrial Replacement Techniques Affect Qualitative or Numerical Identity?', *Bioethics* 31.1 (2017), pp. 20–26.

This also means that the complete biological entity ceases to exist when its capacity to regulate and coordinate the various life processes is irreversibly lost.

Accordingly, in the light of the previous explanations concerning numerical identity and the existence of biological entities, it can be argued that each individual has a specific and unique life trajectory (from creation to death) that begins and ends at a particular three-dimensional place and at a certain time. This implies that the beginning of a life trajectory is especially important for the rest of the life of the biological being, since a specific beginning point in space and time of a life is considered to create a new distinct life trajectory, giving rise to an individual who can never merge with the trajectory of another individual.[73] In short, only one particular life trajectory will ever exist for one individual through time and space. Of course, an individual's life trajectory can change direction over time because of different variables, such as an illness, but it remains the same trajectory and the same individual continues his or her existence. However, creating a totally new life trajectory will always result in the creation of a new individual.

Interestingly, if a biological modification takes place either before or during the creation of an entity, this may also have different effects on numerical identity. For instance, because the particular biological setting at the creation of a living being will always give rise to a specific unique individual with his or her particular complete physical body, any biological change that takes place before or during the creation procedure would result in a (numerically) completely different individual with a distinct body. That is, a new individual with his or her particular beginning and subsequent life trajectory would be created who would be different from the one who would otherwise have existed had the biological change not occurred. In other words, the new individual would have a different body with a different life.

---

[73] For example, even in the rare cases when two early embryos merge to form a new embryo, it can be suggested that either (1) both embryos terminate their life trajectories while a new one begins its own, or (2) one embryo terminates its life trajectory by being incorporated into the second, which continues its own life trajectory.

In a similar way, if an early embryo splits into two, either (1) the original embryo continues its own life trajectory with a new life trajectory splitting off in a new embryo or (2) two new life trajectories begin from the original, which then ends its own trajectory (representing a form of death for this embryo).

Thus, no two life trajectories can be considered to exist in the same place and at the same time if the language and concept of personal identity of a whole being is to be used.

For example, if the X chromosome in a sperm cell, which is used to fertilize an egg to give a one-cell embryo containing XX chromosomes, is exchanged for a Y chromosome, then the individual eventually resulting from this substitution would have a completely different life from the one who would otherwise have existed. The resulting boy (with XY chromosomes) would have an entirely different life trajectory from that of the girl (with XX chromosomes), who would otherwise have existed.

This is true not only for genetic interventions but for any biological modification that takes place before, or at the moment of, the creation process. By this argument, only one individual, with a specific and complete biological body, is considered to arise from a particular biological setting at creation.[74]

More specifically, this means that if the time and place remained unchanged, and only a very small difference in the biological elements used to bring into existence an embryo were introduced, then a particular living entity, which would not otherwise have existed, is once more brought into being, resulting in (all going well) the birth of a specific individual.

In this respect, the American philosopher Matthew Liao explains that a distinct embryonic organism is created through the fertilization of a particular egg by a particular sperm cell. In addition, he notes that if a different second egg is fertilized by a different second sperm cell, then a (numerically) completely different organism is created that is distinct from the first. As a result, Liao argues that if the first egg is fertilized by the second sperm cell, again a numerically distinct organism different from the first is created. This means that different egg and/or sperm cells will create numerically distinct organisms[75] with different life trajectories.

On this account, it may be noted that if an egg or sperm cell is only slightly changed, from a biological perspective, it may persist as the same entity, though this biological modification of the sperm or egg cell would still affect the numerical identity of the resulting embryonic individual created from the coming together of these cells. This is because the beginning of the life trajectory of the individual resulting from the creation of the new embryo using the biologically modified egg or sperm cell would be (and remains) completely different from the one who would,

[74] MacKellar, 'Genome Modifying Reproductive Procedures', pp. 121–136.
[75] Liao, 'Mitochondrial Replacement Techniques', pp. 20–26.

otherwise, have existed had no modification of the egg or sperm cell taken place. This also means that every person's very identity as an individual has its origins in the way this person was brought into existence – in the manner that God created this person. As David Jones says:

> Human beings derive their individual identity at least in part from the circumstances and conditions of their origin. From a theological perspective, this identity of origin is an expression of God's act of creation. It is God who creates the human person and fashions him or her in the womb.[76]

Germline genome editing and discrimination

This all means that making sure only certain possible future children are brought into existence through germline procedures is inherently discriminatory. As already indicated, if parents do decide to avoid having a child affected by a serious genetic disorder (and solely because of this disorder), then in a very real sense such a decision is based on the perceived quality of life of people who already exist and not on the worthiness and inherent dignity of their lives. Moreover, as Hans Reinders explains, it is more than likely that 'in any given case, the only reasonable answer to the question of why a disabled child should not be born is by reference to what one thinks about the lives of people living with the same disorder'.[77] In other words, the indirect message given to persons who have already been born with the same disorder would be that they should also not have been born.

Naturally, it is difficult not to have a lot of sympathy towards parents who have children affected by severe disability and suffering or to recognize the extent of the anguish they are going through. But, as already mentioned, if one asks these parents, it is usually the fact that their child has a disorder and not the very existence of the child with the disorder that has been the cause of so much heartache. Most would never say that they wished their specific child had not existed. They would not indicate that they would have preferred to replace their child with another, healthier, one. They just want to find a treatment for their child.

---

[76] Jones, 'Germ-Line Genetic Engineering', p. 142.

[77] H. S. Reinders, *The Future of the Disabled in Liberal Society* (Notre Dame: University of Notre Dame Press, 2000), p. 8.

In a way, with intentional germline procedures a comparison is made between possible future persons, which then indicates that some of these should not exist, which can clearly be considered as discrimination and thus an undermining of the inherent equality of all human persons in society. On this basis it is very surprising that the International Theological Commission of the Roman Catholic Church argued in its 2004 paper *Communion and Stewardship* that germline genetic engineering, in itself, may be acceptable if other concerns are addressed:

> Germ line genetic engineering with a therapeutic goal in man would in itself be acceptable were it not for the fact that it is hard to imagine how this could be achieved without disproportionate risks especially in the first experimental stage, such as the huge loss of embryos and the incidence of mishaps, and without the use of reproductive techniques. A possible alternative would be the use of gene therapy in the stem cells that produce a man's sperm, whereby he can beget healthy offspring with his own seed by means of the conjugal act.[78]

In this statement, however, an ambiguity seems to exist in that germline procedures are presented as having therapeutic goals that, as already indicated, cannot be accepted since they are clearly selective (and non-therapeutic) in nature. Moreover, a number of Roman Catholic scholars remain unconvinced by the Commission's argument, calling instead for more discussions to take place before any definitive conclusions are given.[79] In addition, as David Jones notes, 'From a theological perspective what is perhaps most striking about all the responses to genetic engineering by the [Roman Catholic] Magisterium and by some groups of Catholic theologians is the absence of theological analysis.'[80] It is also significant that another important Roman Catholic document appears to reject any acceptance of selective germline procedures. The Vatican's 1987 Congregation for the Doctrine of the Faith report *Instruction on Respect for Human Life in Its Origin and on the Dignity of Procreation* states:

78 International Theological Commission (2004), *Communion and Stewardship: Human Persons Created in the Image of God*, para. 90.

79 See e.g. Jones, 'Germ-Line Genetic Engineering', pp. 126–144; A. Moraczewski, 'Germ-Line Interventions and the Moral Tradition of the Catholic Church', in A. R. Chapman and M. S. Frankel (eds), *Designing Our Descendants* (Baltimore: Johns Hopkins University Press, 2003), pp. 199–211.

80 Jones, 'Germ-Line Genetic Engineering', p. 134.

> *Certain attempts to influence chromosomic or genetic inheritance are not therapeutic but are aimed at producing human beings selected according to sex or other predetermined qualities. These manipulations are contrary to the personal dignity of the human being and his or her integrity and identity.* Therefore in no way can they be justified on the grounds of possible beneficial consequences for future humanity.[81]

In addition, if a form of intentional selection is indeed taking place between possible future persons through germline interventions, then one is selecting-out future persons with a disability or selecting-in those with positive traits. This is because any form of selection 'for' automatically means a selection 'against'. And as the Holy See's Pontifical Academy for Life indicated in 1997:

> This selective concept of man will have, among other things, a heavy cultural fallout . . . since there will be a growing conviction that the value of man and woman does not depend on their personal identity but only on those biological qualities that can be appraised and therefore selected.[82]

This implies that because the value and worth of all human beings are not based on their biological qualities but on their imaging of God in an equal manner – any form of germline selection is inherently meaningless and cannot be accepted. Any basis for such selection would be considered as discriminatory as any other selection based, for example, on sex. Thus, in the same way that most men or women build part of their very identity, as men or women, on their embodied sex at birth, many disabled persons build an important part of their identity on their embodied disability at birth.

As a result, society is now before a crossroads with germline genome editing selection procedures. It can either choose to make sure that certain persons are not brought into existence because the value and worth of

---

[81] Congregation for the Doctrine of the Faith, *Instruction on Respect for Human Life in Its Origin and on the Dignity of Procreation: Replies to Certain Questions of the Day* (1987) (emphasis original).

[82] Pontifical Academy for Life, *Reflections on Cloning* (1997), para. 3; retrieved 13 February 2020 from <www.vatican.va/roman_curia/pontifical_academies/acdlife/documents/rc_pa_acdlife_doc_30091997_clon_en.html>.

their lives are considered to be unacceptable. This would then mean that society would begin to classify the worth of all lives and start going down a eugenic road. Or, it could choose to believe that all lives are equal in value and worth, which is the very basis of civilized Christian society, making any selection and classification meaningless.

Genetic modifications of sperm and eggs and during fertilization

In the specific context of a genetic modification that takes place either in the sperm and egg cells before they are used for conception or during fertilization, resulting in the formation of a one-cell fertilized egg, a new individual, who would otherwise not have existed, is brought into being. This would happen because, as already noted, any change (no matter how small) of any of the variables in bringing an individual into existence would result in a very different individual existing in time. In other words, any individual brought into existence through one of these procedures would be a totally different person, from a numerical identity perspective, from the one who would otherwise have existed.[83]

If such a conclusion is accepted, then this again has a clear eugenic element, since a new individual is brought into existence in preference to another who may, for example, have qualities seen as less valuable than those of the new individual. What is being proposed, therefore, is not a form of therapy. No existing person is being treated for a disorder. Instead, it is making sure that only certain kinds of persons are brought into existence based on the quality of their genomes.[84] But here again it is worth noting that the modification of sperm and eggs cells may be acceptable under international regulations but only as a secondary effect of the main genetic treatment of an existing person for clinical reasons.

What do the egg and sperm cells represent?

Again, it is important to remember how sperm and egg cells may be understood from an ethical, cultural, philosophical and theological perspective. As already mentioned, they may be seen, in a way, as representative bodies or even ambassadors of the person taking part in the

---

[83] D. Parfit, 'Rights, Interests and Possible People', in S. Gorovitz, A. L. Jameton, R. Macklin, J. M. O'Connor, E. V. Perrin, B. P. St. Clair and S. Sherwin (eds), *Moral Problems in Medicine* (Englewood Cliffs: Prentice Hall, 1976), pp. 369–375.

[84] MacKellar, 'Genome Modifying Reproductive Procedures', pp. 121–136.

bringing into existence of the embryo. Thus, both the sperm and the egg cells may represent the man and woman, respectively, in the act of bringing into existence an embryo. This means that if one of the reproductive cells did not entirely originate from one of the reproductive partners but was significantly modified after it had been produced, it could be seen as no longer fully representing this original partner.[85] As a result, ethical questions may arise that are similar, though not identical, to those that occur in the use of donor sperm and eggs in reproduction.[86] On the other hand, if a procedure such as gene therapy modified the sperm and egg cells in combination with all the other cells of the person being treated, then the sperm and egg cells might continue to be seen as representing the whole person.

Genetic modifications of very early embryos

Interestingly, if a genetic modification takes place in a very early post-conception human embryo (such as a two-cell embryo), a number of additional ethical challenges arise. Indeed, it would be difficult to know whether any significant genetic change would bring about a completely new individual or whether the original embryonic individual continues to exist and is simply modified. In other words, whether the procedure would have a numerical or only a qualitative effect on identity.

In a way, this philosophical conundrum is not new and comes in many different forms. It is similar to the one mentioned by the Greek historian Plutarch (c. 46–120) in his *Life of Theseus* (the mythical founder king of Athens). Here Plutarch questions in a thought experiment whether a ship that is restored by replacing every one of its wooden parts remains the same ship. This is especially relevant if the old parts are then used to build another ship. In the same way, it is possible to ask whether an embryo in which a certain number of genes have been edited remains the same embryo or whether a completely new embryo has been created, meaning that a change in numerical identity has taken place.

From an ethical perspective, if the genetic modification does not significantly change the already existing embryo, it would no doubt be

85 C. MacKellar, 'Representative Aspects of Some Synthetic Gametes', *The New Bioethics* 21.2 (2015), pp. 105–116.

86 Naturally occurring spontaneous genetic disorders affecting the germline, such as those that give rise to Down syndrome, would also have to be studied in this regard.

seen as being similar to classical (somatic) gene therapy in which the original individual remains, and the masterpiece is restored. However, if the genetic modification substantially modifies the genome of a very early embryo, more questions relating to the continued existence of the original embryonic individual could be asked. The genetic modification could even be considered to end the life of the original embryo (a form of death) while creating another. Indeed, if this were to happen, then a clear eugenic element would exist since it would mean preferring one new being over another based on the quality of his or her genome.

Maternal spindle transfer and pronuclear transfer

As already noted, the desire of most parents to have children 'of their own', or at least as much as possible 'of their own', is the driving force behind the popularity (and financial success) of fertility clinics throughout the world. Indeed, it may be the reason why most reproductive technologies were developed in the first place.[87] The deep sense of loss or incompleteness felt by many parents unable to be directly responsible for the procreation of the life of their child is one of the underlying reasons for them to seek assisted reproduction.

In this context, it has been intimated that new research could eventually be useful in preventing some forms of inherited mitochondrial diseases that may be debilitating or even fatal in offspring. Mitochondria are extremely small entities found in all the cells of the human body, constituting 15 to 35 per cent of a cell's total mass. Depending on its function, a cell may contain a few hundred to several thousand mitochondria. They are considered to be the power source of the cells, giving them the energy to survive. But for a cell to function and replicate properly, the thirty-seven genes in all the mitochondria must interact correctly with the 20,000 to 30,000 genes in its chromosomes. Individuals generally only inherit their mitochondria from their mother, since they are already present in the egg when it is fertilized by the sperm cell. Thus, they are received by the children in a different manner from the genes in the chromosomes, which are inherited equally from both father and mother.

---

[87] Nuffield Council on Bioethics, *Novel Techniques for the Prevention of Mitochondrial DNA Disorders: An Ethical Review* (London: Nuffield Council on Bioethics, 2012), p. 68.

Mitochondrial disorders arise when mutations in the genes of the mitochondria or of the chromosomes limit the energy supply in the cell. In the UK recent studies indicated that while 1 out of 200 children is born with a potentially dysfunctional mitochondrial mutation, about 9 out of 100,000 have mutated mitochondria that could give rise to disorders including muscle weakness, neurological problems, issues with sight and/or hearing, kidney disease, diabetes or heart disease. Only 1 child in 6,500, on average, is affected by a serious mitochondrial disease that may, in some instances, lead to death in infancy.[88]

In this regard, the new procedures being proposed to address such mitochondrial disorders consist of two possible, but similar, techniques called maternal spindle transfer and pronuclear transfer, which are sometimes defined as 'mitochondrial donation'. As such, they enable a woman to have a child that she may consider to be 'her own' and who is free from some forms of mitochondrial disorders.

Maternal spindle transfer

With maternal spindle transfer, a transfer of chromosomes takes place from an *unfertilized* egg with defective mitochondria into an *unfertilized* egg, which has been emptied of its own chromosomes, with healthy mitochondria, originating from a donor woman. In other words, the procedure involves the following stages:[89]

- eggs from the woman wanting a child but who is affected by dysfunctional mitochondria are removed from her ovaries;
- next, the small spindle-shaped entity containing the chromosomes (and most of the genes) in the unfertilized egg is removed and this remaining emptied egg discarded;
- the egg of a second woman, who agreed to donate her eggs, which contain healthy mitochondria, is then taken and its own spindle (containing all the chromosomes) removed and discarded;
- the spindle from the first woman is subsequently transferred to this emptied egg of the second woman;

[88] C. Giles, 'Mitochondria', *Wellcome News*, spring 2012, p. 24.

[89] C. MacKellar; *GM Babies with 3 or 4 Parents: Maternal Spindle Transfer and Pronuclear Transfer, an Ethical Discussion* (Newcastle upon Tyne: The Christian Institute, 2012).

- once this new egg is obtained it is then fertilized by the sperm of the first woman's partner or a donor to form an embryo;
- this embryo is finally transferred back into the uterus of the first woman wanting the child with the hope that it may develop into a child without any mitochondrial disorders.

Pronuclear transfer

With pronuclear transfer, chromosomes are transferred from a *fertilized* egg with defective mitochondria into a *fertilized* egg that has been emptied of its own chromosomes, with healthy mitochondria originating from a donor woman. In other words, the procedure involves the following stages:

- eggs from the woman wanting a child but who is affected by dysfunctional mitochondria are removed from her ovaries;
- one of these eggs is fertilized with the sperm of her partner. Once this happens all the chromosomes (and most of the genes) of the egg are regrouped into the female pronucleus and all the chromosomes of the sperm are regrouped into the male pronucleus;
- these pronuclei are then removed and the remaining fertilized egg (with the dysfunctional mitochondria) discarded;
- an egg of a second woman, who agreed to donate her eggs, which contain healthy mitochondria, is subsequently taken and fertilized with the sperm of her partner or a donor;
- the pronuclei (containing the chromosomes) of this second fertilized egg are then removed and discarded;
- once this has taken place, the pronuclei of the first couple (who want to have the child) are transferred into the emptied fertilized egg of the second couple;
- the fertilized egg from the second couple containing the chromosomes (and most of the genes) from the first couple is then left to develop and transferred back into the uterus of the first woman wanting the child with the hope that it may develop into a child without any mitochondrial disorders.

Again, it is worth emphasizing that maternal spindle transfer and pronuclear transfer would create new and therefore distinct individuals.

This is because the new unfertilized or fertilized eggs used in the procedures eventually bring new individuals into existence who are (numerically) completely different from the one who would, otherwise, have existed had maternal spindle transfer and pronuclear transfer not been considered.[90]

Thus, since a deliberate selection is being undertaken between two numerically different possible future persons, serious concerns can be raised as to the eugenic nature of maternal spindle transfer and pronuclear transfer. In other words, an element of discrimination is present through the decision to select one possible future child over another.

Cytoplasmic transfer

With cytoplasmic transfer a small amount of cytoplasm (all the material enclosed by a cell membrane – except for the chromosomes) containing healthy mitochondria from a healthy donor egg is injected into the egg of a woman who has defective mitochondria in her own eggs. The procedure thus enables a mixture of different mitochondria with different genes to exist in the reconstructed egg, which is then fertilized with the sperm of the intended father or a donor and implanted either into the woman wanting a child or into a surrogate. Again, with cytoplasmic transfer, because the new egg is biologically dissimilar to the one that would, otherwise, have existed had the procedure not taken place, a new numerically distinct person is brought into existence, who would not otherwise have come into existence.[91]

Again, because the genome of any future descendants may be modified in this way in a manner considered to be positive, this is a kind of germline intervention through genetic modification. In other words, cytoplasmic transfer may be considered an unacceptable eugenic procedure.[92]

---

90 MacKellar, 'Genome Modifying Reproductive Procedures', pp. 121–136.

91 Ibid.

92 S. A. Newman, 'The British Embryo Authority and the Chamber of Eugenics', *The Huffington Post*, 11 May 2013; retrieved 15 April 2013 from <www.huffingtonpost.com/stuart-a-newman/mitochondrial-replacement-ethics_b_2837818.html>.

5
Conclusion

In many respects, eugenic policies are about control and enhancing autonomy so that parents can choose what kinds of children they want. This is generally expressed in making sure these children are not disabled and have a good quality of life. Such a decision reflects, in a sense, the basic values of a modern liberal society that may increasingly consider the disappearance of disabled children as a beneficial development. As David King indicates, 'Eugenicists argue for "improvement" of the overall human gene pool, but what really appals them is that the whole business of human reproduction is out of rational control, and is left to chance.'[1] In other words, there is a widely accepted argument that the reproductive autonomy of prospective parents should always be respected, especially if the aim is to reduce the suffering of any future child and even if others disagree. As a result, any restrictions or criticism of eugenic selection procedures are often seen as unacceptable and offensive. But this position may also create difficulties, since concepts of agency, including 'choice', 'freedom' and 'self-determination', which are the default position in liberal societies, ignore other essential aspects of human existence, such as solidarity and mutual dependence. As a result, it makes it more difficult for persons with disability to be accepted as full members of society, in their own right, when they do not meet contemporary expectations.[2]

But the position of wanting to 'take back control' is not new. The American geneticist Hermann Muller (1890–1967), the 1946 Nobel Prize winner for Physiology or Medicine, suggested that it should be humanity, and not any 'mythical divinity', who should decide its future through, among other things, eugenic procedures. In his book, written in 1925 but

---

[1] D. King, 'Eugenic Tendencies in Modern Genetics', *Ethics and Medicine* 14.3 (1998), pp. 84–89 (p. 85).

[2] H. S. Reinders, *The Future of the Disabled in Liberal Society: An Ethical Analysis* (Notre Dame: University of Notre Dame Press, 2000), p. 205–206.

first published in 1935, *Out of the Night*, Muller explained that humanity is right to defy accepted norms and take back control of its destiny:

> And so we foresee the history of life divided into three main phases. In the long preparatory phase it was the helpless creature of its environment, and natural selection gradually ground it into human shape.
>
> In the second – our own short transitional phase – it reaches out at the immediate environment, shaking, shaping and grinding to suit the form, the requirements, the wishes, and the whims of man.
>
> And in the long third phase, it will reach down into the secret places of the universe of its own nature, and by aid of its ever growing intelligence and co-operation, shape itself into an increasingly sublime creation – a being beside which the mythical divinities of the past will seem more and more ridiculous, and which setting its own marvellous inner powers against the brute Goliath of the suns and the planets, challenges them to contest.[3]

Without any doubt, therefore, a lot of pride in humanity may exist in demonstrating that it is in control – that it has become like God in being able to decide and direct what kinds of future persons should exist. Because of this, and as the abuses that took place in the first half of the twentieth century slowly become an ever-older memory, pressures are now returning for a new kind of control – a new eugenics. For example, James Watson wrote in 1995:

> But diabolical as Hitler was, and I don't want to minimize the evil he perpetuated using false genetic arguments, we should not be held in hostage to his awful past. For the genetic dice will continue to inflict cruel fates on all too many individuals and their families who do not deserve this damnation. Decency demands that someone must rescue them from genetic hells. If we don't play God, who will?[4]

---

[3] H. J. Muller, *Out of the Night: A Biologist's View of the Future* (New York: Vanguard, 1935 [repr. 1984]), p. 37.

[4] J. Watson, 'Values from a Chicago Upbringing', in D. A. Chambers (ed.), *Deoxyribonucleic Acid: The Double Helix – Perspective and Prospective at Forty Years* (New York: New York Academy of Science, 1995), p. 197.

But if God is seen as incompetent in his creation of humankind or if he is considered inexistent or pronounced dead, then the words of the Holy See's Pontifical Academy for Life become relevant:

> The proclamation of the 'death of God', in the vain hope of a 'superman', produces an unmistakable result: the 'death of man'. It cannot be forgotten that the denial of man's creaturely status, far from exalting human freedom, in fact creates new forms of slavery, discrimination and profound suffering . . .
>
> Man, to whom God has entrusted the created world, giving him freedom and intelligence, finds no limits to his action dictated solely by practical impossibility: he himself must learn how to set these limits by discerning good and evil. Once again man is asked to choose: it is his responsibility to decide whether to transform technology into a tool of liberation or to become its slave by introducing new forms of violence and suffering.[5]

But it is still possible to ask what is ethically wrong in choosing to select and deciding that only healthy, and not disabled, children are brought into existence. Why not make sure that children who will have a short and difficult life of suffering are not brought into existence?

In response, this study has suggested that it is important first to understand why parents may actually want a child and, if they do, what value system they are using if they decide to select for a certain kind of child. In this connection, this investigation has proposed that self-interested parental aims should never be at the centre of wanting a child and that unconditional love and acceptance of the other should always be at the very core of the desire to procreate. In this regard, Stanley Hauerwas wrote:

> Now who knows what we could possibly want when we 'want a child'? The idea of want in that context is about as silly as the idea that we can marry the right person. That just does not happen. Wanting a child is particularly troubling as it finally results in a deep distrust of mentally and physically handicapped children. The

5 Pontifical Academy for Life, *Reflections on Cloning* (1997), para. 3; retrieved 13 February 2020 from <www.vatican.va/roman_curia/pontifical_academies/acdlife/documents/rc_pa_acdlife_doc_30091997_clon_en.html>.

> crucial question for us as Christians is what kind of people we need to be to be capable of welcoming children into this world, some of whom may be born disabled and even die.[6]

Christians are, therefore, called to welcome unconditionally, without choosing, every kind of child into existence, irrespective of their biological characteristics, even if they have very short and challenging lives of suffering. Of course, to many this may seem unreasonable and difficult to accept, even in the Christian church. Indeed, it is likely that some Christians will express strong opposition to this stance. But this is not new – even at the beginning of the twentieth century Christian US commentators who resisted eugenic ideology were often considered to be unreasonable. As the biomedical science journalist Christine Rosen notes, members of clergy and laypersons in that period 'who clung stubbornly to tradition, to doctrine, and to biblical infallibility opposed eugenics and became, for a time, the objects of derision for their rejection of this most modern science'.[7] In this regard, it is possible to query whether history will repeat itself in the twenty-first century and beyond.

But if this study has, in some manner, been convincing from a Christian and biblical perspective, rational reasons have been initiated and presented concerning the following arguments.

God's creation of the child

To begin with, the creation of another person by God through a human couple expresses the wonderful act of unity of love in the Trinity. The creation of a child becomes, in this way, the symbol and reality of the love and unity of the Father, the Son and the Holy Spirit participating in the act of creation. As already mentioned, it means that love is the source of creation reflecting the existence of love between the persons in the Trinity – a love that results in the creation of human beings. This implies that creation and love express the same action.

---

[6] S. Hauerwas, *Abortion, Theologically Understood*, Lifewatch (Dothan: Taskforce of United Methodists on Abortion and Sexuality, 1991); retrieved 22 November 2016 from <www.lifewatch.org/abortion.html>.

[7] C. Rosen, *Preaching Genetics: Religious Leaders and the American Eugenics Movement* (Oxford: Oxford University Press, 2004), p. 5.

But what is wonderful is that this creative power of love in the Trinity is also expressed at the level of humankind in the same form. As the Father, Son and Holy Spirit created the universe and humankind, God continues to create through the trinity of the persons in the Godhead and his two created procreators (the husband and the wife) an ever-increasing number of human beings.

Thus, a man and woman joined in matrimony become cooperating partners under God, the sole creator, in an act of bringing forth new human life through procreation.[8]

However, this also means that in creation (1) the unconditional love and acceptance of the Trinity always expands onto the new resulting child, and that (2) the unconditional love and acceptance of the parents for each other should also expand onto this child. This unconditionality is central to any ethical understanding of procreation but is also crucial to the argument against eugenic selective procedures.

Unconditional acceptance in procreation

In order to develop a discussion on the ethical implications of a voluntary eugenics, the US philosopher Robert Nozick (1938–2002) examines the futuristic existence of a possible child supermarket where future parents are free to decide what kinds of children they want.[9] One can then query whether such a supermarket in which the pictures and expected characteristics of possible future children are presented can be seen as challenging society in some way. In response, it is important for society first to acknowledge that such selective practices are already present, and that urgent reflection is, therefore, required. It then needs to investigate with courage and purpose the very real ethical concerns raised by the new eugenics while examining the significant risks that may exist. For example, it will be important to study whether eugenic selection procedures of possible future children may lead to unexpected consequences for the way parents and their children interact or how society will view selected children. Furthermore, it will be crucial to consider whether parental

[8] John Paul II, *Evangelium Vitae* (1995), para. 43; retrieved 3 December 2007 from <www.vatican.va/holy_father/john_paul_ii/encyclicals/documents/hf_jp-ii_enc_25031995_evangelium-vitae_en.html>.

[9] R. Nozick, *Anarchy, State, Utopia* (New York: Basic, 1974).

acceptance of disabled children may diminish so that there is eventually no tolerance for disorders.

As already discussed, it is vital for a child's psychological well-being that he or she is brought into existence in a context of unconditional love and acceptance. Michael Sandel shares his concern about developing selection procedures in his book *The Case against Perfection*. At the centre of his argument is the understanding that each human life is a gift and should be accepted for its own sake. Sandel summarizes the risks of rejection when children are not brought into existence from unconditional acceptance, which he characterizes as unconditional love:

> Parents bent on enhancing their children are more likely to overreach, to express and entrench attitudes at odds with the norm of unconditional love . . . We would do better to cultivate a more expansive appreciation of life as a gift that commands our reverence and restricts our use.[10]

This means that if preconditions in the biology of the future child need to be fulfilled before he or she is brought into existence by prospective parents, then in many cases this cannot be seen as a form of unconditional love. Indeed, the development of selection procedures may open the door to parents eventually feeling a sense of disappointment or even regret concerning their choice at a later stage in the child's life. Instead of being delighted with the mere existence of their child, they may eventually regret that they did not choose a different child. Where choice exists, there is always the possibility of later regretting the choice made! While this form of regret may be seen as deplorable in itself, it is particularly disturbing from the child's perspective, who will be aware that his or her parents regret his or her very existence.

On this account, another significant concern with all eugenic selection procedures is that they endanger the holistic well-being of children brought into existence by appending conditions to their very existence. A number of children may even experience a really challenging life if they sense that they have to earn their parents' love, approval and acceptance. Of course, it is impossible to predict how possible future children may

[10] M. J. Sandel, *The Case Against Perfection: Ethics in the Age of Genetic Engineering* (Cambridge, Mass.: Harvard University Press, 2007), pp. 49, 127.

value their selection. However, there is a real risk that some may eventually experience a diminished sense of self-acceptance and value of their lives, even though they were brought into existence with superior characteristics such as good physical health. This is because if children realize that their existence is dependent on the fulfilment of certain preconditions, it is possible that some may end up questioning whether they have an unconditional place in society, since any sense of 'who one is' includes more than physical characteristics. In addition, the way in which people accept themselves in their very identity is crucial to their flourishing and well-being. This means that selection procedures may also undermine a child's experience of self-acceptance.

Moreover, because selection procedures may now enable parents to accept a child only if he or she meets certain expectations, some parents may begin to see a child as a solution to their own needs and requirements, resulting in him or her becoming intrumentalized. In other words, he or she is transformed into a mere means to an end, becoming only the instrument of another person.

In 1980 Swiss child psychologist Alice Miller (1923–2010) wrote, 'As soon as the child is regarded as a possession for which one has a particular goal, as soon as one exerts control over him, his vital growth will be violently interrupted.'[11] She argues that for children to develop into psychologically healthy adults, they should begin their lives with a firm knowledge of their parents' unconditional love and acceptance.

The immeasurable worth and value of all individuals created in the same image of God

This book also argues that the image of God is fundamental in seeking to understand the new eugenics – an image reflected in all human beings because God created them in the same special way. It follows that this image of God cannot be reduced to a feature of human nature, such as genetics or qualities such as intellect, rationality or function.

Moreover, it is because human beings are created in the image of God and out of his love that each member of humanity has immeasurable value

[11] A. Miller, *Prisoners of Childhood* (New York: Basic, 1980), p. 75.

while being completely equal in worth. This also means that the value and worth of a human being do not rest on his or her ability to do anything, such as being able to reason, experience autonomy or communicate. Instead, they originate in God, who embraces the bearer of his divine image during all the stages of his or her existence on earth through death and beyond. When God looks on his human creatures, the first thing he sees and loves in them is not what they can do but his own reflection, which affirms the supernatural and transcendent origins of genuine human worth and value.

In addition, the importance and uniqueness of humankind are wonderfully expressed in the birth and death of Jesus Christ, whereby God demonstrated that he loves humanity to such an extent that he was prepared to go to the cross for them. The reality that the eternal Son of God became incarnate in Jesus and took on humanity is the ultimate and transcendent origin of the immeasurable order of *agapē*-love which is behind the creation of each human being.[12] Moreover, that Jesus Christ is the 'image of the invisible God' (Col. 1:15) attests to the inherent dignity and immeasurable moral worth of that image not only by sharing in it, but by revealing its very origins and foundations. No hesitation was present when Jesus Christ, the Word of God, became existentially involved in humanity while treating all those he encountered, including the weakest and most vulnerable, with an immeasurable love and dignity. Christ, as the perfect human being, was also the perfect image of God.

Furthermore, it is worth noting that real value, worth and meaning can come only from the love of God, whose existence will never be logically demonstrated. This means that it will never be possible to prove scientifically that an adult human person has any value and worth or that he or she is equal in worth to all other individuals. Christian theology has always been challenged to understand what makes human persons special, but it does recognize that persons are a unity created by the transcendent God as embodied souls and ensouled bodies – a unity that also reflects the image of the unity in love of the divine persons of the Trinity. As a result, trying to understand or determine in a reductionist manner what makes human beings so special from both a scientific and a theological

[12] T. F. Torrance, *The Being and Nature of the Unborn Child* (Edinburgh: Handsel, 2000 [published for the Scottish Order of Christian Unity]), p. 4.

perspective is impossible. Human beings will always remain a mystery because they are created in the image of God, whose very nature will always remain a mystery.

The ethics of the new eugenics

That all possible future and existing human beings should be considered equal in value and worth because they all reflect the same image of God, however, is slowly being undermined in modern society, where a growing consensus seems to be developing that children with a disability should not be brought into existence. Such a position has already reached a stage at which some couples decide to terminate a pregnancy because the foetus is affected by a disorder such as Down syndrome, without even addressing the crucial question of what they are actually doing. In many ways, public opinion has already told these expectant couples what is expected of them. Few are also prepared to really compare the ideology behind the current eugenic developments to that which was responsible for the abuse and horrors that took place at the beginning of the twentieth century. There is no willingness to heed the warning of past eugenic programmes and how they undermined both the (1) immeasurable and (2) equal value and worth of human beings.

This is especially relevant because the ideology that inspired past eugenics programmes has not changed. Of course, coercive policies are generally absent, but the goals remain the same, with a wish to control the genetic heritage of all members of society. The eugenic ideologies have just returned under the compassionate guise of 'therapeutic genetic selection' and other forms of 'vocabulary cleansing'.

Certainly, the suggestion that a new eugenic ideology is now developing has been questioned by many, who argue that parents have a right to make their own decisions. Defenders of selection argue that procedures such as preimplantation embryonic selection are simply a matter of parental choice and that the voluntary nature of such decisions must be considered acceptable. In other words, the widespread use of selection procedures, particularly in making sure children with genetic disorders are not brought into existence, should be seen as a form of humanitarian assistance that society should welcome.

The manner in which eugenic selection may take place will also certainly develop with time from seeking to select-out children with disability to selecting-in those with enhanced traits. As Lee Silver explained in 1999, in the context of using genetics in reproduction (reprogenetics):

> It will begin in a way that is most ethically acceptable to the largest portion of society, with the treatment of only those childhood diseases . . . that have a severe impact on quality of life. The number of parents who will desire this service will be tiny, but their experience will help to ease society's trepidation.
>
> As fear begins to subside, reprogeneticists will expand their services to nullify mutations that have a less severe impact on a child, or an impact delayed until adulthood. Predispositions to obesity, diabetes, heart disease, asthma, and various forms of cancer all fall into this category. And as the technology spreads, its range will be extended to the addition of new genes that serve as genetic inoculations against various infectious agents, including . . . [the one] that causes AIDS. At the same time, other genes will be added to improve various health characteristics and disease resistance in children who would not otherwise have been born with any particular problem.[13]

This means that in the future prospective parents may eventually want to express their choice by not only selecting against a disabled child but deciding what kind of positive characteristics their future child should have. Furthermore, confronted with the challenge of deciding where to draw the lines, some may argue that no lines can or should be drawn. This is because it may become increasingly difficult to distinguish healthy from unhealthy lives or differentiate treatment from enhancement. As Leon Kass wrote, 'once one blurs the distinction between health promotion and genetic enhancement, between so-called negative and positive eugenics, one opens the door to all future eugenic designs'.[14] It has even been suggested that only self-regulatory unenforceable guidelines from professional bodies should be considered – guidelines already being used to implement a number of eugenic selection procedures in a number of countries.[15] Thus, it should be recognized that selective eugenic practices are here to stay.

13 L. M. Silver, *Remaking Eden* (London: Phoenix [Orion], 1999), pp. 277–278.

14 L. R. Kass, 'The Wisdom of Repugnance: Why We Should Ban the Cloning of Humans', *Valparaiso University Law Review* 32.2 (1998), pp. 679–705 (p. 699).

15 Ibid., p. 699.

Therefore, the question is no longer whether society will accept eugenic selection, but which forms of procedures are going to be accepted. Of course, not all decisions involving a eugenic element may be associated with the same concerns. For example, if a woman is attracted to a man because, among other reasons, she is unconsciously drawn to the possibility of rearing certain kinds of children with him, this cannot be considered as being unethical. It is also possible to ask whether it is even possible for prospective parents not to make a choice between a new eugenic germline reproductive procedure that becomes available and natural procreation. This is because whatever is decided will bring a different person into existence (a numerically different person). On this account, what may be important for the parents to consider is whether they may see the new procedure as ethically acceptable in itself (without any consideration of selection). For example, whether some significant advantages for the woman herself are associated with the process. In this case a beneficial procedure could probably be considered in a positive manner even though it might have a secondary and unwanted effect on numerical identity. But any eugenic selection used solely to intentionally control the genetic heritage of a possible future child may be seen as undermining the inherent and equal value and worth of all human beings in society.

Risks of discrimination

One of the main problems with eugenic selection when the aim is to prevent bringing into existence a certain kind of future child who may, for example, be disabled is also the indirect message such selection gives to society. This is because the message implied, even if unspoken and indirect, can only be that people with a similar disability who already exist should not have been born. As a result, some eugenic selection procedures undermine the important Christian principle that all human lives have equal value. To be sure, many arguments have already sought to distinguish between the disorder itself, seen as a negative, and those affected by the disorder, who should be considered equal in value to any other existing individual. As Julian Savulescu argued in 2012:

> Testing [to deselect] for cystic fibrosis or Down syndrome is said to send the message that such lives are less valuable, that those

> people are of lower status. This is deeply mistaken. To say that a disease is bad is not to say that a person with that disease is less equal or bad in some way. The problem is some people identify with their disease, disorder or some other characteristic about themselves, like sex.[16]

Similarly, Mary Warnock said in 2018:

> [T]here were those [who] . . . suggest that it was wrong to try to find ways to remove or alleviate the sufferings of those who have genetically determined disabilities. To suggest that one might hope to eliminate disability was the same as to hope to eliminate disabled people. And this was discrimination.
>
> But this argument, though I have frequently encountered it, often put forward with passion, seems to me very weak. To say of someone that his life would be better if he were not disabled is not the same as to say that it would be better if he did not exist.[17]

However, as already mentioned, such arguments remain unconvincing for the very reason that Savulescu mentions and because he does not differentiate between persons who are created with a disorder and those who are affected by the same disorder later in life. Indeed, many disabled persons consider their disorder as part of who they are, especially when they were brought into existence with their disability. In a way, they know that they would not have existed without the congenital disability and that another person would have existed instead. When a decision between bringing a disabled or a non-disabled possible future child into existence is considered, it is indeed impossible to divorce these individuals and their very identity from their physical traits. This implies that when a person *born* with a certain disability becomes aware that possible future individuals with similar disabilities are being selected-out, they will rightly believe that their very existence is being questioned. In other words, a real risk of discrimination exists when it is suggested that disabilities, which

[16] J. Savulescu, 'Should We Decide Which Breed of Human to Create?', *News Limited Network*, 9 October 2012; retrieved 25 October 2012 from <www.news.com.au/news/should-we-decide-which-breed-of-humans-to-create/story-fnepjsb4-1226492003389>.

[17] M. Warnock, 'We need to Use Gene Editing Wisely but also Embrace Its Vast Potential', *The Guardian*, 11 March 2018.

are always embodied in persons, should not be brought into existence. In the same way that femininity is a set of attributes, behaviours and roles generally associated with girls and women, a disability cannot be dissociated from the very existence of the disabled person born with the disorder. In short, saying that femininity or a disorder should not exist always means that a person born with such femininity (a woman) or a disorder (a disabled person) should also not be brought into existence, which undermines equality in society. Thus, any reproductive selective decision that is made public will certainly be considered as disturbing to many in the disabled community.

It is also difficult to see how the same individual with the same value system can, in any rational way, discriminate between possible future persons by prioritizing the concept of quality of life over the inherent and equal worth of life, while at the same time indicating that all existing persons have the same inherent and equal worth irrespective of their quality of life. In other words, it is inconsistent and contradictory to say that certain possible future persons should not exist while at the same time indicating that all existing persons should have existed and are equal in worth. This also means that it is the making of any kind of choice between possible future persons that is the real problem in eugenic selection – for example, a choice to make sure that a non-disabled possible future child exists instead of a disabled one (or the reverse). In other words, if all possible future persons have exactly the same value and worth, no choice between them can ever be made – any choice would be based on the wrong reasons.

Society will also need to be mindful of the risks of developing a position whereby it would be seen as irresponsible not to select for only healthy future children. Indeed, such a society might begin to accept that every possible future child had a 'right' to be genetically healthy and that the very existence of a disabled child was the result of a selective mistake. This battle of values becomes important in the current discussion about the new eugenics, especially if a society is challenged by difficulties such as financial limitations in the health sectors. In this regard, Diane Paul observed:

> One clear lesson from the history of eugenics is this: what may be unthinkable when times are flush may come to seem only good common sense when they are not. In the 1920s, most geneticists

> found the idea of compulsory sterilization repugnant. In the midst of the Depression [1929 to 1939], they no longer did.[18]

A further argument occasionally heard supporting certain forms of eugenic procedures is the emphasis that future parents should never be obliged to accept a disabled and suffering child whose birth could have been avoided. A significant amount of resentment, and even anger, is sometimes expressed towards such a limitation of choice, which is considered unacceptable and cruel – something that should never be countenanced. In this regard, it is true that disabled children are sometimes seen as the cause of deep suffering in a family, which may even undermine its unity. But such statements cannot refute the reality that, from a Christian perspective and in a civilized society, every life has equal as well as inherent value and worth. Consequently, if any human life is ever considered unworthy of life, then critical questions can be asked about the way such a society values all human life. As the US Protestant ethicist Scott Rae explained:

> [A]ssuming that the degree of deformity experienced can be predicted with certainty, it is presumptuous to suggest that the lives of genetically or otherwise disabled persons are not worth living. That is a value judgement, not a medical fact, and no one should have the right to impose that kind of value judgement upon another person . . . Not even parents should have the right to set the standard of a life worth living for their child. In many cases in which abortion is contemplated, the parents may confuse the burden of life for the child with the burden of the parents caring for the child.
>
> Though society should not underestimate the challenge of a life-time of caring for these children, the notion of a life not worth living for the child should not be used to disguise what is often the real reason the child is being aborted: the burden on the parents. The hardship on the parents does not justify ending the pregnancy, any more than the financial hardship of a poor woman justifies her ending her pregnancy.[19]

---

[18] D. B. Paul, *Controlling Human Heredity: 1865 to the Present* (Amherst: Humanity, 1998), p. 34.

[19] S. B. Rae, *Brave New Families: Biblical Ethics and Reproductive Technologies* (Grand Rapids: Baker, 1996), p. 200.

This means that instead of accepting the new eugenics, a more responsible and compassionate way forward would be for society to properly support and assist parents to look after children affected by a severe disability. Such an approach would neutralize the temptation of ensuring that children with serious genetic disorders are not brought into existence, while valuing them for who they are when they are born.

Of course, if prospective parents really want to have a child but believe they are incapable of looking after a disabled child, for a number of reasons such as their psychological health or lack of societal support, they may eventually seek to avoid having a child with a significant disability. For example, these parents may finally decide not to have any, or any more, children (parents may decide not to have children for all sorts of reasons). But this would not be a decision based on eugenic considerations. Had they been able, such a couple would have welcomed *any* child, irrespective of his or her biological characteristics. However, it would be a very sad society that enabled parents only to choose a healthy child because these parents would not receive the support necessary to look after a disabled child. In this respect it is impossible to blame such parents who make a choice not to have a disabled child. But no parents should have to make a decision not to have such children just because they, themselves, cannot cope. If this happens, society should do all it can to address the concerns of prospective parents concerning the kind of support they would receive if they brought a disabled child into existence.

On the other hand, it is difficult to see how parents can decide not to have certain kinds of children without making a value judgment that some children are less desirable. It follows that when parents decide that only a certain kind of child should be brought into existence, based solely on genetic factors, this can only mean making a eugenic choice and preferring one possible future child over another.

From a Christian perspective this is very important, since the inherent as well as equal value and worth of each human life are based on the reality that every human being is created to reflect the same image of God and called to a future eternal destiny with him. From God's perspective every possible future person has the same value and worth regardless of his or her state of health or how long or short a time a person may live and no matter how much suffering or pleasure he or she may experience during life on earth.

The value and worth of life versus the quality of life

Some of the most important arguments supporting eugenic developments are based on the ethical theory of consequentialism, which weighs the overall amount of pleasure versus suffering an action may cause. In a similar way to earlier programmes in the twentieth century, the new eugenics promises to reduce the amount of suffering experienced by whole population groups, families or individuals. For instance, Derek Parfit suggested the following consequentialist principle for eugenic selection: 'If in either of two possible outcomes the same number of people would ever live, it would be worse if those who live are worse off, or have a lower quality of life, than those who would have lived.'[20] But in weighing up the different outcomes, Parfit positioned an individual's quality of life over the equality in worth and value of every human person that is one of the pillars of civilized societies.

To quote Roberto Andorno again:

> In reality, eugenic ideology presupposes stepping from a 'worthiness of life' culture to a 'quality of life' culture, in other words, to the idea that not every life is worthy of being lived, or to put it more bluntly, that there are some lives that do not have any worth.[21]

This is the basis of the fundamental disagreement concerning the new eugenics. On one side, quality of life and the reduction of suffering are seen as having top priority; on the other, the equal worth of all human life is considered to be the most important factor, even though the alleviation of suffering is also imperative. Interestingly, such a difference is not new. In 1922 the English science fiction author H. G. Wells (1866–1946) highlighted the obvious tension that existed between the different world views in society when he discussed eugenic birth control in the context of creating fewer and better children in the UK:

---

[20] D. Parfit, *Reasons and Persons* (Oxford: Oxford University Press, 1986), p. 360.

[21] R. Andorno, 'Fondements philosophiques et culturels de l'eugénisme sélectif', in J. Laffitte and I. Carrasco de Paula (eds), *La génétique, au risque de l'eugénisme?* (Paris: Edifa-Mame, 2010), p. 140 (tr. C. MacKellar).

> When we realize clearly this possibility of civilizations being based on very different sets of moral ideas and upon different intellectual methods, we are better able to appreciate the profound significance of the schism in our modern community, which gives us side by side, honest and intelligent people who regard Birth Control as something essentially sweet, sane, clean, desirable and necessary, and others equally honest and with as good a claim to intelligence who regard it as not merely unreasonable and unwholesome, but as intolerable and abominable. We are living not in a simple and complete civilization, but in a conflict of at least two civilizations, based on entirely different fundamental ideas, pursuing different methods and with different aims and ends.[22]

Regrettably, Wells's comments on a divided society remain just as valid at present. There is a conflict between those who believe (and it is only a belief) in the inherent equality of all human beings, as in Christianity, and those who seek to reduce moral reasoning to science and tangible experiences, such as pleasures and the reduction of suffering. However, by suggesting a purely naturalistic explanation of humanity there is a danger that it may be reduced to biological science.[23] But this would imply that any inherent equality no longer exists between human beings since science, by itself, cannot give any basis for this equality. From this perspective, making sure that those who are deemed of lower value and worth are not brought into existence in society in order to improve human well-being would be consistent with this new morality based on science. Indeed, it is as a result of the scientific strength of the above arguments that eugenic ideology was so successful at the beginning of the twentieth century among some of the medical and scientific elites around the world.[24]

But as Roberto Andorno rhetorically asks, 'Does human selection not contradict the principle according to which all human beings have the same worth, regardless of their state of health?'[25]

---

22 H. G. Wells (introduction) in M. Sanger, *The Pivot of Civilization* (New York: Humanity, 2003 [originally published in New York in 1922 by Brentano's]), p. 39.

23 The French anthropologist George Vacher de Lapouge went even further by suggesting that it is science that will give society its new morality as well as its new politics; Y. Conry, *L'introduction du darwinisme en France* (Paris: Vrin, 1974), pp. 245–246.

24 R. Weikart, *From Darwin to Hitler: Evolutionary Ethics, Eugenics, and Racism in Germany* (New York: Palgrave Macmillan, 2004), p. 232.

25 Andorno, 'Fondements philosophiques et culturels', p. 131.

In view of this, any selection decision between children made by a person or a society may reveal their genuine, and unacceptable, moral values. Children are valued either for their inherent worth because they reflect the image of God or, instead, for their quality of life. Moreover, if persons are valued because they reflect the image of God, which is radically equal among all individuals, then the act of selection becomes meaningless since everyone is equal, and choosing among them becomes pointless. On the other hand, if a person's quality of life is seen as the most important basis for considering whether a life is valuable or meaningful, then eugenic programmes will become attractive. But then a risk exists that the value and worth of a life will be reduced to whether an individual can experience a certain amount of happiness and pleasure.

In this reflection on the dangers of the new eugenics everyone must consider all the different issues for themselves, carefully examining the relevance of the different ethical arguments. But in so doing they should also consider the lessons of history and not believe that the abuse cannot return. Moreover, since a number of the selective reproductive procedures presently being developed will eventually affect all of humanity, it is also for democratic society as a whole to consider, discuss and decide on the challenges arising from the developments of eugenics. This means that any weighing up of the benefits and risks relating to eugenic procedures should not be restricted to just a few individuals or a small community.

From a Christian perspective, as already mentioned, it is worth remembering that God really does welcome all individuals into existence, no matter who they are, and is calling all existing persons to do the same with possible future children. This is the only way a Christian civilized society can survive. As the Holy See's Congregation for the Doctrine of the Faith indicated in 2008:

> The question of using genetic engineering for purposes other than medical treatment also calls for consideration. Some have imagined the possibility of using techniques of genetic engineering to introduce alterations with the presumed aim of improving and strengthening the gene pool. Some of these proposals exhibit a certain dissatisfaction or even rejection of the value of the human being as a finite creature and person.
>
> Apart from technical difficulties and the real and potential risks involved, such manipulation would promote a eugenic mentality

> and would lead to indirect social stigma with regard to people who lack certain qualities, while privileging qualities that happen to be appreciated by a certain culture or society; such qualities do not constitute what is specifically human.
>
> This would be in contrast with the fundamental truth of the equality of all human beings which is expressed in the principle of justice, the violation of which, in the long run, would harm peaceful coexistence among individuals.
>
> Furthermore, one wonders who would be able to establish which modifications were to be held as positive and which not, or what limits should be placed on individual requests for improvement since it would be materially impossible to fulfil the wishes of every single person. Any conceivable response to these questions would, however, derive from arbitrary and questionable criteria.
>
> All of this leads to the conclusion that the prospect of such an intervention would end sooner or later by harming the common good, by favouring the will of some over the freedom of others.
>
> Finally it must also be noted that in the attempt to create a new type of human being one can recognize an ideological element in which man tries to take the place of his Creator.
>
> In stating the ethical negativity of these kinds of interventions which imply an unjust domination of man over man, the Church also recalls the need to return to an attitude of care for people and of education in accepting human life in its concrete historical finite nature.[26]

Of course, it is possible to challenge this statement by emphasizing that certain forms of prenatal selection are already taking place, including with preimplantation embryonic selection, whereby only the 'best' embryos resulting from IVF are selected for implantation in a woman. Moreover, it can be argued that such procedures have not given rise to any perceived damage to the equality between persons. But these procedures are, in effect, already sending the message that all persons are not equal in value and that some possible future individuals should not be born. And the more the vulnerable edifice of equality of worth in civilized society is

[26] Congregation for the Doctrine of the Faith, *Dignitas Personae (Instruction on Certain Bioethical Questions)* (2008), para. 27.

undermined by decisions that weaken its very foundations, the more likely it is that this equality may eventually collapse and disappear – a situation that will threaten the very personhood of certain members of society. One of the leading American bioethicists, Joseph Fletcher (1905–91), who was ordained as an Episcopal Christian priest but later identified himself as an atheist, was already arguing in 1968:

> People . . . have no reason to feel guilty about putting a Down's syndrome baby away, whether it's 'put away' in the sense of hidden in a sanitarium or in a more responsible lethal sense. It is sad; yes. Dreadful. But it carries no guilt. True guilt arises only from an offense against a person, and a Down's is not a person.[27]

Such a statement may then highlight how eugenic ideology can lead to the denial of personhood of certain members in society and a complete breakdown of civilization. Indeed, it is not possible to overestimate the dangers for society of the new eugenics, and society must remain vigilant as to its development. The Christian bioethicist Agneta Sutton is therefore correct to argue that:

> Any form of eugenics involves discrimination based on the view that some individuals are either unwelcome or less welcome than others. Eugenics, in whatever form it takes, means usurping powers of the lives – and deaths – of others, while failing to recognize our creaturely limitations and the fact that true perfection is not of this world.[28]

Because of this, Christians must learn to welcome all possible future children into existence in an attitude of humility and gratitude that reflects their unconditional and equal value and worth, whoever they are, including both the suffering and the happy child. Society will then continue to maintain and protect the inherent, as well as equal, value and worth of all human beings. God will never prefer some persons over others no matter how able or disabled they may be or how much pleasure

---

[27] B. Bard and J. Fletcher, 'The Right to Die', *The Atlantic Monthly* 221 (April 1968), pp. 59–64; retrieved 2 October 2019 from <www.riverbendds.org/index.htm?page=fletcher.html>.

[28] A. Sutton, 'A Case Against Germ-Line Gene Therapy', *Ethics & Medicine* 29.1 (2013), pp. 17–22 (p. 21).

or suffering they experience during their lives. Instead, each one is created to reflect his amazing image and express the wonderful, immeasurable and unconditional love that exists in God.[29]

[29] C. MacKellar, *The Image of God, Personhood and the Embryo* (London: SCM, 2017), pp. 32–50.

Further reading

C. MacKellar and C. Bechtel (eds), *The Ethics of the New Eugenics* (New York: Berghahn, 2014). An interdisciplinary study from the Scottish Council on Human Bioethics, bringing together research from embryology, genetics, philosophy, sociology, psychology and history. It constructs a thorough picture of the procedures emerging from today's reproductive developments, including a rigorous ethical argumentation concerning the possible advantages and risks related to the new eugenics.

D. J. Kevles, *In the Name of Eugenics* (Cambridge, Mass.: Harvard University Press, 1995). Traces the study and practice of eugenics from its inception in the late nineteenth century to its most recent manifestation within the field of genetic engineering. It is rich in narrative, anecdote, attention to human detail and stories of competition among scientists who have dominated the field.

E. Black, *War Against the Weak* (New York: Thunder's Mouth, 2004). Documents how American corporate philanthropies launched a national eugenic campaign in the USA at the beginning of the twentieth century and then created the modern movement of human genetics. It also examines how some eugenic policies were implemented, such as the sterilization of some 60,000 Americans in twenty-seven states of the USA.

C. Rosen, *Preaching Eugenics: Religious Leaders and the American Eugenics Movement* (Oxford: Oxford University Press, 2004). Studies how American Protestant, Catholic and Jewish leaders confronted and, in many cases, enthusiastically embraced eugenic ideology in the first half of the twentieth century. In this regard, the author argues that a number of religious leaders became attracted to eugenic policies precisely when they distanced themselves from traditional religious positions. The liberals and modernists (those who challenged their churches to embrace modernity) played an important part in the success of the eugenics movement in the USA.

D. B. Paul, *Controlling Human Heredity: 1865 to the Present* (Amherst: Humanity, 1998). Examines whether the eugenic ideology has now returned, since the abuse that took place in Nazi Germany, under the guise of medical genetics. In so doing, the author aims to bridge the gap between expert and lay understanding of the history of eugenics and thereby to enrich the debate on the perplexing contemporary choices of genetic medicine.

N. Agar, *Liberal Eugenics, in Defence of Human Enhancement* (Oxford: Blackwell, 2004). In this controversial book, philosopher Nicholas Agar seeks to defuse the anxieties over past eugenic policies while defending the idea that parents should be allowed to enhance their children's characteristics. In other words, he argues that parents can use new technologies to realize their reproductive goals without harming the people they will bring into existence, while suggesting that certain risks related to eugenic developments can be resisted.

R. Cole-Turner (ed.), *Design and Destiny: Jewish and Christian Perspectives on Human Germline Modification* (Cambridge, MA: MIT Press, 2008). Approaches the question of germline genetic modifications from the perspective of traditional Jewish and Christian teaching. In so doing, the study reflects upon the meaning and destiny of human life in a technological age and whether such genetic modifications could be welcomed provided certain moral challenges are addressed.

Glossary

Note: Some of the terms in this glossary do not appear in the text but are included in order to help readers when they come across them elsewhere.

aneuploidy A condition in which the number of chromosomes in a cell differs from the normal number.

assisted reproductive technologies (ARTs) The collective name for all biomedical procedures used to assist women to have children.

cell differentiation The process by which cells achieve specialized function in an organism.

cell nuclear replacement (also called **somatic cell nuclear transfer**) The procedure of replacing the cell nucleus (containing the chromosomes) of an egg with the nucleus from another cell.

chimera An organism composed of cells derived from at least two genetically different cell types. The cells could be from the same or separate species.

chromosome A feature of all plant and animal cells composed of DNA and protein. Chromosomes carry the information necessary for the development and functioning of the body. Humans normally have forty-six chromosomes in the nucleus of their non-reproductive cells (twenty-two pairs plus two sex chromosomes, denoted X or Y), which contain the 20,000 to 25,000 human genes.

clone A cell or organism derived from, and genetically identical to, another cell or organism.

commodification Term used to describe the treatment of a human being or an entity as an interchangeable marketable commodity that can give rise to commerce. A commodity has a price and only an instrumental value.

congenital Refers to a characteristic present at birth, though not necessarily evident at birth. Often used in the context of negative traits, such as 'congenital malformations', deformities, diseases and so on, but positive conditions are also congenital.

diploid Having the normal two sets of chromosomes, usually one paternal and one maternal.

DNA Deoxyribonucleic acid – part of the cell's and the body's genetic material.

donor Donors are people who consent to allow their sperm, egg cells or embryos to be given to others. If the procedure is provided in a licensed centre in the UK, they are not the legal parents of the resulting children. The legal parents are the woman giving birth and usually her partner if she has one.

egg The reproductive cell produced by a woman during her monthly cycle. The nucleus of an egg always contains an X chromosome, having twenty-three chromosomes in all.

embryo biopsy Removal and examination of one or more cells from a developing embryo for diagnostic purposes.

embryo (human) A human being during the first fifty-six days (eight weeks) of his or her development following his or her creation, excluding any time during which the development has been suspended.

embryonic stem cells (ES cells) Embryonic cells that can proliferate indefinitely and differentiate into many different tissues.

enucleated Where the nucleus, containing all the chromosomes, has been removed from a cell (usually an egg cell).

eutelegenesis A positive eugenic procedure in which sperm from specially selected 'high quality' men is used in donor insemination.

fertilization Fertilization is the joining of an egg with a sperm cell to form an embryo. Naturally, fertilization occurs in the woman's body (in vivo) but it can also occur in the laboratory (in vitro).

foetus The gestating prenatal human person between eight weeks and birth.

gametes The common name for eggs and sperm cells.

gene The genetic information required to form a protein.

genetic counselling Guidance regarding genetic disorders. Genetic counsellors can provide information about a range of issues, from risks to treatments.

genetic testing A procedure geared towards detecting the presence or absence of, or change in, a gene or chromosome.

genome The complete genetic heritage or make-up of an individual.

germline The cells of an organism that, during the usual course of reproduction, may pass on their genetic material to progeny.

haploid Having one set of chromosomes as normally carried by a sperm or egg cell.

implantation Process that lasts about one week, beginning when the embryo attaches to the wall of the uterus of the woman and ending when it is fully embedded in this wall, or exceptionally in an extrauterine place.

insemination The introduction of sperm into a woman's body to create a pregnancy. Artificial insemination can be done using either freshly ejaculated sperm or sperm that has been frozen. Generally, however, where the sperm of a donor is used (donor insemination), this will have been frozen to allow time for the donor to be screened for transmissible diseases before insemination takes place.

instrumentalization Term used to denote the transformation of a person or an entity into a mere means to an end. The person or entity then becomes only the instrument of another person.

in vitro fertilization (IVF) A common technique for overcoming infertility whereby eggs are collected from the woman and fertilized with sperm in the laboratory. Generally, up to two resulting embryos are then transferred to the woman's uterus to begin a pregnancy.

in vivo fertilization Introduction of sperm into a woman's reproductive system for the purpose of reproduction. This can happen through sexual intercourse or in other ways, such as by artificial insemination, in which the sperm is injected directly into the woman's reproductive system through the use of a syringe.

karyotype Analysis of the number, size and shape of an individual's chromosomes.

late-onset disorder Disorders that normally become symptomatic in later life, such as in adult life.

mitochondria Present in all cells, they are sometimes described as 'cellular power plants' because they convert organic materials into energy. They do not form part of the nucleus (containing the chromosomes) of a cell but contain thirty-seven genes in humans.

monogenic disorders Disorders arising from defects in a single gene.

monozygotic Derived from one zygote.

multifactorial condition A condition caused by the joint effect of several genes and environmental factors (dissimilar to a polygenic condition).

multiple birth Birth of more than one baby from a pregnancy.

mutation The change in a gene or chromosome that causes a disorder or the inherited susceptibility to a disorder.

nucleus A cellular organelle enclosed in a membrane that contains the chromosomes of a cell.

numerical identity Reflects what is necessary for a relationship that a being has to himself or herself to remain over time, enabling him or her to be numbered. In other words, it considers whether an individual at a certain time is identical to the one existing at a later time. In this way, it examines the number of individuals who exist and whether they are distinct.

For example, numerical identity considers whether the continuous sense of a living being remains as the same being throughout his or her life trajectory (from creation to death) in the three dimensions of space and over time.

objectification Term used to describe the treatment of a human being as a thing or an object, disregarding his or her personality and inherent dignity.

oocyte The mature oocyte, also called an ovum or egg, is the female reproductive cell, possessing a genome reduced by half (haploid genome). In other words, it normally contains twenty-three chromosomes in humans.

oocyte in the process of fertilization The result of the penetration of a male sperm cell into an oocyte; it contains a male pronucleus, containing the set of chromosomes of the male sperm cell, and a female pronucleus, containing the set of chromosomes of the female egg.

penetrance factor The frequency with which persons carrying a genetic characteristic responsible for a disease show signs of the disease.

polygenic condition A condition caused by the effects of several genes (dissimilar to multifactorial condition).

posthumanism The idea that the human body can be substantially replaced or upgraded to no longer even resemble, in any way, that of a human person. In other words, it is an ideology in which possible future beings would originate from humanity but their basic capacities would so radically exceed those of present humans as to no longer be considered human in any significant degree.

preimplantation genetic diagnosis Use of genetic testing on a live embryo to determine the presence, absence or change in a gene or chromosome prior to implantation of the embryo in the uterus of a woman.

prenatal diagnosis A test providing a genetic diagnosis of a foetal condition. There are two primary types:

1 *Amniocentesis* – this method involves examining foetal cells taken between fifteen and sixteen weeks of pregnancy from the amniotic fluid that surrounds the foetus. The foetal cells are cultured and the genetic make-up of the foetus determined. This allows testing for chromosomal abnormalities such as Down syndrome and other birth defects.
2 *Chorionic villus sampling (CVS)* – this method involves the removal of a small sample of placental tissue between nine and eleven weeks of pregnancy, which is tested for genetic abnormalities.

prenatal screening A public health service that offers pregnant women a test to examine whether the future baby is at an increased risk of having a disorder such as Down syndrome. If a screening test reveals an increased risk, it is followed by the offer of a diagnostic test to clarify the cause of the screening results and any implications for the health of the future baby.

pronucleus (pronuclei) The haploid nucleus (containing only half the chromosomes) of the egg and the sperm cell after fertilization but before the dissolution of their membranes and the first division of the fertilized egg.

qualitative identity Examines similarities in qualities or properties in the same individual in different settings (such as at two different times) or between distinct individuals. For example, two beings may be similar from a biological perspective but exist in different settings of space and/or time. In this way identical twins are qualitatively identical (for the most part) but numerically distinct. Each twin exists in a different setting of the three dimensions of space, though they generally live at the same time.

RNA Ribonucleic acid – genetic material that complements the work of DNA and is essential in various biological activities, such as in the regulation and expression of genes.

social Darwinism Theory that suggests that natural selection in a society will eventually enable superior groups to outcompete inferior ones.

somatic cells All body cells that are not reproductive cells.

sperm The gamete produced by the male, usually through ejaculation. Millions of sperm cells are present in each ejaculate and roughly half of these will carry X chromosomes, the other half carrying Y chromosomes.

sperm sorting The separation of sperm carrying X chromosomes from those carrying Y chromosomes prior to fertilization in order to select the sex of offspring.

stem cell A cell that has the ability to divide for an indefinite period in vivo or in culture and to give rise to specialized cells.

syngamy The mingling of the male and female haploid chromosomes following the breakdown of the pronuclear membranes approximately twenty-four hours after the fusion between the sperm cell and the egg. This results in the formation of the zygote.

teleology Describes the doctrine of the end of history or the interpretation of history with respect to its ends, purpose or goals.

teratoma An uncontrolled growth of cells that are the result of an abnormal fertilization without any potential to develop into an embryo proper.

totipotent Demonstrates the ability of a cell to develop into every cell type required for human development, including extra-embryonic tissues, to produce a fertile, adult individual. An individual cell that is totipotent can also be considered a one-cell embryo. In other words, a cell that is capable of generating a globally coordinated developmental sequence.

transhumanism The idea that the human body can be substantially upgraded though some elements would remain. Transhumanism is different from the concept of enhancement in that it seeks to create beings that have never previously existed in the history of humankind. These beings would retain some human characteristics, such as with human-nonhuman interspecies beings or cyborgs that combine the human with the robot. Transhuman persons should, however, be distinguished from posthuman individuals.

uterus The woman's womb, in which the embryo develops into a baby.

X-linked disorders Disorders due to a mutation on the X chromosome. X-linked disorders usually affect only males, but the disorders can be transmitted through healthy female carriers.

zygote The final stage of fertilization, the single cell formed when the two sets of chromosomes, one from the male sperm cell, the other from the female egg, have joined.

General index

ableism 94
Agar, Nicolas 117
Amphilochius (Saint) 52
Andorno, Roberto 61, 71, 85, 192–3
Aquinas, Thomas (Saint) 33
Archard, David 51
Aristotle 38, 153
Asquith, Herbert 2
Augustine (Saint) 41

Baker, Graham 16
Balfour, Arthur 17
Barth, Karl 43
Baylis, Françoise 59
Bayne, Tim 92
Benatar, David 51
Benedict XVI (Pope) 47
Blocher, Henri 30
Brave New World 9, 10
Brock, Dan 67
Brown, Ivan 94

Cairns, David 30
Calvin, John 33–4
Canada 12, 59, 94
Caplan, Arthur 122
Catholic (Roman) 14, 17, 25, 37, 44, 127, 159, 169, 198
Chamberlain, A. Neville 17
Charter of Fundamental Rights (EU) 163
Chesterton, Gilbert K. 4
Christian Medical & Dental Association 86
Churchill, Winston (Sir) 2, 17
Club feet 105
Cohen, Cynthia 8
Cokley, Rebecca 84
conditional parenthood 59
Congregation for the Doctrine of the Faith (Holy See) 169, 194
Convention on Human Rights and Biomedicine (Council of Europe) 162–3
Council of Europe 107, 162–3
Crick, Francis 7, 18, 23, 153
CRISPR–Cas9 156
Cystic fibrosis 83, 187

Darwin, Charles 2, 120
Darwin, Leonard 120
designer babies 163
Down syndrome 57, 59, 91, 94, 101, 105, 139, 142, 185, 187, 196

Edwards, Robert 19
Eichrodt, Walther 41
Eugenics Education Society (EES) 15–17, 121,
Eugenics Society 17–18
euthanasia 13–14, 23, 122, 152

Feast, Julia 72
Feinberg, Joel 64
Fletcher, Joseph 196
Francis (Pope) 62, 141
Frankenstein (Monster) 73
Frankenstein, Victor 72
Free Church of Scotland 37
French National Consultative Ethics Committee 92

Galton Institute 18–19
Galton, Francis (Sir) 1–2, 7, 11–12, 15
genome editing 156–7, 159–64, 168, 170
German Ethics Council 83
Germany 3, 6–7, 12, 14, 22, 119, 122, 126, 128
germline genetic modification 26, 156, 158–9, 162–4, 168–70, 176, 187
Glover, Jonathan 65
Graham, Robert 136
Gregory of Nyssa (Saint) 43
Groningen Protocol 152
Gunton, Colin 46

Habermas, Jürgen 111–12
Harris, John 113, 154
Hauerwas, Stanley 50, 179
Health Council of the Netherlands 133
Herzfeld, Noreen 42
Himmler, Heinrich 126
Hitler, Adolf 12–13, 178
House of Lords ((UK) 105
Howe, David 72
Human Fertilisation and Embryology Authority 157
Humphrey, Hubert Jr. 124
Huxley, Aldous 9–10, 18
Huxley, Julian (Sir) 18

Immigration Restriction Act 1924 (USA) 21
Inge, William R. 15–16
International League of Societies for Persons with Mental Handicaps 97
International Theological Commission (Holy See) 39, 169
intracytoplasmic sperm injection (ICSI) 136
Irenaeus (Saint) 32, 33

Jesus Christ 29, 37, 39, 117, 184
Jewish 28, 82, 126–7, 198
John Paul II (Pope, Saint) 45, 47, 52, 80, 140, 155
Jones, David A. 37, 159, 168–9

Kass, Leon 45, 104, 111, 142, 150–1, 158–9, 164, 186
Katz Rothman, Barbara 60
Kilner, John 39, 41, 43–4
Kim, Scott 89
King, David 109, 122, 177
Kings College (London) 18
Kitcher, Philip 115
Koch, Lene 3
Kristol, Elizabeth 93

Lewis, Clive S. 25, 112
Lewontin, Richard 82
Liao, Matthew 167
life unworthy of life 13, 67, 82, 85–7, 142, 190
Luther, Martin 33

MacIntyre, Alasdair 75
Macrae, Ian 97
Magisterium 159, 169
maternal spindle transfer 173–6
Matthews, Pia 44
Mehlman, Maxwell 114
Meilaender, Gilbert 45, 53–4
Mental Deficiency Act 1913 (UK) 16
Miller, Alice 183
Mitchell, Ben 40
mitochondrial disorder 174–5
Muller, Hermann 177–8

National Academies of Sciences, Engineering, and Medicine (USA) 164
National Socialism (Nazi) 3, 6–7, 12–14, 22, 82, 119, 122, 126, 128
natural humility 55, 146

Nobel Prize 4, 7, 19, 136, 177
non-identity argument 65–6, 68, 74
Noyes, John 20
Nozick, Robert 181
numerical identity 160–2, 164, 166–7, 171–2, 187

O'Donovan, Oliver 92
Obasogie, Osagie 122
open future argument 110–14
Orthodox 25–6, 56, 159
Orwell, George 57

Parfit, Derek 65, 192
Parkinson's disease 89
Pattinson, Shaun 109
Paul, Diane 9, 189
Peters, Ted 24, 103–4
Pius XI (Pope) 17, 55
Plato 11, 115, 153
playing God 4, 102–4
Plutarch 172
Polio 83
Pontifical Academy for Life (Holy See) 142, 151, 170, 179
preimplantation genetic diagnosis 143
President's Commission on Bioethics (USA) 93
President's Council on Bioethics (USA) 106
Procreative Beneficence 118
pronuclear transfer 173–6
Protestant 20, 24–5, 30, 33, 36, 39, 40–7, 50, 92, 159, 190, 198

qualitative identity 161–2, 165

Rae, Scott 190
Ramsey, Paul 48
Rapp, Emily 78–9
Reinders, Johannes (Hans) 76–8, 89–91, 152, 168
Repository for Germinal Choice 136
Roosevelt, Theodore 21
Rosen, Christine 180

Saintôt, Bruno 141
Sandel, Michael 116, 182
Sanger, Margaret 121
saviour sibling procedure 147–8
Savulescu, Julian 118, 146, 187–8
Second World War 3, 14, 17, 19, 136
serious disorder 1, 65, 80, 83, 105–8, 129, 158
Shelley, Mary 72
Sicard, Didier 92
Silver, Lee 8–9, 185
Singer, Peter 154
Smith, Ellison D. 21
Smith, Kevin 70
somatic genetic modification 158–9, 161–2, 164, 173
Sparta 11
SS (Schutzstaffel) 126
Stăniloae, Dumitru 56
Stott, John 42
Sutton, Agneta 196

Tay-Sachs 79, 82
Torrance, Thomas F. 36

United Kingdom (UK) 2, 12, 15–17, 20, 51, 57, 83, 96, 105, 115, 122, 145–6, 154, 157, 174, 192
United Nations Educational, Scientific and Cultural Organization (UNESCO) 18, 163
Universal Declaration of Human Rights (UN) 56
Universal Declaration on the Human Genome and Human Rights (UNESCO) 163
University of Munich 12
USA 12, 20–2, 119, 124, 135, 147, 198

von Galen, Clemens August (Graf) 14

Warnock, Mary (Baroness) 82, 122, 188
Waters, Brent 47
Watson, James 4, 7, 153–4, 178
Wells, Herbert G. 192–3
Wilkinson, Stephen 66, 81
Williams, Glanville 18, 121
Wright, Christopher 35
Wyatt, John 36, 44, 93, 95, 162

Yazdani, Farhan 123

Index of Scripture references

OLD TESTAMENT

Genesis

1:1–3 *26*
1:26–28 *26*
1:26 *27, 38, 53*
1:27 *40*
1:28 *48, 51*
2:18 *47–48*
2:24 *48*
5:1–2 *30*
5:1–3 *52*
5:1 *53*
9:6 *30*

Psalms

139:13–15 *47*
139:13–16 *49–50*
139:15 *37*

Leviticus

18:6 *127*

NEW TESTAMENT

Matthew

7:12 *117*
19:4 *48*

John

1:14 *36*